Published by

Pedigree Books Limited, Beech Hill House, Walnut Gardens, Exeter, Devon EX4 4DG

YOURS is a monthly magazine for the young at heart. Look out for it in your local newsagent.
YOURS, Bretton Court, Bretton, Peterborough PE3 8DZ

*Compiled by Caroline Chadderton, designed by David Reid. Sub edited by Christine Curtis.
Additional writing, Sanchia Gorner and Bridget Davidson. Heartfelt thanks to all the readers who
contributed so magnificently to this annual by sending in their letters, tips, stories, recipes and photos.*

Hello!

We're so pleased you are spending another Year with YOURS. For this, our third edition, we've brought together more fascinating nuggets from past and present to inform and amuse you throughout the year.

As well as being a handy calendar, I like to think of A Year with YOURS as a 12-month bran-tub, which you can keep dipping into whenever you need a little bit of inspiration.

I'd like to thank YOURS' Features Editor, Caroline Chadderton for all her hard work and creative inspiration in compiling this issue.

And look out for two old friends from the monthly magazine – Dr Roger Henderson and gardening expert Phil McCann – who've provided year-long advice to keep both you and your garden in tip-top shape!

It just remains for me to say once again – have a wonderful year with YOURS!

Our best wishes for 2004

Valery

Valery McConnell
Editor

Valery McConnell   Caroline Chadderton   Phil McCann   Dr Roger Henderson

January 2004

PIC/REX FEATURES

A flavour of the month

Welcome to the 2004 YOURS Annual and a very Happy New Year to you all! Have you made any New Year resolutions? Now's the time for a fresh start, so here are a few ideas to get you going!

Make this the month to organise yourself for the year ahead and commit your plans to paper. Book your annual eye test, doctor and dentist check-ups. Buy a diary, or simply use the diary pages of this annual to record all your appointments for the year. Transfer all your birthdays, anniversaries and special dates from last year's diary into your new one.

January is also a good time to clear out the old. Anything gathering dust should be thrown away or, better still, recycled or given to charity.

Send old specs to the World in Sight Appeal, Help the Aged, Freepost LON 13109, London EC1B 1JY, where they will be cleaned and sent to help visually impaired people in the developing world. Your unwanted hearing aids can be refitted for someone who really needs it in Nepal. Send them to Adam Shulberg, 25 New Cavendish Street, London W1M 8LP.

Used stamps equal sterling, too. Send them to The RNIB Fundraising Group, 20 Bowers Road, Benfleet, Essex SS7 5PZ, where they will help raise money for RNIB services.

THURSDAY	1	New Year's Day Bank Holiday
FRIDAY	2	Bank Holiday (Scotland)
SATURDAY	3	
SUNDAY	4	
MONDAY	5	
TUESDAY	6	Epiphany
WEDNESDAY	7	
THURSDAY	8	
FRIDAY	9	
SATURDAY	10	
SUNDAY	11	
MONDAY	12	
TUESDAY	13	
WEDNESDAY	14	
THURSDAY	15	
FRIDAY	16	
SATURDAY	17	
SUNDAY	18	

MONDAY	19	
TUESDAY	20	
WEDNESDAY	21	
THURSDAY	22	Chinese New Year
FRIDAY	23	
SATURDAY	24	
SUNDAY	25	Burns Night
MONDAY	26	
TUESDAY	27	Holocaust Memorial Day
WEDNESDAY	28	February YOURS on sale
THURSDAY	29	
FRIDAY	30	
SATURDAY	31	

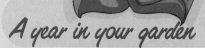

A year in your garden

Being in the depths of winter doesn't mean that the garden need be forgotten. Nor does it mean a bleak month, as flowers can cheer our spirits, even in January. Spread around the garden they may become lost, but concentrated in a hanging basket, they will have the most impact.

Winter flowering pansies are the best of the bunch as they are bred to produce colour throughout the winter. It's a good tip when buying winter flowering pansies to buy only plants showing a little bit of flower. This way you're guaranteed to have a great winter display.

Winter flowering heather is another favourite but most varieties do require ericaceous compost. Bear this in mind if you're making up your own basket.

Ivy is a terrific trailer for winter baskets or containers, and a small shrub called Gaultheria is lovely if you want small, shiny berries.

Bulbs are indispensable when creating a winter display as crocus will push through the compost surface and delight for weeks in January. Snowdrops grow well in baskets, and once the show is over are easily transferred to the garden.

Planting is easy, but it isn't a case of hoping the winter rain will do all your watering. Baskets hang near the wall, and walls create rain shadows. A dense canopy of leaves will also stop water from reaching the compost. Water whenever the compost feels dry, and this could be weekly.

PIC: EMAP GARDEN PICTURE LIBRARY

✣ READER'S TIP ✣
Marjorie Lockwood in Barnsley, South Yorkshire recommends hanging your baskets on a swivel hook, or a dog lead connector. They allow 360 degrees of movement of the basket letting you get the most from a confined planting space.

January 1-4

WHAT'S COOKING?

PIC: HULTON ARCHIVE

▲ It may be below freezing but the family tobogganing on Hampstead Heath in 1945 look to be having far too much fun to worry!

Trout with Orange and Mustard Sauce
(Serves 4)

- 4 trout, approx. 8 oz/225 g each
- Juice 1 lemon
- 2 oz/50 g butter
- 2 Seville oranges, grated rind of 1 and juice of 2
- 1 tbs Dijon mustard
- 2 tbs chopped parsley
- 1 egg yolk
- Salt and freshly ground black pepper
- Segments of orange
- Fresh dill or parsley

1 Place the fish in a greased, shallow ovenproof dish. Season well and pour on the juice of the lemon.
2 Cover and bake at 180°C/350° F/Gas Mark 4 for 30 minutes.
3 To make the sauce: Melt the butter, taking care not to burn it. Add the grated rind of one Seville orange and the juice of both, whisking into the butter. Add the mustard and the parsley. Simmer for 2 minutes. Stir the egg yolk in a small bowl and drop in the hot sauce, beating continuously.
4 Return the sauce to the pan on a low heat to thicken a little. Do not boil.
5 Remove fish from the oven and place in a warm serving dish. Spoon over some of the sauce and serve the rest separately.
6 Decorate with peeled segments of orange and fresh dill or parsley.

PIC: FRESH PRODUCE CONSORTIUM

ON GROWING OLDER
'I'm not ageing – I'm marinating.'
Anon

OLD WIVES' TALES

To cure a cough, take a hair from the coughing person's head, put it between two slices of buttered bread, feed it to a dog, and say: "Eat well you hound, may you be sick and I be sound."

Dr Henderson replies: If you believe this one, you probably also think the earth is flat and that the moon is made of green cheese. Witchcraft and hogwash (and that's being kind). However, it made me chuckle and I'm sure my dog would appreciate the bread!

AT THE MOVIES

Who said?
'I'm sorry sir. I could never answer to a whistle. Whistles are for dogs and cats and other animals but not for children and definitely not for me. It would be too humiliating.'   (Answer below)

Answer: Julie Andrews getting indignant with Christopher Plummer in The Sound of Music

Such a surprise awaited Della Rowe from Falmouth…

For my 80th birthday, my daughter invited me to her house for lunch.

When my friend Barbara collected me from church I was taken on a round about route which I thought was rather strange. We arrived at the church hall, where all my family and friends had gathered and there was a sight to behold – it was decorated and there was a banquet fit for a queen. I was dumbfounded but enjoyed a wonderful party which I shall remember all my life.

PAUSE FOR THOUGHT

'*I cut this snippet from a newspaper and I have always tried to live by it*', **writes C Guy of Co Durham:**

I have to live with myself and so
I want to be fit for myself toknow.
I want to be able as days go by
Always to look myself straight in the eye.
I don't want to stand with the setting sun
And hate myself for the things I've done.
                                        Edgar A Guest

Top tip

An umbrella sleeve fits perfectly over a folding walking stick and prevents it from opening when not in use.

DID YOU KNOW THAT

A caterpillar grows to about 27,000 times the size it was when it emerged from its egg.

OUT & ABOUT TO...

Alnwick Garden, Northumberland

See in the New Year with a stroll around this delightful garden. Originally planted in the 18th century by the first Duke of Northumberland, who was a keen botanist and avid collector of exotic species, it fell into disrepair after the Second World War and has recently been revamped by the present Duchess, Jane Northumberland. With the help of renowned designers Wirtz International, she's created an ornamental garden, rose garden and spectacular Grand Cascade. The garden has been cleverly planned so that in winter, even if there's snow on the ground, the ice makes patterns on the water features and the vegetation creates an interesting, sculptural effect.

A woodland walk in the garden by the banks of the River Aln is the perfect antidote to a couch potato Christmas. Once you've had enough fresh air, head for The Garden Café for a feast of delicious hot chocolate, soups and cakes made by local farmers' wives. And if the sight of nearby Alnwick Castle gives you a sense of déjà vu, that could be because it had a starring role in the recent Harry Potter film, Harry Potter and the Philosopher's Stone.

- *Adults £4, concessions £3.50, children free*
- *Excellent licensed café catering for special diets (phone ahead if possible); gift shop*
- *Wheelchair access (call in advance to borrow a wheelchair)*
- *Tel: 01665 511350 (Internet: www.alnwickgarden.com)*

January 5-11

WHAT A COINCIDENCE

In 1951 I was living in Beryl Street, Broken Hill, New South Wales. I'd lived in other parts of Australia but never met anyone who had been to Broken Hill, never mind lived there.

After I returned to the UK, I got a job repping, having to call at public houses. I went into The Jolly Sailor just outside Ripley in Surrey and found that the current licencees were Australians from – you've guessed it – Broken Hill.

But that wasn't the end of the story. I found out they'd stayed in the same house in Beryl Street that I'd had – 14 years ago and 12,000 miles away!

Sheila Wright, Bournemouth

Top tip

To kick-start a fading ballpoint pen, run the tip under boiling water

DID YOU KNOW THAT

Einstein couldn't speak fluently until he was nine. His parents thought he might be retarded.

A DAY TO REMEMBER

Charles and his son in 1945

Absence made my heart grow fonder, recalls Lilian Willcocks from Kent...

At 1.10am on December 12, 1945 my husband Charles arrived home after nearly five years away, having been a prisoner of war for three-and-a-half years.

After being found by Australians in September of that year, he was taken to Perth Military Hospital for several weeks and came home on HMS Maidstone.

I heard the taxi arrive; we just looked at each other after not having seen each other for five years. His first words were: "Where's the boy?" We went upstairs and there was our son looking over the sheet, who said: "My Daddy".

There followed lots of fuss! He was put back to bed and we went downstairs. Charles decided to show me what he'd brought home – and he emptied two large kit bags on to the floor. What goodies from Australia – dried fruit, silk stockings...

I didn't know whether to laugh or cry but hugs and kisses were the order of the day. It took a little while to adjust but we shared 37 years together, some good, some bad but I wouldn't have had it any other way.

OLD FASHIONED REMEDIES

What memories the two words 'goose grease' conjure up. When I had a cough, out would come a square of strong brown paper liberally coated with the grease, then pinned across my chest. I think I was the only child in the class whose mum believed in 'grandma's remedies'. The horror of the crackling when I moved and the 'aroma' as I warmed up. What a joy when the paper disintegrated – I vowed never to cough again!

Mrs E Potter, Halifax

Dr Henderson replies: A common old remedy this one, but not one with any great medical facts behind it. This was guaranteed to embarrass rather than help, I think, although at least it would have done you no harm – an important point with old fashioned treatments!

Out & About To...

Newarke Houses Museum, Leicester

Most of us eat too much at Christmas, but some indulge more than others. If you're feeling a little flabby after overdoing it on the turkey sandwiches, plum pudding and chocolates, spare a thought for what life must have been like for Daniel Lambert, who at his heaviest weighed more than 52 stone!

Born in Leicester in 1770, 'Fat Dan' was so huge he couldn't sink, and used to float along the River Soar with children on his stomach. By the age of 30 he was too large to carry on with his job at the town jail, so spent his remaining years charging people for the privilege of gawping at his girth. At the time, he was Britain's biggest man, and measured 9ft 4in around his waist. To find out more about Fat Dan, head for Newarke Houses, which has a room devoted to Lambert's clothes, chair and other personal effects. If nothing else, it'll make you feel incredibly slender…

- Admission free
- Wheelchair access
  Tel: 0116 225 4980

PIC: NEWARKE HOUSES MUSEUM

What's Cooking?

QUICK SNACK
Fish Rounds
(Serves 4)

- ½ lb/225 g mashed potatoes
- 2 eggs
- 1 lb/450 g cooked fish
- 1 oz/25 g butter or margarine
- 2-3 chopped chives
- Salt and pepper
- Breadcrumbs

1. Heat the butter in a saucepan. Add the coarsely chopped cooked fish, potatoes, chives, yolk of 1 egg, salt and pepper.
2. Stir over a low heat for a few minutes, then turn on to a plate and allow to cool.
3. When cold, shape into round flat cakes.
4. Brush with beaten egg, coat with breadcrumbs and bake in the oven for 15 minutes (190 C/375 F/Gas Mark 5).

My Advice Is...

'Never put off until tomorrow what you can do today'. The older I get, the more I believe this to be true.
Vera Mabberley, Wiltshire

At The Movies

Who said?
'What is it you want, Mary? What do you want? You – you want the moon? Just say the word, and I'll throw a lasso around it and pull it down. Hey, that's a pretty good idea. I'll give you the moon, Mary'.
(Answer below)

Answer: James Stewart sweet-talking Donna Reed in Frank Capra's It's A Wonderful Life

January 12-18

ON GROWING OLDER

When we're 20 we don't care what the world thinks of us. At 30 we start to worry about what it thinks of us. At 40 we realise that it isn't thinking of us at all.

Anon

WHAT A COINCIDENCE

Some years ago we were visiting Bernkastel in Germany on a coach tour. As we walked by a group of workmen digging a hole in the road, my friend called to me: "What's the time?, to which I replied: "Twenty to…." From the depth of the hole a voice shouted: "That runs from Homerton to Putney."

Everyone looked round in surprise but, by sheer coincidence, I'd worked in Homerton for years and had lived in Median Road, Clapton, on the route of the number 22 London bus! So I knew immediately that this was what he was referring to, and so was able to make a swift jocular remark back. A surprised head popped up out of the hole!

Maude Tulk, Suffolk

WHAT'S COOKING?

SUPPER DISH
Tangy Orange Chicken

(Serves 4)

- 4 chicken quarters
- 1 large onion, chopped
- 6 oz/175 g orange juice
- 1½ oz/40 g butter
- 2 tbs oil
- 1 pt/570 ml water
- 1 chicken stock cube
- ½ oz/10 g cornflour
- 5 oz/150 g carton soured cream
- Fresh parsley

1. Pre-heat the oven to 180°C/350° F/Gas Mark 4.
2. Melt half the butter and oil and brown chicken quarters.
3. In a separate pan, saute the chopped onions gently for 2-3 minutes in the rest of the butter and oil. Stir in concentrated orange juice, water and stock cube. Bring to boil.
4. Transfer to a casserole dish and add chicken. Cover with lid and bake for 1½ hours until the chicken is tender. Baste occasionally with orange sauce.
5. Remove chicken and skim any excess fat from the sauce. Blend the cornflour with 2 tablespoons water and add to the sauce. Return to the boil and cook for 2-3 minutes, stirring continuously. Cool slightly and stir in the soured cream. Pour over chicken and decorate with fresh parsley.

DID YOU KNOW THAT

At US President Andrew Jackson's funeral in 1845, his pet parrot was removed for swearing.

AT THE MOVIES

Who said?
'Why don't you get out of that wet coat and into a dry martini?'
(Answer below)

Answer: Robert Benchley getting familiar with Ginger Rogers in Billy Wilder's The Major And The Minor

OLD WIVES' TALES

A spider's web is most efficacious for an open wound.

Dr Henderson replies: Dating back centuries this really belongs in the Middle Ages and is only for the gullible. It is interesting to look back and see how these beliefs arose and I can only assume it was felt that because of how a spider's web looked, it may have been of use in closing wounds. Interesting but useless.

Janet Brown from Fife casts her mind back to a Royal visit 40 years ago…

Crowds walking the Forth Road Bridge in 1964

On September 4, 1964, I stood alone among hundreds of people waiting at the south end of the Forth Road Bridge to greet the Queen's car making the inaugural crossing of the bridge, after she'd performed the opening ceremony.

After she passed, some of the crowds started to walk back over the bridge, so I decided to do the same. I was one of many that day to have the chance to walk the length of the bridge on the motorway, as the sidewalks were not finished for people to walk on. A truly unforgettable experience!

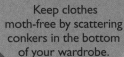
Top tip

Keep clothes moth-free by scattering conkers in the bottom of your wardrobe.

PAUSE FOR THOUGHT

The Doctor's lot
I always look up to my doctor
As someone set apart
I depend on him to cure my ills
From head to toe, to heart.

Lined up outside his surgery
We await his call
Then he listens carefully
As we tell him all.

He hands me a prescription,
Take this three times a day.
I make my way towards the door,
Thank you, doctor, I gratefully say.

We should all look up to our doctor,
He has so many demands.
He may be under the weather
But still has our ills on his hands.

So give him a thought at the end of the day,
It's our duty to respect him.
Remember him in your prayers tonight,
And may the good Lord protect him.
                    Dorothy M Titley, Tamworth

OUT & ABOUT TO…

The Great Glasshouse, National Botanic Garden of Wales, Llanarthne, Wales

Escape from the long, dark days of winter into the welcoming warmth of the Great Glasshouse, the largest single-span greenhouse in the world. Controlled by computer to vary the climate in different parts, it's around the size of a football pitch and houses some of the most threatened species of plants on the planet, from Chile, California, Western Australia, South Africa and the Mediterranean. Plus you can see the rarest tree in Britain, the Ley's Whitebeam.

Don't miss The Physicians of Myddfai, an indoor exhibition and outdoor garden that explains how plants have been used for medicinal purposes from the past to the present. It's based on the legend of the lady of the lake, who taught her sons to use herbs to heal the sick. Mirroring the tale, more recently three brothers founded the famous Myddfai dynasty of apothecaries, from which this part of the garden takes its name, and their descendants became doctors.

Weather permitting, there are also 568 acres of grounds to explore!
● *Adults £6.95, concessions £5, children £3.50*
● *Meals, snacks; shop; disabled access*
Tel: 01558 668768 (Internet: www.gardenofwales.org.uk)

PIC: NATIONAL BOTANIC GARDEN OF WALES

January 19-25

WHAT A COINCIDENCE

During the war I was accepted into the RAF in May 1944 and one of my fellow aircrewmen, Geoff, became my special friend.

After training, Geoff went off as an Airgunner/Wireless Operator and I went on to become a Flight Engineer. We corresponded for some time, then lost touch.

In May 1994 my wife and I were on a conducted tour of Eastbourne, when we stopped at Burwash. I remember Geoff telling me his father owned a butcher's shop there. Imagine my disappointment when I got to the shop to find it was early closing day but then a tradesman rang the bell and who should come to the door but my friend Geoff!

I couldn't stay long as the coach was waiting but we exchanged addresses and promised to write. We have kept in touch ever since and both our wives get on as if they were old friends.

D W Hobbs, Essex

Top tip

Get rid of water stains caused by dripping taps by rubbing them with a little lemon juice and salt paste.

A DAY TO REMEMBER

A daughter to be proud of for Barbara Hunter of N Yorks…

The day I'll never forget is the day my eldest daughter, Pamela, graduated from university. A first in our family and how proud I was of her.

It was wonderful to be among all the caps and gowns, and the learned professors chatting to us. Then, after the presentations, a parade back to campus for a buffet tea; photos were taken and futures discussed. To many nothing out of the ordinary but to me (a single mother) a day to remember forever.

Barbara and Pamela on graduation day

DID YOU KNOW THAT

In Switzerland, it is illegal to mow your front lawn while dressed as Elvis.

OLD FASHIONED REMEDIES

Friday night was not only bath night but also the night of the dreaded Gregory Powder! Mother stood over me and my brother, with strict instructions to, 'open your throat and get it down'. Next was the Mint Imperial to take away the taste, then I'd bury my face in the roller towel on the back of the kitchen door! I asked mother once what it was for and she said: "If nothing else, it's good for the complexion." Mother had a lovely complexion but I never saw her take a dose of Gregory Powder!

Margaret Whitmore, Shropshire

● *Gregory's Powder was a mixture of pulverised rhubarb, ginger and magnesia, prescribed as a laxative*

Dr Henderson replies: Any mixture with magnesia and rhubarb in it could easily have a gentle laxative effect so Gregory's Powder may have been useful in this respect if you had been constipated as a child (although I would not have recommended it myself). As for the complexion, I am afraid your mum was stretching the imagination a bit here! It would have had no effect on this.

OUT & ABOUT TO...

Eden Camp, Malton, North Yorkshire.

PIC: NICK HILL, EDEN CAMP

Contemporary wars, fought by professional armies on foreign soils, often have little impact on those left at home. In complete contrast, Eden, set in an original prisoner-of-war camp, tells the story of how World War Two touched the hearts and minds of the troops who put their lives on the line, plus ordinary men, women and children.

What makes this museum seem special from the outset is the fact that the vast majority of the exhibits on display – from brass buttons to an armoured car – have been donated by members of the public.

The action takes place in 'huts', each covering a different aspect of the war. The themes include rationing, propaganda, life in the trenches, the holocaust and women at war, all brought to life in realistic tableaux, with moving figures, authentic sounds and smells. Eden Camp is a fascinating day out for all ages, and as it's undercover, you don't need to worry about the weather.

● *Adults £4, concessions £2, children £3*
● *Refreshments; wheelchair access (available on loan); Braille sheets and tapes available*
Tel: 01653 697777

WHAT'S COOKING?

A MEAL ON A BUDGET
Crusty Cheese and Onion Pie

(Serves 6-8)

● Shortcrust pastry (using 8 oz/225 g flour and 4 oz/110 g margarine)
● 3 onions
● ¹/₂ oz/10 g flour
● Salt and pepper
● 4 oz/110 g cheese, grated
● 2 tbs milk

1 Parboil the onions while making the pastry.
2 Line an 8 in/20 cm heatproof plate with half the pastry.
3 Mix the salt and pepper with the flour.
4 Slice the onions and dip in the seasoned flour. Spread them over the pastry, sprinkle with cheese and add the milk.
5 Wet the edge of the pastry and cover with pastry lid, pressing the edges firmly together. Brush over with milk.
6 Bake in a hot oven (220°C/425°F/Gas Mark 7) for 40 minutes.

MY ADVICE IS...

'Always leave things as you would like to find them'.
Diane Clark, Bristol

AT THE MOVIES

Who said?
'Marry me and I'll never look at another horse'.
(Answer below)

Answer: Groucho Marx proposing to Margaret Dumont in A Day At The Races

OUT & ABOUT TO...

Sheffield Winter Garden, Sheffield

PIC: SHEFFIELD CITY COUNCIL

A welcome oasis in the heart of the city, this exotic indoor space provides a great opportunity for you to take a break from the hustle and bustle of the January sales. As you relax in the natural beauty of Sheffield's surprisingly green and pleasant retreat, you'll be amazed to see more than 2,500 plants – some familiar and others you're unlikely to have seen before. Mainly from the southern hemisphere, you'll encounter gigantic palms from Central America, Madagascar and China, grass trees from Australia and pines from Norfolk Island.

The garden has become an important part of community life in this busy city, and is much loved by visitors and locals alike. So next time you're in Sheffield and feel in need of a little peace and quiet, this is where to find it.

- *Admission is free*
- *Refreshments; wheelchair access Tel: 0114 221 1900 (Internet: www.sheffield.gov.uk)*

WHAT A COINCIDENCE

Violet with brother John

I was blessed with six brothers but the one I was closest to was John. He was born when I was 12 years old, so I was a second mother to him.

After 31 years of married life, my husband died suddenly, aged 49. All my family rallied round, and especially John. Trying to live on my own, I wanted to see John more but this caused ill-feeling and led to a falling out. I didn't see him or his family for more than a year, which broke my heart.

In an attempt to get on with my life, I went on holiday to Benidorm. One night we went into a bar and who should be there dancing but John and his wife!

We hugged and cried buckets, and spent the rest of the holiday together. We are now closer than ever – and I hope we won't fall out again!

Violet Ingham, Bradford

WHAT'S COOKING?

Butter Bean Snack
(Serves 2)

- 1 large tin of butter beans
- 4 oz/110 g cheese, grated
- 2 tomatoes, sliced
- 2 oz/50 g mushrooms, sliced

1 Drain the beans and place them in an ovenproof dish.
2 Spread mushroom and tomato slices on top. Sprinkle with salt, pepper and grated cheese.
3 Bake at 190°C/375° F/Gas Mark 5 for 20-30 minutes.

Mrs J Condon, Hornchurch, Essex

 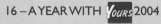

A DAY TO REMEMBER

Florence's Emma and James

Two surprises in one day for Florence Scott of Herts...

I was thinking how wonderful it would be to spend my 60th birthday with my family, especially listening to my two grandchildren Emma and James (seven and five years old) singing Happy Birthday to me.

Two days before my special day, my husband told me to pack a suitcase and off we went in the car. I found myself on the M25, then the M3, finally the M27. Still having no idea of my destination, I noticed a signpost to Bournemouth and we eventually arrived at an exclusive hotel for the weekend.

Sitting in the bar before dinner, although I was thinking how lucky I was to be in such delightful surroundings, I was still missing my family and wishing they could be here with me.

It was if I had rubbed a genie's lamp when suddenly through the door walked my two sons, daughter-in-law and two excited grandchildren.

What a wonderful surprise! It left me with tears of joy when my grandchildren, having kept the secret, yelled out: "We tricked you, didn't we, Nan?" A magician could not have performed a better one!

Top tip

A stubborn zip will run more smoothly if wiped with a little candle wax.

DID YOU KNOW THAT ?

Early mattresses were filled with straw and held up with a rope stretched across the bed frame. If the rope was tight, sleep was comfortable – hence the phrase, 'sleep tight'.

ON GROWING OLDER

'Age is something that doesn't matter – unless you're a cheese'.

Burke

OLD WIVES' TALES

Rub a gold ring on a stye to rid yourself of the beastly blemish.

Dr Henderson replies: Styes are small infected spots just under the eyelid and gold has no effect on them. However, in a small proportion of styes the very act of rubbing them may cause them to burst and so appear to be removed. I would not advise this though, as it more often just makes them more reddened and uncomfortable.

AT THE MOVIES

Who said?
'I've aged, Sidney. There are new lines in my face. I look like a brand-new, steel-belted radial tyre.'
(Answer below)

Answer: Maggie Smith scrutinising the mirror in Neil Simon's California Suite

PAUSE FOR THOUGHT

Jill Logan of Farnborough has these thoughts to share:

● *Do not complain that there are thorns on roses. Be thankful there are roses on thorns.*
● *God always answers our prayers but sometimes he says no.*
● *You can shed tears that he has gone, or you can smile because he has lived.*

PIC CREDIT: GORDON LANGSBURY

Watch the birdie!

Take some time out to watch our feathered friends and it could be the beginning of a fascinating hobby

Glance out of your kitchen window and what do you see – shrubs, trees, flowers, a lawn? Very likely, but can you also see some birds? Perhaps there is a Robin singing, a Blackbird foraging on the lawn or a Blue Tit searching a bush for insects.

Birds are our most commonly seen wild creatures and the best place to watch them at close quarters is in your garden – your private patch. Gardens are perfect for anyone starting birdwatching and once you are confident you can learn more about them by watching their behaviour.

Birds have three basic needs:

Food, water and shelter and these are easy to provide. Most gardens have a hedge, a few shrubs or trees or a fence covered by climbers such as clematis, roses or honeysuckle. Any of these will provide shelter for roosting and nesting, or a place to hide if a predator, such as a cat or a Sparrowhawk, is around.

Natural food such as seed heads, pollen, berries, fruit, insects and grubs occur in gardens and if you provide food on a bird table or hanging feeder you will encourage more birds to visit. Water for bathing and drinking can be in a shallow dish – the type of saucer that goes under patio pots is ideal.

Blue, Great and Coal Tits, Robins, Blackbirds, Greenfinches, Goldfinches, Chaffinches visit gardens. If you live near a wood a Great Spotted Woodpecker or a Nuthatch may visit. The countryside is no longer the bird-friendly habitat it used to be, so our gardens are important.

Once common species, such as the House Sparrow and Starling have seriously declined in the last 25 years. So, if you have these in your garden, feed and encourage them and if you spend a few minutes watching them you may be hooked on an activity enjoyed by millions – garden birdwatching.

Carol Debney

The things we miss

Washday

Monday was washday – and who remembers what a performance it was years ago? First, the whitewashed copper kettle had to be heated in the scullery with a fire underneath, started early Monday morning.

And the floor was covered with mini mountains of sorted laundry waiting to be done. Then all the clothes were washed by hand before throwing them into the copper and boiling them.

And stirring this strange Monday 'soup' with a stick, heads grew blurred in clouds of steam and cheeks glowed pink with exertion and heat. Gradually the smell of

laundry on the boil seeped throughout the house.

Now the whites had to be 'blued' in a bath with a bag of Reckitt's Blue to make them come up bright as new. After blueing, out came the mangle, the machine groaning and protesting as item after item was passed between its rollers. And mind your fingers, children!

In dry weather the clothes were pegged out to flap damply in back yards and gardens, or if it rained they were draped around the house. Dad would have to fight his way through a maze of damp sheets when he came home from work!

Memories of washday remain strong, especially for Gwen Downey from Devon who wrote the following poem:

Monday memories

Mum's not the same on Mondays,
Her temper's always frayed,
Amid the steam she's toiling there
With crimson cheeks and harassed air,
The whitewashed copper 'on the boil',
And laundry all around.

Mum's hard to please on Mondays,
She wields the copper stick,
So if you're saucy, woe betide!
You'll get a 'belter' round your hide,
Just leave her to her 'washday blues'
Within her steamy world.

Mum hasn't time on Mondays
To cook a decent meal,
She blues and rinses, mangles hard,
Then staggers, loaded, to the yard,
So don't complain of mash and mince
And pray it doesn't rain!

Mum's not herself on Mondays
From morn till night she toils,
But when in bed, she tucks us snug,
With tender kiss and loving hug,
We're reassured she hasn't changed,
We smile and understand.

Puzzles

Missing links

The three words in each clue have a fourth word in common – and that's your answer. For instance, clue 1 Across gives you the answer SNOW (snowboarding, snowdrop, Peter Snow).

ACROSS
1 ~~Boarding, Drop, Peter (4)~~
4 Cat, File, Right (4)
7 Hand, Pipes, Tea (3)
8 Award, Fame, Military (7)
10 Fast-food, Retail, Sewage (6)
12 Computer, Restaurant, Set (4)
13 Price, Sink, Trust (4)
15 Holy, Last, Marching (6)
19 Class, Drive, False (7)
20 Aboard, Fours, Hold (3)
21 Lever, Pressure, Spare (4)
22 Licence, Running, Show (4)

DOWN
2 Mare, Shift, Stag (5)
3 Blue, Bone, Killer (5)
4 Apple, Spider, Stick (4)
5 Cod, Meal, Rate (5)
6 Decree, Power, Silence (8)
9 Enjoy, Please, Suit (8)
11 Parking, Whole, You (3)
12 Bath, Guard, Pack (3)
14 Coast, Merchant, Tower (5)
16 Ark, Family, Flush (5)
17 Details, Replica, Science (5)
18 Ceiling, Hip, Rambling (4)

Solutions on Page 159

Logic problem

Give your powers of deductive reasoning a work-out.

Present	Sister	Reason for return	Reason for refusal
Scarf			
Socks			
Tie			

Wally and his sisters Dolly, Molly and Polly are notoriously unsentimental about the gifts they exchange, and this January, as ever, saw Wally queuing in the department store to return all his Christmas presents. From the seven clues, can you work out the present he received from each sister, why he wanted to return it, and the reason the shop assistant refused?

1 The tie was a present from Polly.
2 Dolly's present could not be returned because it had been bought in the sale.
3 Molly's was not the present Wally tried to return because of its hideous colour.
4 One present could not be returned because it was old stock.
5 The socks were unwanted for being two sizes too big.
6 Wally tried to exchange one present as he was allergic to its material.
7 The scarf was unreturnable as it had been marked as damaged stock.

Solutions on Page 159

Smile please

By Mary Bristow-Jones

"I'd like you all to smile more," said the manager. "Smile when a customer asks you a question; smile when you give change at the till; smile, smile, smile, even if some customers are rude or glum-looking."

We girls were crowded into his office, summoned there one rainy morning. Nobody felt particularly like smiling non-stop but we all smiled obediently and chorused: "Yes, Mr Partridge."

"Right!" he answered, "Now off back to work." We all smiled from ear to ear until we were outside his door.

"That man!" exploded Angie. "I'm always polite to customers but it would be insincere to smile the way I feel now." Poor Angie had just come through a divorce and was trying to pick up the pieces. Lynne had joined a dating agency and met one unsuitable man after another, which didn't encourage much jollity. And as for me, I was heartbroken and in the depths of despair. Peter had left me after what I'd thought were six happy months. Just said he'd met someone else and that was it!

Smile indeed!

The other girls went off nattering. Angie, Lynne and I were best mates and always stuck together through thick and thin. We all followed Mr P's instruction. He was quite a popular manager – not only that, but he would be walking about the store snooping for non-smilers.

"Oh, my cheeks are aching!" groaned Lynne at the end of the day.

"I'd better get my front tooth crowned," said Angie.

I had now lost my smile and felt more like tears as I went home to a lonely flat.

Next day was as dull and wet as ever. I was in charge of biscuits and chocolates and I had to go up to the storeroom and collect more to fill up some shelves. I met dear old Violet in the service lift. She was one of the early morning cleaners and very energetic with her mop, although in her late seventies. She looked a bit down.

I'd grown used to smiling at everybody and I gave her a large, sunny beam. She smiled back and seemed encouraged to tell me her troubles. She had to go into hospital for an operation and couldn't find anyone to look after her cat, Billy.

I'm a sucker for cats so I said: "D'you think he'd come to me?"

"Would you really have him?" She looked so filled with relief and gratitude that I put my arm around her and said: "Of course I will, Vi. I'll come and fetch him whenever you like."

Angie was sitting smilingly at the checkout, dazzling away while she handed out change. A very tall, French-looking man smiled back at her and asked her if she would accept his business card. He said he was a movie director and was looking for a girl just like her for a film.

"Someone gamine with a broken tooth in front. When you smile eet ees so sweet. Please, please phone."

Angie's smile was now genuine as she looked into his dark eyes and said: "Yes," before he was pushed along by a tutting woman who had unloaded an overflowing trolley.

Lynne was working upstairs in the underwear department and she saw a young man hovering by some slips and examining them with an air of puzzlement.

"Do you need any help?" she asked, smiling.

"Well," he said, half grinning, but looking flummoxed. "My mother said she'd like a slip for her birthday and it's so

"I'm always polite to customers but it would be insincere to smile the way I feel now"

and yowled all the way to my flat but, after hiding behind the sofa for a while, he stalked out and went to his dish. I smiled at him and he seemed to sense my friendliness and came over to be stroked.

A few days later I went to the hospital to see Violet. She was sitting in a chair beside her bed, looking pale, but happy.

'This is my son, Jamie," she said, as a good-looking young man approached with a vase of flowers which he placed on her locker.

'This is Millie," said Violet, and, of course, I smiled at Jamie who smiled back at me.

When the time came for Violet to leave hospital, Jamie and I both took some leave from work and drove her and Billy home. Billy toured around every room to make sure everything was in order.

We called round every day to cook Violet a meal and clean the bungalow and get her settled in bed before we left in the evening. Jamie and I became great friends and as time went by we knew that we wanted to be together forever.

Violet was over-joyed.

We sometimes hear from Angie, who is now a movie actress, and we often visit Lynne and Tom and talk about the old days at the store.

Jamie said: "The first thing I fell in love with was your beautiful smile."

PS We invited Mr Partridge to our wedding.

difficult to choose. There seem to be so many different types. Mum can't get out to shop herself, you see," he added, losing his nervousness as Lynne gently smiled at him.

She asked him about his mum, her size and colour preferences and together they settled on a slip.

"You can always change it if you like," said Lynne.

The young man returned next day but not for a refund; he asked Lynne for a date.

The French director invited Angie out to dinner. She insisted that Lynne went with her as she felt he was a bit too good to be true. But it turned out that he was quite famous and he offered her a small part in his film. Soon

they fell in love and before long they were married and Angie eventually went to live in France.

Lynne's date was called Tom. He took her to meet his mum and then out dancing until 4am. She arrived at work next morning with a smile to beat all smiles! They went out on many dates after that and nowadays live in a neat little house and have twin girls.

Violet received a letter at last, giving the date of her operation, and I went round to her bungalow to collect Billy, an important-looking old tabby. I loaded up my little car with cat food and his litter tray, basket, cushion, toy mouse and teddy bear. He didn't like being in the car

February 2004

A flavour of the month

PIC: REX FEATURES

February may traditionally be the time of giving and receiving gifts from a special sweetheart. But, this year, why not treat yourself to a pampering present?

Rich Christmas food has probably had an effect on your skin and energy levels, so eat plenty of fruit and vegetables (at least five portions a day) to maximise your vitamin, mineral and fibre intake. Also, drink two to three litres of water daily to prevent dehydration, which can zap energy and make skin appear sallow. If you feel thirsty you are already dehydrated.

As the ultimate boost have a new haircut, a manicure, pedicure or a massage.

If you don't want to splash out on a pampering session at a salon, have a go at home. These homemade treats cost almost nothing to make and most of the ingredients will already be in your kitchen cupboards.

● For shiny, glossy hair mix two tablespoons of honey with four tablespoons of olive oil and warm through. Apply to hair and leave for 20 minutes before washing thoroughly.

● Soothe dry skin with a banana face mask. Mash together a banana, 3 tablespoons of honey and a small tub of yoghurt. Apply to face and neck for about 15 minutes before rinsing.

PIC: REX FEATURES

SUNDAY	1	
MONDAY	2	
TUESDAY	3	
WEDNESDAY	4	
THURSDAY	5	5-8 Cheltenham Folk Festival
FRIDAY	6	
SATURDAY	7	
SUNDAY	8	
MONDAY	9	
TUESDAY	10	
WEDNESDAY	11	
THURSDAY	12	
FRIDAY	13	
SATURDAY	14	St Valentine's Day
SUNDAY	15	
MONDAY	16	
TUESDAY	17	
WEDNESDAY	18	

THURSDAY	19	
FRIDAY	20	
SATURDAY	21	
SUNDAY	22	
MONDAY	23	
TUESDAY	24	Shrove Tuesday
WEDNESDAY	25	Ash Wednesday (Lent begins)
THURSDAY	26	
FRIDAY	27	
SATURDAY	28	March YOURS on sale
SUNDAY	29	

PIC: EMAP GARDEN PICTURE LIBRARY

A year in your garden

February can be an awkward one for plants in containers. Chances are we'll see and feel the coldest temperatures of the year, but damage to pots and plants growing in them can be minimised. Moving pots to a frost-free place is the obvious way of keeping things healthy but a little insulation wrapping can work wonders.

Hessian sacking is a great insulator and wrapped around the outside of pots, it will stop a few degrees of frost and could save the plant roots. And that's the reason why plants in containers often die before the same plants growing in the soil. Roots are frozen, wind still blasts over the top of the plant and the whole thing dries up.

If you have a really sensitive plant, you can insulate the inside of the pot. This can be a simple lining of black polythene or bubble insulation.

The containers, too, can be damaged by the winter — cheap, machine manufactured terracotta pots are the first to flake and crack. Sturdier, hand made, but usually more expensive clay pots stand up to the weather better, but plastic rules when it comes to fighting the frost. They never crack, and new ranges are looking more and more like the real thing than ever.

If, after all your insulation tricks, your plants still get frozen solid, it's best to move them to a semi-shaded spot where they can defrost slowly. It's the speed of thawing that often causes damage — you must have experienced mushy magnolia buds at this time of year. A fast thaw means the plant cells rupture and never recover.

But it isn't all doom and gloom, as in a few weeks time spring flicks over on the calendar and plants can wait no longer.

✻ **READER'S TIP** ✻
Sarah Barber in Farnborough always covers her seedlings with a sheet of newspaper. It keeps young seedlings warm enough to survive, but remember to remove the paper once the sun is up in the morning and things start to warm up in the greenhouse.

February 2-8

A DAY TO REMEMBER

Little Nancy on that perfect wedding day in 1932

AT THE MOVIES

Nancy Lowther from Kent was a reluctant bridesmaid...

My mother's cousin, Elsie, was to be married to John, in the summer of 1932, with her two sisters as bridesmaids. Mother was asked if I would be the third. Mother said, 'Yes', I said, 'No!

My friend at school said her sister had been a bridesmaid and was sick afterwards. However, it was a lost cause and the fittings began.

The voile (or vile, as I called it) was too long, too tight, too short, too awful, I thought. White gloves, socks, white buckskin shoes but, worst of all, a Dutch bonnet with little 'wings' on it. I felt very silly in it and hated everything. But came the day...

It was perfect; the sun shone, nobody laughed at me but said I looked very pretty in my outfit – and all the gentlemen twirled me round the dance floor. Best of all, I had a sip of Champagne, lots of strawberries, lashings of ice cream, plus a lovely bracelet from John.

I was never a bridesmaid again. Shame about that, I'd just got the knack of it. Oh, and I wasn't sick – and the bride and groom lived happily ever after!

DID YOU KNOW THAT

The octopus is an expert at camouflage. It can change colour in less than a second.

OUT & ABOUT TO...

The Real Mary King's Close, Edinburgh

PIC: THE CONTINUUM GROUP

As you walk through the City Chambers, through an ordinary wooden door and down some steps in search of Edinburgh's new, underground tourist attraction, it's impossible to imagine what lies ahead. The scene that unfolds before your eyes is 17th century Edinburgh: A guide dressed as a character from the past, who once lived on the close, will lead you down a narrow, pot-holed street where the houses loom up to seven storeys high on either side. Your guide will tell of ghosts and other unfortunate residents, who struggled to subsist in the slum-like conditions of this warren of hidden streets. As the past is brought to life with subtle lighting and sound effects, you'll find out how people really lived. Among those you'll encounter are the Craig family, who were struck down by the plague, and the doctor who treated them, wearing a mask stuffed with sweet-smelling herbs to help cover the smell and ward off the disease.

● *Adults £7, children £5*
● *No children under five; unsuitable for wheelchairs*
Tel: 0870 243 0160 (Internet: www.realmarykingsclose.com)

WHAT'S COOKING?

PIC: HULTON ARCHIVE

▲ Shrove Tuesday in the 1950s and the ladies of Olney, Buckinghamshire toss their pancakes as they race towards the finishing line

Rhubarb Soufflé Omelette
(Serves 1)

- 2 sticks rhubarb, washed and diced
- Juice of ½ orange
- 1 tsp caster sugar
- 2 eggs, separated
- 1 tbs milk
- Finely grated zest of ½ orange
- Butter for frying
- ½ tsp brown sugar
- 1 tbs Greek yoghurt
- 1 tbs flaked almonds
- Icing sugar

1 Poach the rhubarb in orange juice and caster sugar until tender.
2 Whisk the egg yolks, milk and orange zest until stiff. Separately, whisk up the egg whites. Fold the mixtures together carefully.
3 Heat the butter in an omelette pan and pour in the soufflé mixture.
4 Cook over a low heat until the base has set.
5 Sprinkle over the rhubarb, brown sugar and yogurt.
6 Cook for a further 1 minute then flip over to enclose filling. Serve sprinkled with almonds and icing sugar.

PIC: FRESH PRODUCE CONSORTIUM

Top tip
Firmly tap the bottom of your screw-top bottles and containers to make them easier to open.

ON GROWING OLDER
'The best thing about growing older is that it takes such a long time'.

Unknown

MY ADVICE IS...
'If you can't pay for something, you can live quite happily without it'. My mother said this to me when I was 12 – and I've never had a credit card and I always pay by cash or cheque.

Noreen Pratt, Leics

OLD FASHIONED REMEDIES

When we were children, if my brothers or I had a cold, my mum would warm up camphorated oil and rubbed it on our chest, then covered it with an old piece of flannel.

Joan Lewer, London

Dr Henderson replies: Camphor and camphor-like rubs are still available today and remain popular with some people in helping the symptoms of colds and 'flu. The aroma when warmed up is said to help with blocked or stuffy noses. The old piece of flannel was useless here though!

February 9-15

A DAY TO REMEMBER

This was really A night to Remember says Margaret Urban from Cambs…

Today I am quite happy to sit at home watching snooker on TV because my arthritic legs are painful when walking. But in 1995, at the age of 82, I was still able to walk freely and I travelled to the places I hadn't seen. Rome, Sorrento, Assisi, Florence and Venice.

While staying in Rome I joined our happy companions to see 'Rome by night'. After a lovely meal, we sauntered along to see the Trevi Fountain and make a wish.

Passing a group of young Italians who were joking and laughing with their young ladies – and having parked their scooters alongside the fountain – I spotted a beautiful red one.

The longing in my heart to sit on a scooter once more overpowered me – for I have had three different motor scooters in my lifetime and had criss-crossed England many a time.

So I asked the young Romeo if I could sit on it. "Si, si, mama mia," said he, and quick as a flash, one of our companions had her camera ready.

I can hardly describe the happiness I felt on that scooter and then, at the Trevi fountain, I threw in my coin and made a wish.

Now my wish has been granted – I now have transport driving an electric scooter. It's simply heavenly!

Margaret back at the wheel again!

ON GROWING OLDER

'Old age is like everything else. To make a success of it, you've got to start young'.

Fred Astaire

WHAT'S COOKING?

QUICK SNACK
Fluffy Potato Soufflé

(Serves 2)

- 1 lb/450 g cooked potatoes
- 1 leek finely chopped
- Salt and pepper
- Grated nutmeg
- 1 oz/25 g butter
- 3 eggs
- 2 oz/50 g cheese, grated
- 1/4 pt/150 ml cream

1 Sieve the potatoes before mixing with the salt, pepper and nutmeg.
2 Melt the butter and add to the potatoes and lightly fried leeks, then add the beaten egg yolks and the cream. Whisk the whites stiffly and fold lightly into the mixture.
3 Pour into a greased pie-dish or soufflé case and top with grated cheese. Bake in a moderate oven (180°C/350°F/Gas Mark 4) for 30 minutes.

AT THE MOVIES

Who said:
'Well, you look like the kind of angel I'd get. Sort of a fallen angel, aren't you? What happened to your wings?'
(Answer below)

Answer: James Stewart berating his heavenly messenger in Frank Capra's It's A Wonderful Life

OUT & ABOUT TO...

Sunderland Winter Gardens, Sunderland

PIC: SUNDERLAND WINTER GARDENS

Oranges and lemons might seem unlikely residents of Sunderland, but along with bananas, giant yuccas and palm trees they thrive in this glass-roofed urban jungle. A winter garden since Victorian times, it was bombed during World War Two, and has only recently been rebuilt. The spectacular glass and steel building houses more than 1,500 exotic plants from 146 species, arranged in three different tropical 'climates'. The plants have been chosen to appeal to all five senses, and you can follow special trails to discover how plants such as eucalyptus, camphor and ginseng are used for medicinal purposes; and see how tea, coffee, sugarcane and pepper grow.

The best vantage point in the garden is the tree-top walkway – an open-decked area nine metres above the floor, which provides a fabulous view of the park. There are intriguing water features, including a waterfall sculpture, koi carp pool and streams stocked with water-loving plants.

● *Admission is free*
● *Refreshments, gift shop, toilets, wheelchair access, facilities for people with hearing and visual disabilities*
Tel: 0191 553 2323 (Internet: www.twmusums.org.uk/sunderland)

OLD WIVES' TALES

A cure for chilblains: Immerse your feet in a chamber pot early morning. (Preferably one at a time to avoid soaking the carpet).

Dr Henderson replies: Gosh – you're brave if you want to do this. No use at all, and simply anti-social for you and your bedroom carpet!

Top tip

Make a resolution to fix those leaky taps! Just one drip per second wastes more than four litres of water everyday.

DID YOU KNOW THAT

At the Poles, the rainbow is seen as a complete circle.

WHAT A COINCIDENCE

A colleague went on holiday to Bangkok with her husband. On his return, he was called out to a house in north east England to mend a washing machine.

The lady who opened the door was the singer at the hotel where they had been staying. She had been sent home to recover from a bout of flu!

Keith Gregson, Sunderland

PAUSE FOR THOUGHT

'Here are the words of wisdom that I have lived by for a long time', writes Gladys Mitchell, who is 91 and comes from Leicestershire:

Serenity
God grant me the serenity to accept the things I cannot change; Courage to change the things I can and wisdom to know the difference.

February 16-22

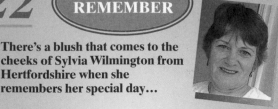

MY ADVICE IS...

'There's no such word as can't'. My granddad told me this and, although some things are impossible for mere mortals, this advice ensured that I never gave up easily!

Cynthia Brown, Suffolk

WHAT'S COOKING?

SUPPER DISH
Fish Parcels
(Serves 4)

- 1 lb/450 g frozen puff pastry
- 1 oz/25 g butter
- ½ lb/225 g cod fillet
- 1 tablespoon chopped parsley
- 1 egg
- Salt and pepper
- Juice of ½ lemon
- Wedges of lemon to serve

1. Roll out pastry thinly. Cut out four 8 in/20 cm squares, place on baking sheet.
2. Melt butter in pan. Add chopped cod plus salt, pepper and lemon juice.
3. Mix well, cover and cook for 5 minutes. Beat the egg, add half to the fish and mix well. Divide the mixture between the pastry squares.
4. Dampen the edges of the pastry and bring the four corners to the centre, pressing well to seal. Brush with remaining egg.
5. Bake in a preheated oven (230°C/450°F/Gas Mark 8) for 10 minutes. Serve with lemon wedges, a piping jacket potato and seasonal vegetables.

Top tip
To make candles burn longer pop them in the freezer for a few hours before use.

There's a blush that comes to the cheeks of Sylvia Wilmington from Hertfordshire when she remembers her special day...

It was the day before I got married. I was 17 and worked as the post girl in a paperware factory.

When I got back from lunch, I got the surprise of my life. My desk was decorated with paper doilies, different colour serviettes, strung together cake cases, even toilet roll paper hung about in big bows. I'd never seen anything like it.

When we'd finished work, my bike was missing and I cried to my friend that it had been stolen. She offered to help me look for it and led me to the back of the bike sheds where I discovered it all done up in doilies and toilet rolls!

As I laughed with relief, the girls jumped out of hiding and threw what must have been a sackful of confetti in the air over my head. I had never seen anything so pretty as the hearts and horseshoes, and silver and gold glinting in the sun.

I cycled home but I scatted confetti everywhere I went. People tooted on their horns and I felt so special.

ON GROWING OLDER

'Years may wrinkle the skin but to give up interest wrinkles the soul'.

Douglas MacArthur

AT THE MOVIES

Who said?
'*I now pronounce you men and wives*'.
(Answer below)

Answer: Ian Wolfe performing the finale wedding in Stanley Donen's Seven Brides For Seven Brothers.

OLD FASHIONED REMEDIES

When we had teenage spots, my mother said we needed, 'a spring clean'. So she did what her mother did, and got a saucer full of black treacle and mixed a teaspoonful of sulphur in it and gave us all a dose. It was horrible but she did give us a boiled sweet afterwards, to soften the blow!

Emily Turton, Widnes

Dr Henderson reples: Ugh! Not only would this have been useless for your teenage acne, but as you say it would have tasted horrible. The boiled sweet would have been better medicine! Treacle and sulphur sounds a frightening combination – don't try it!

WHAT A COINCIDENCE

I was born and brought up in Stockport, Cheshire, then spent two years at secretarial college in Didsbury, Manchester.

In the late '60s I moved to Fife, Scotland and in 1997, enrolled on a new opportunities course at the local college.

One of the courses included a weekly swimming session and one day, chatting to a fellow student, I was astonished to learn that not only was she from a nearby town in Cheshire but had gone to the same secretarial college in Manchester! Gill and I remain good friends to this day.

Carol Massey, Fife

DID YOU KNOW THAT

The discovery of yeast in 6000BC made the production of bread, cheese, beer and wine possible

PIC: NATIONAL RAILWAY MUSEUM

OUT & ABOUT TO...

National Railway Museum, York

If you're looking for somewhere special to take small grandchildren with a penchant for Percy and pals, this A Day Out With Thomas event should be just the ticket (call first to check dates). With plenty of rides to take and familiar friends to see, it's heaven for tiny trainspotters who need to let off steam.

As well as the Thomas experience, you'll be able to make tracks to all the usual attractions, including a replica of Stephenson's Rocket, a section of the Chunnel (Channel Tunnel) and Queen Victoria's royal railway carriage. There's also a collection of 1.4 million photographs dating from the 1850s to the present day, which chart the cultural, social and technological changes sparked by the transport revolution.

● *Admission is usually free; during special events adults £6, concessions and children £4*
● *Refreshments; gift shop; excellent facilities for the disabled (including wheelchairs available for loan)*
Tel: 01904 621261 (Internet: www.nrm.org.uk)

February 23-29

DID YOU KNOW THAT

One issue of a broadsheet newspaper contains around 100,000 words. To read it all, the eyes must travel 1km.

Top tip

Cover the inside of your letterbox flap with a square of material — it'll help keep heat in and draughts out!

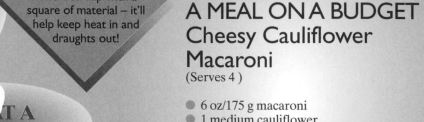

WHAT'S COOKING?

A MEAL ON A BUDGET
Cheesy Cauliflower Macaroni
(Serves 4)

- 6 oz/175 g macaroni
- 1 medium cauliflower
- 1½ oz/37.5 g flour
- 1½ oz/37.5 g margarine
- 1 pt/570 ml milk
- A pinch of dried mixed herbs
- 6 oz/175 g grated cheese

1. Cook the macaroni as instructions on the packet.
2. Cut the cauliflower into small florets and boil until tender. Make a sauce with the margarine, flour and milk and stir in the mixed herbs and 4 oz/100 g of cheese.
3. Place the macaroni in an ovenproof dish, top with cauliflower, and coat with sauce. Sprinkle with the rest of the cheese and brown under a hot grill.

WHAT A COINCIDENCE

I listen to YOURS on tape and a few years ago there was an article in the magazine about a lady who bought an embroidered tablecloth at an auction.

In the 1950s, we lived in Quorn, Leicestershire, but before we moved down south, I started an autograph tablecloth which all my friends signed.

When I heard the item my mind immediately went back to one particular name – Mary Setchfield. Later I was listening to the tape and came to the Bygones section, which listed a Badge Collectors Club. I could hardly believe my ears when the name of the Hon Secretary was read out – Mary Setchfield – and still living in Quorn! Needless to say, I wrote to Mary and we still keep in touch.

Audrey Watson, Surrey

ON GROWING OLDER

'I've given my memoirs far more thought than any of my marriages. You can't divorce a book'.
Gloria Swanson

AT THE MOVIES

Who said?
'And will you be happy, Charlotte?'
'Oh, Jerry, don't let's ask for the moon. We have the stars'.
(Answer below)

Answer: Paul Henreid and Bette Davies reaching a romantic understanding in the last lines of Irving Rapper's Now, Voyager.

OLD WIVES' TALES

Rub yourself with dog oil for aches and pains.

Dr Henderson replies: Dog oil is a rather general term for liniment-type embrocations and there is no question that many people can find these beneficial. However, the current thinking is that it is the actual rubbing or massage itself which causes the benefit rather than the embrocation, although if these warm the skin that can feel pleasant too.

OUT & ABOUT TO...

Anglesey Abbey Gardens & Lode Mill, Lode, Cambridge

Spring is always a joy at the Abbey, thanks to its stunning display of snowdrops. People come from far and wide to admire the collection, which grew almost by accident. When the first Lord Fairhaven laid out the gardens in the 1930s, no expense was spared in creating extensive formal gardens, interspersed with elements of surprise.

In the Seventies, the gardens were devastated by Dutch Elm disease, which killed more than 4,000 mature elms. However, in a stroke of luck, when the gardeners cleared away the debris, they discovered 15 varieties of snowdrop, including an unusual double one with inner petals, which has been named after the present Lord Fairhaven and is called Galanthus Ailwyn. Since then, the collection has gone from strength to strength, and galanthophiles (people who have a passion for snowdrops) have contributed new varieties in return for bulbs – rather like stamp collecting.

There's a circuitous winter walk (open 10.30am-4pm), which follows a gravel path, planted with trees, shrubs and bulbs, chosen for their coloured and textured bark, or winter flowering habits. Look out for the fabulous hyacinths in spring, plus, on the first Saturday each month, you can see the restored watermill in action – it still produces flour.

- *Adults £3.75, children £1.60 (winter prices for the garden only)*
- *Restaurant; shop; plant centre.*
- *Wheelchair access (powered mobility vehicles available); Braille guide.*

Tel: 01223 810080
(Internet: www.nationaltrust.org.uk)

A DAY TO REMEMBER

Our granddaughter is such a joy, writes Jeanne and Charles Gapp from Cambs...

Our only granddaughter, Zoe, was born on April 17, 1982. Her mum had had problems during pregnancy, owing to long-term diabetes, so her birth was our day to remember.

Zoe was so precious and still is, she too having become a diabetic on insulin at 15 months old. She has achieved so much in spite of this and is loved and treasured by us, her grandparents and thankfully lives only 40 minutes' drive away.

Zoe, who allows nothing to hold her back

PAUSE FOR THOUGHT

'This is a verse I have carried in my purse for many years,' writes Enid Dunscombe from Cardiff:

However many burdens
Not of your own making
Have been thrust upon you.
However much grief or trial
You have had to bear; the way
You react is your own decision and
Your own choice.
Free will to make our own choice is what
God gave us.
You may not always be the master of your fate
But remember this, you are always the
Captain of your soul

Sounds like heaven!

Gardening is a sensory experience, so increase your pleasure by making these simple windchimes

Car boot sales, charity shops and flea markets – we all love to have a good browse – and even better if we find a bargain! Odd pieces of cutlery crop up all the time and both spoons and forks can make a great starting point for windchimes.

What you need

Selection of spoons and forks
Clear nylon line
Glass beads
Pliers
Silver charms (from a charm bracelet)
Gas burner
Drill with a metal bit

Method

● Take the cutlery and, using a drill with a metal drill bit, make a small hole in the end of each implement.

● Wearing heat-resistant gloves hold each fork so its prongs are suspended over the flame of the gas burner.

● When the prongs are hot, bend them outwards in different directions (north, south, east and west) using a pair of pliers. These will act as the arms of the windchime from which the chimes can be suspended. Bend the very end of each prong upwards again so that you can tie a length of nylon line to each one securely

● Take the other forks and heat their prongs. When they're hot,

bend them around a glass bead until they hold them tightly.

● Cut several lengths of clear nylon line and tie one end to the prongs of the central fork and the other to the chimes, either a spoon or a fork with a decorative glass bead

● Customise your windchimes with a silver charm (you can buy these for only a few pounds from a jeweller's shop)

● Hang the windchimes where they catch the breeze and enjoy the gentle tinkling sound they make. Now relax.

Gareth Salter

PIC: GA PICTURE LIBRARY

The things we miss

Horses and carts

Before cars clogged the roads and filled the air with fumes, the sight of a horse and cart clopping slowly down the street was common – most things were delivered or collected in this way.

Huge, powerful Shires pulled the brewers' drays loaded with barrels of beer or the coal cart with its lumpy bags. Then there was the open cart, which collected the rubbish and the chariot-shaped vehicle of the milkman, pulled by a pony. It carried a churn or two of fresh milk, with the metal measures and the cans the milk was sold in, hung round the sides, clanking as the milkman passed by. He would stop and dole out a measure of milk for you into the can, or your own jug, before plodding off on his rounds.

Summer saw the arrival of the ice cart, which delivered huge blocks to the butchers and to the sweetshops that made ice cream.

The baker had a covered cart with high sides, drawn by a small horse. As you went up to it your nostrils would be filled with the heavenly smell

PIC: HULTON ARCHIVE

of freshly baked bread and as the baker handed you your loaf, it was often still warm from the oven.

Then there were the handcarts: Fishmongers had big, flat ones, drawn by a small donkey or horse, and piled high with sprats or other fish. Housewives would go out into the street with their plates on which he would weigh out a pound of fish.

Even what the horses left behind was useful. Manure was quickly scraped up with a bucket and shovel by those gardeners eager to give their rose bushes a boost.

Memories of grandma

Maureen Spring loved her grandma but wishes she'd known her better. Now she's a grandma herself and knows what joy she and her granddaughter bring each other

Whenever I think of my grandma (which is, surprisingly, often since I became a grandmother myself) the first thing that comes to mind is a corset.

Not her grey-white hair, the natural curls stretched out straight into the tight little bun in the nape of her almost non-existent neck (which I've inherited – thanks, gran) or her round rosy-cheeked story-book granny face.

Though, on second thoughts, it wasn't as story-book as all that because she rarely smiled; when she did allow the corners of her mouth to flick upwards, I remember now, how her eyes stayed sad. I wish I knew why. I wish she was still here so that I could ask her. I know nothing about her life, her longings or the reason for those sad eyes.

Mind you, it could have been the corsets. Grandma was short, rather stout and softly bosomed ,but there the softness abruptly ended. From bust to just below her hips she was rigid. It was like cuddling a large stone pillar, even stiffer where the whalebone supports stuck out. I daresay they stuck in as well but as a small child, anxious for a cuddle, my prime concern was finding something pliable enough to cling on to so I wouldn't slip off her narrow little lap. One memorable day I clutched a bosom. "You mustn't touch ladies there," she said softly, removing my hand and holding it.

I knew she wore corsets – or stays as she called them. I'd seen them every Monday, palest pink and skeletal, on our clothes-line.

I was only three years old when grandma came to live with us. She had our middle bedroom as a bedsit. A small room with her bed, chest of drawers and a dressing table cluttered with mementoes of her life.

Every opportunity I had I was in there, fiddling with her things, trying on the wire-framed spectacles, making her dainty porcelain ladies play ring-a-roses, spilling face powder, holding the gold pocket watch that had belonged to the granddad I never knew, to my ear to listen to the strong heartbeat of its tick. Having a tantrum when she took it out of my hand to place it carefully back on the lace-edged mat where it lay next to a faded snapshot of him in uniform. I wish I could ask her how they met; had she loved him very much? And did she sometimes still sit and weep with her memories? I'd really like to know that now.

She didn't often go out, my grandma. She sat for hours in her armchair quietly reading while I stood behind her on a footstool un-pinning her bun letting the long wavy hair cascade down her back so I could endlessly brush and plait it or pile it on top of her head to make a pony tail tied with ribbons from mine.

I have that footstool in my bedroom; the gold brocade covering a little more faded now, and that tear I made with my sandal buckle is fraying badly. I was 'showing off' as mum used to call it, in other words, screaming like a banshee while grandma held my nose and shoved the spoonful of cough mixture into my wide open mouth. So shocked, I fell off the stool into a heap on gran's pom-pommed slippers. Very wise, my grandma. She knew mum's gentle persuasion would never work on such a wilful child. However, I do remember cuddling the corsets for an especially long time afterwards though.

I hope my new granddaughter will remember me as wise when she's grown up. I'd like that. Most of all I want her to know me. Not only as the grandma who whispered: "Who's grandma's precious girl?" in her ear every time we met.

No, I want her to know the grandma who pretended to be the dragon or fairy godmother talking to her Cinderella, the grandma who played Snakes and Ladders 25 times and only won once, who sat curled up in a plastic Wendy House on boiling hot summer afternoons and made up stories about her and Princess Rhiannon the Welsh rabbit. The Grandma who longs for her husband to have lived to see his grandchild dancing in fairy wings.

Perhaps, she'll recall these childhood scenes – just as I'm doing these days. When she's a little older I shall tell her stories of my life. Where I went, what I thought about, boyfriends I thought I loved and how I fell head over heels in love with her the first moment I saw her face.

My granddaughter is going to know the real me. The only thing missing will be a corset.

March 2004

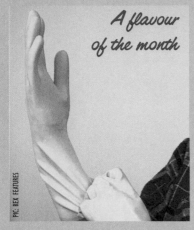

A flavour of the month

PIC: REX FEATURES

Roll up your sleeves and grab the rubber gloves, the dusters and the polish – March is the month for your house's annual MOT!

A good spring clean is essential and most of us are guilty of hoarding but don't be afraid to let go of items you don't want. As a rule, if you haven't touched it for six months you probably won't again! Donate your unwanted items to charity or hire a stall at a car boot sale and sell them.

You don't need to invest in expensive cleaning fluids and utensils to get your house squeaky clean. Some of the traditional methods are still the best. White vinegar, salt and baking soda all make economical cleaning agents. Try these…

● Clean windows with a mixture of white vinegar and water with a squirt of liquid soap.

● Clean out the kitchen sink with an abrasive solution of 50g/2oz table salt to 600ml/1 pint water.

● To shift hard water deposits from the base of bathroom taps, scrub gently with an old toothbrush dipped in vinegar.

● Treat your mould and mildew with neat white vinegar. Leave for half an hour before wiping off.

● To remove stains on your carpets, sprinkle with baking soda. Leave for a minute and vacuum up.

MONDAY	1	St David's Day
TUESDAY	2	
WEDNESDAY	3	
THURSDAY	4	
FRIDAY	5	
SATURDAY	6	
SUNDAY	7	7-10 Crufts Dog Show, NEC, Birmingham
MONDAY	8	
TUESDAY	9	
WEDNESDAY	10	
THURSDAY	11	
FRIDAY	12	
SATURDAY	13	
SUNDAY	14	
MONDAY	15	
TUESDAY	16	
WEDNESDAY	17	St Patrick's Day (Bank Holiday in N Ireland)
THURSDAY	18	

FRIDAY	*19*	
SATURDAY	*20*	
SUNDAY	*21*	Mothering Sunday
MONDAY	*22*	
TUESDAY	*23*	
WEDNESDAY	*24*	
THURSDAY	*25*	
FRIDAY	*26*	
SATURDAY	*27*	
SUNDAY	*28*	British Summer Time begins, clocks go forward
MONDAY	*29*	April YOURS on sale
TUESDAY	*30*	
WEDNESDAY	*31*	

PIC: EMAP GARDEN PICTURE LIBRARY

A year in your garden

You can keep your cuckoos, because primulas are the true harbingers of spring. Sitting all winter, buds at the ready, all they need is a few warm days and, kapow, the delicate yellow flowers burst forth and we're on our way. Cowslips are one of the nation's favourite flowers, with the rosettes of green leaves supporting the stalks of yellow flowers. Oxlips have collections of yellow blooms that are deliciously scented. But the primula show doesn't stop there, as there are many other varieties in this amazing group of plants.

Auriculas are real showstoppers, and there are two main types. Show auriculas, once the doyenne of cotton workers in Lancashire, have unbelievably beautiful blooms in a variety of colours. Look out for the sensational 'Lucy Lockett' with her yellow and white blooms, and try to get any of the rich velvets in red, purple and green. Border auriculas are equally good-looking, but don't mind being bunged in the border and left to fend for themselves.

Then, of course, you have the blousy blooms of polyanthus. Produced on tall stalks, the oranges, reds, yellows or pinks will add zest to any flagging container, not to mention dull borders.

Looking after primulas isn't difficult if you remember most are natives of woodlands or at least have a parent who once lived there. Semi shade is best and plenty of water is a necessity. Drainage is important as the roots soon rot in waterlogged conditions. And if you're going to have a go at showing auriculas, please keep water and your fingers off the leaves. That powder, or farina, is beloved of auricula growers and it would be a shame to ruin the overall appearance of these superb plants.

✳ READER'S TIP ✳
Frank Sealy in Birmingham is a dervish when it comes to deadheading. Picking off flowers as soon as they fade is a sure way to encourage the plants to keep producing more blooms. Unless, of course, you want to collect seed from your own plants.

March 1-7

A DAY TO REMEMBER

Let me out, shouted Beryl Watts…

My husband was sitting reading, so I decided to go down the garden and tidy the greenhouse. As I shut the door behind me, the bolt dropped down, locking me inside.

After about an hour my husband — looking down the garden and seeing me still in the greenhouse working (so he thought!) — decided to have a bath. Three quarters of an hour later, he came down to see what I was doing, only to find me in tears, very hot, nothing to sit on except the floor and desperate to get out!

We laugh about it now but it wasn't funny at the time!

AT THE MOVIES

Who said?
'I wanted to marry her when I saw the moonlight shining on the barrel of her father's shotgun'.
(Answer below)

Answer: Eddie Albert explaining his sudden liking for matrimony in Fred Zinnemann's Oklahoma!

DID YOU KNOW THAT

In a lifetime, an average person eats 50,000kg of food.

Top tip

Attach a paperclip to the end of your sticky tape to make the end easier to find.

OUT & ABOUT TO…

The Judge's Lodging, Presteigne, Mid Wales.

The Judge's Lodging was described as 'the most commodious and elegant apartments for a judge in all England and Wales' by Lord Chief Justice Campbell when he stayed there in the 1850s, and when you visit you'll see that little has changed since his time. The house, along with its gas-lit servants' quarters, kitchens, damp, rat-infested cells and vast, echoing courtroom – has been painstakingly restored to its former glory.

You can wander through the judge's apartments, study his books and sit in his chair – and even pump water in the kitchen. With an audio tour of voices from the past, featuring actor Robert Hardy, it's easy to conjure up a vision of times gone by. You'll find out about the rural Radnorshire Constabulary, and hear the tragic tale of Mary Morgan, reputedly the last woman to be hanged in Wales. Gripping stuff – and it's set in the town of Presteigne, which boasts beautiful countryside and has recently been hailed as one of the top ten places to live in Britain.

● *Adults £3.95, concessions and children £2.95, people with disabilities free*
● *Gift shop*
Tel: 01544 260650 (Internet: www.judgeslodging.org.uk)

▲ It's Mothering Sunday in 1955 and a little girl is about to give Mummy a kiss and surprise her with a bunch of flowers

OLD FASHIONED REMEDIES

This is a cough mixture that we used to make up: 2oz glycerine, 2 drops essence of peppermint, 2 drops Ipec wine, ¼lb honey. Add one pint of boiling water to it.

Christine E Touhig, Nottingham

Dr Henderson replies: This is not bad advice at all really. Ipec wine was known as a cough suppressant and the honey and glycerine would help to soothe tickly coughs and sore throats, too. I still hear of this remedy being used sometimes these days and have no problems with it if I do.

MY ADVICE IS...

'Learn to hold your tummy in'. I was told if I got used to doing that, my tummy would always be flat. I taught all my four daughters the same thing.

Mrs D Moore, Co Durham

WHAT'S COOKING?

Banana and Date Bread
(Serves 8-10)

- 4 oz/100 g plain flour
- 4 oz/100 g wholemeal plain flour
- 1 tsp baking powder
- 4 oz/100 g butter or margarine
- 3 oz/75 g soft brown sugar
- 4 oz/100 g pitted dates, chopped
- 1 lb/450 g ripe bananas
- 2 (size 2) eggs, beaten

1 Heat the oven to 180°C/350°F/Gas Mark 4. Grease and line a 2 lb/1 kg loaf tin with greaseproof paper.
2 Sift the flours and baking powder into a bowl, rub in the butter until the mixture has a fine texture.
3 Stir in the sugar and dates. Peel the bananas and mash, add to the dry ingredients with the eggs. Mix together until well blended and the mixture has a soft consistency. Spoon into the prepared tin and spread level.
4 Bake for 1-1¼ hours until risen and golden. Cool for 10 minutes before turning out on to a cooling rack. Store for 24 hours before slicing.

PIC: FRESH PRODUCE CONSORTIUM

ON GROWING OLDER

'The secret of staying young is to live honestly, eat well and lie about your age'.

Lucille Ball

March 8-14

OUT & ABOUT TO...

Kew Gardens Orchid Festival, Royal Botanic Gardens, Richmond, Surrey

PIC: KEW GARDENS. DIGITAL IMAGES.

With their sensuous, exotic looks, orchids have always inspired passion, and in Victorian times, the people who sought out these rare plants were renowned for their tales of derring-do in the face of botanical adversity.

In mid-March (phone first to check dates), The Princess of Wales Conservatory will be turned into a steamy tropical paradise for Kew Gardens' 10th annual Orchid Festival. The colourful display will include half a million orchids – hanging from trees, gathered around rock pools and peeping out from behind the foliage. There will also be an exhibition of Victorian orchid hunters' illustrations, letters and paintings, plus fascinating stories about their hunting trips in dangerous locations.

● *Entry to the exhibition is free, as are guided tours of the orchids*
● *There will also be two orchid evenings (£15 per person; call for dates and details), which will include a glass of wine, canapés and access to a shop selling a wide range of orchids.*
Tel: 020 8332 5000

Top tip

A dropped egg is easy to pick up if you sprinkle it with plenty of salt, which will absorb much of the liquid and make it easy to scoop.

WHAT A COINCIDENCE

On a visit to Pitlochry Theatre, my attention was drawn to one of the props, a wedding group photograph on the wall of the set. The more I looked at it, the more familiar it became.

After the show, I asked to see the manager and I was proved right! The picture was of my late aunt's wedding, at which I was the tiny four-year-old flower girl. The wedding took place in 1931 and I am the only one alive from the group.

The manager thought the picture may have been bought from a house clearance sale room in Dundee; and later he sent it to me. Our friends who were with us that night were very impressed with my sharp eyes!

Isobel Gay, Perthshire

OLD WIVES' TALES

Eating green potatoes can poison you.

Dr Henderson replies: Poison? No. Best to avoid? Yes. A simple truth in this one – eat your fruit and vegetables as fresh as possible to get the maximum benefit out of them, and green potatoes are obviously not this.

WHAT'S COOKING?

QUICK SNACK
Peppery Welsh rabbit
(Serves 2)

- ¼ red pepper, finely sliced
- 1 tsp mixed mustard
- Few drops of Worcester sauce
- 4-6 oz/110-175 g grated strong cheese
- Salt and pepper
- 1 oz/25 g margarine
- 1 level tbs flour
- 5 tbs milk
- 4 slices of buttered toast

1. Heat the fat in a pan and stir in the flour. Cook for several minutes, stirring well.
2. Add the milk and stir well over the heat until a smooth thick mixture, then add the mustard, pepper, Worcester sauce, cheese and a good pinch of salt and pepper.
3. Spread on the slices of buttered toast and grill until golden brown. Serve immediately with salad.

PAUSE FOR THOUGHT

'A lady doesn't smoke, drink or swear. My father gave me these words of wisdom', writes I E Joel from Essex. *'I've never smoked, I drink very little but must admit to the odd swear word or two – but not very bad ones!'*

DID YOU KNOW THAT

A law in the State of Indiana, USA, prohibits people from travelling on a bus within four hours of eating garlic.

AT THE MOVIES

Who said?
'Mr Kane was a man who got everything he wanted and then lost it. Maybe Rosebud was something he couldn't get or something he lost… No, I guess Rosebud is just a piece in a jigsaw puzzle – a missing piece'.
(Answer below)

Answer: William Alland giving up on the mystery of Orson Welles in his Citizen Kane.

A DAY TO REMEMBER

Ivy Wood from Powys remembers a day from her childhood…

Ivy, the little girl who couldn't tell a lie

I was brought up as a child by my grandparents and before I started school, I had a fall and had a very bad knee for a long time.

During that period, in 1927, the then Prince of Wales came to open the new bridge over the River Trent at Gunthorpe. My grandfather wanted to take me, so he borrowed a pushchair with a carpet bag seat and off we went.

I don't remember the Prince but I do remember a gentleman coming up to us and saying: "Hello Bill, this must be the little girl who never tells a lie." To this day I just cannot tell a lie.

March 15-21

Top tip

To conserve heat, erect shelves above radiators – it helps direct warm air into the room as it rises.

MY ADVICE IS...

'Take one step and one day at a time'. Words to remember when you are going through difficult days.

Mrs L Carter, Surrey

A DAY TO REMEMBER

A wedding far away for Ivy Spavins of Cirencester...

In March 1999 my late husband Leonard and I travelled to Seoul in South Korea to see our eldest son, Lee, marry Mihee, a Korean girl.

Although the bride wore a Western dress, she asked me if, like her mother, I would wear a Korean dress. I was honoured and the dress was made in a few days after we arrived.

Although the ceremony was in Korean, it was then immediately repeated in English for our benefit, and as neither we nor the bride's parents could speak one another's language, we smiled and bowed. Later I sent a letter, to be translated, to say how much we loved and welcomed Mihee to our family.

Top: Bride Mihee with her mother-in-law Ivy, both looking radiant
Above: The happy bride and groom, Mihee and Lee

DID YOU KNOW THAT

False teeth were made from ivory, whalebone or porcelain in the early 1800s.

WHAT'S COOKING?

SUPPER DISH
Piped Chicken and Potato Pie
(Serves 4)

- 1 large packet instant potato
- 2 oz/50 g Edam cheese, grated
- 1 oz/25 g butter
- Eight pieces of chicken
- 1 large tin condensed vegetable soup

1 Fry the chicken in the butter until brown. Transfer to a heatproof dish. Add the soup and quarter can of water.
2 Mix well, cover the dish and oven cook for 30 minutes (190°C/375°F/Gas Mark 5).
3 Make up the potato as directed on the packet. Put into a piping bag and pipe over the top of the chicken mixture. Sprinkle with cheese.
4 Grill until the top is golden brown.

AT THE MOVIES

Who said?
'You know what your trouble was Willie? You always took the jokes too seriously. They were just jokes. We did comedy on the stage for 43 years. I don't think you enjoyed it once.'
(Answer below)

Answer: George Burns berating his former partner Walter Matthau in Herbert Ross's The Sunshine Boys

PIC: CUMBERLAND PENCIL MUSEUM DIGITAL IMAGES.

OUT & ABOUT TO...

Cumberland Pencil Museum, Greta Bridge, Keswick, Cumbria.

Did you know the first pencils ever made were produced in Keswick in about 1550, following the discovery of Cumberland graphite (used for the pencil lead)? A real draw on a wet afternoon in the Lake District, this museum takes you on a journey through the history of pencils and pencil making.

The shepherds who originally found lead used it for marking sheep. Pencil making quickly sprang into a cottage industry, and the first factory opened in 1832, beginning the long tradition of Derwent pencils, now regarded as one of the best brands of fine art pencils in the world. You can walk through a replica of a graphite mine; watch a video extract from Raymond Briggs' animated cartoon The Snowman, which was drawn with Cumberland products; see the world's longest pencil; and try brass rubbing and other artistic techniques.

● *Adults £2.50, concessions and children £1.25*
● *Gift shop; wheelchair access. No café on site, but the museum is just five minutes from the town centre*
Tel: 017687 73626

OLD FASHIONED REMEDIES

Surgical spirit applied between the toes will cure the itching caused by athlete's foot. And for 'digestive therapy', stir a pinch of cayenne pepper into a small glass of hot water. Sweeten with a teaspoon of honey and swallow.

Margaret Rowling, County Durham

Dr Henderson replies: Odd though it may sound, surgical spirit undoubtedly has helped patients of mine with nasty cases of athlete's foot infection.

With the digestive tip, hot water has long been known to ease indigestion in some people and this is why this remedy may work, although I suspect the pepper is of little use in this mixture.

WHAT A COINCIDENCE

Margarita-Kathleen as a young girl

It had been a boiling hot day during World War Two and my friend and I couldn't sleep indoors after coming off ATS night duty, so we went into Kensington Gardens.

Two Canadian soldiers started talking to us and one of them remarked how alike his mate and I looked. When he told me his name was LeRoy, I was amazed because my surname was King, and his name was a corruption of the French for King, le roi.

We compared pay books and our descriptions were exactly the same: Height, 5 ft 8½ in; hair, fair; eyes, hazel. We were born on the same day, June 1, 1921 and found our likes and dislikes very similar. He called me 'Twinny' all afternoon.

Neither my friend and I thought of keeping in touch but I often wonder what happened to Charles Le Roy, my 'twin'.

Margarita-Kathleen Abbott, Cambs

ON GROWING OLDER

'There are three signs of old age. The first is your loss of memory. The other two I forget'.
Unknown

March 22-28

PAUSE FOR THOUGHT

Pam Lawrance from Leicestershire goes back to her schooldays: 'In 1947 one of my teachers wrote in my autograph book:

If a task is once begun
Never leave it, till it's done
Be the labour great or small
Do it well or not at all.

'This has stayed with me all these years, and I quoted this to my children and as they grew older they knew what I was going to say, so often finished these words of wisdom with me'.

OLD WIVES' TALES

Everyone knows that cracking your knuckles gives you arthritis.

Dr Henderson replies: Everyone seems to, and everyone is, unfortunately, wrong! This is a very common one that has in fact been looked at in a little detail by the medical establishment, and there is no proven link whatsoever between cracking your knuckles and developing arthritis in them. A genuine old-wives' tale this one!

Top tip

Rub soap along the hinges to silence a creaky door.

OUT & ABOUT TO...

Dymock Woods, Gloucestershire

In mid-March during the 1930s, the area between the villages of Newent, Dymock and Ledbury was described as the Golden Triangle and special trains ran from London, packed with tourists keen to see the stunning display of wild daffodils.

Not called narcissi for nothing, these stunning yellow blooms now form the focus of the Daffodil Way, a circular walk from Dymock which takes in a wealth of woods and orchards, ponds and streams, meadows and fields. The walk covers ten miles in total, but don't worry if you're not up to it – simply get a friend to pick you up after a couple of miles, then head back to Dymock. In this pretty village surrounded by rolling hills, you can enjoy a well-deserved drink

PIC: REX FEATURES

at the village pub. The Norman church is also worth a look – a corner of it is dedicated to a display on the famous Dymock poets – Rupert Brook, John Drinkwater, Lascelles Abercrombie and Wilfred Wilson Gibson, who lived and wrote in the area before the World War One.

● *For a leaflet about the Daffodil Way walk, write (enclosing stamps to the value of 50p) to Newent Tourist Information Centre, 7 Church Street, Newent, Gloucestershire GL18 1PU or tel: 01531 822468*

● *During the daffodil season, home-made teas are available at Kempley Village Hall, just off the Daffodil Way*

WHAT A COINCIDENCE

My sister had left England for a new life in Australia, selling her lovely home named Summer Place – a tune that was always a favourite with her. Many years later she died and I was unable to go out for her funeral. Consequently, I felt that I had never wished her a proper farewell.

Some time passed and I was able to visit Australia. I asked my sister's grown-up children to show me where their mother's funeral had taken place. Just as we entered the gate of the crematorium, we realised that the tune being played on the car radio was Summer Place. It was unbelievable but very poignant and, having seen her memorial plaque in the garden of remembrance, I felt I had at last said a fond farewell.

Shirley Read, Bucks

ON GROWING OLDER

'Old age comes at a bad time'.

Unknown

DID YOU KNOW THAT

The first practical submarine was invented in America in 1776.

WHAT'S COOKING?

A MEAL ON A BUDGET
Perfect Pizzas
(Serves 1)

- 2 crumpets
- 1 tomato
- Pinch of mixed dried herbs
- Salt and pepper
- 1 oz/25 g cheese, grated
- 4 anchovy fillets

1 Toast the crumpets on both sides.
2 Slice the tomato and place on the crumpets. Sprinkle with herbs and season with salt and pepper.
3 Place the cheese on the tomato and top with the anchovy fillets.
4 Grill until the cheese is bubbling.

A DAY TO REMEMBER

Sheila (below left) achieving her dream, with her friend Joyce

Sheila Pottinger of South Shields gets into the saddle…

I collect Beswick horses and have quite a collection. But I've always wanted to ride a real horse.

Eventually, on my 73rd birthday my friend Joyce took me on a surprise visit to a riding school. I'm partially disabled but with help I got into the saddle – and here I am sitting on a lovely horse. I felt like Princess Anne!

AT THE MOVIES

Who said?
'Then close your eyes and tap your heels together three times. And think to yourself, There's no place like home'.
(Answer below)

Answer: Billie Burke telling Judy Garland how to get home to Kansas in Victor Fleming's The Wizard Of Oz

The nesting instinct

When is the best time and where is the right place to put up a nestbox? Carol Debney gives us the answers

PIC: BIRDWATCHING

The nesting season is a secretive time when birds are busy with one of the most important aspects of their lives – mating, egg-laying and rearing their chicks. Usually this begins in late March or April when the weather warms up, and is timed to coincide with the hatching of insects and caterpillars to feed the nestlings.

Birds build their nests in hedges, bushes, holes in trees, old buildings, under the eaves and in the roof space. Different species have different needs but, if you'd like them to breed in your garden, a nestbox may entice them.

Nestboxes come in all shapes and sizes but the most common type of box is a closed one with a hole in the front for Blue or Great Tits or an open-fronted box which is the kind Robins and Spotted Flycatchers prefer.

Place your box in a sheltered spot away from the prevailing wind and where it will not get too much sun. Also make sure it is not accessible to cats. Some cover from a tree or a climbing plant is a good idea. Then just leave well alone. It may take some time – perhaps, even a year or so – for birds to discover it but when they do you'll see some fascinating bird behaviour and may even witness the fledglings leave the box.

Even when the birds have left you should not disturb the box until the autumn. Then you can clear out the old nesting material and see if the box needs any minor repairs. Woodcrete boxes are excellent and need little maintenance except cleaning. Use gardening gloves and take care when cleaning boxes as they may contain parasites and insects.

It's a good idea to erect boxes in the later autumn. This allows birds to find them before the nesting season and also to use them for roosting during the cold winter nights.

The things we miss

Childhood foods

Dripping
Just thinking of the tastes and smells of your youth brings back vivid memories, especially for the foods you can't find now. Remember thick doorsteps of crusty bread plastered with beef dripping and a sprinkling of salt? Under the opaque white fat was a layer of delicious, rich, brown jelly. The two would mingle as you spread them on bread or toast, browned in front of the fire on the end of a long toasting fork. The taste of that just-melting dripping would be worth the red face you had to endure to get the toast golden-brown.

Muffins
If you wanted muffins to spread your dripping on, you had to catch the muffin man as he went on his rounds on Sunday afternoons in time for tea. He would walk up and down the streets with his tray balanced on his head covered by a white cloth, and ringing his bell to attract customers.

Broken biscuits
Buying biscuits was a pleasure; you would go to the local shop and choose your selection from large jars with glass lids. You could pick and mix the biscuits to make up a pound, which was handed over in a paper bag. Nothing was wasted, so if you couldn't afford whole biscuits you could buy broken ones at a third of the price.

Ice cream
Every child would stop their games as soon as they heard the sound of the Wall's 'Stop Me And Buy One' ice cream man's bell. He would ride by on his bike with the huge cold compartment on the front filled with frozen treats (if you could persuade your mum to give you the money!) There was Snowcream or Snowfruit, a triangular lolly in a blue and white checked wrapper.

PIC: HULTON ARCHIVE

Skeleton

With just the bare bones of a grid, see if you can work out the grid pattern, which is fully symmetrical, and complete the crossword.

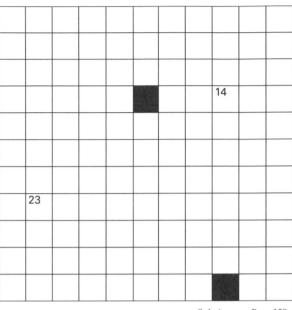

ACROSS
2   Planet's course
6   Block of bread
7   Ship's steering apparatus
8   Riotous comedy
11 Collar extension
13 Likeness
16 Judge
17 Pole
18 Spike of corn
19 Muslim month of fasting
22 Soft brushed leather
24 Avoid paying
26 Lower leg joint
28 Profound
29 Remainder
30 Secret meeting

DOWN
1   Duty list
2   Bid
3   Drinking venue
4   Topic
5   Stopper
9   Egg-white
10 Stronghold
11 Nocturnal primate
12 Army chaplain
14 Amphitheatre
15 Spooky
20 Alter to suit
21 Ward off
23 Second-hand
25 Office table
27 Essential

Solutions on Page 159

Cryptograms

In a cryptogram, each letter of the alphabet is substituted by another. Can you crack these coded quotes to reveal two remarks by the actor Peter O'Toole about his work and the film world? Each quote is in a different code and, to help you start, we can tell you that the words 'AND' and 'ARE' can be found in both.

1   NJPDP HDPL'N HLW DPHY BQITP BHZPDR HLW BQDP. NJP OXRTLPRR TR DXL OW NJP UQDLGYHZPR BPL HLC NJPW HDP QLYW TL TN GQD NJP KTDYR.

2   B'I CP OPLOWLCBPOW. LNBR BR IS QXM. LNOWO CWO IOP, YXIOP, VNBFAWOP CPA RXFABOWR MOBPJ TBFFOA WBJNL PXY. IS QXM BR LX VNOWW LNOI ZE.

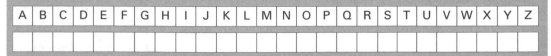

Short story

The dream house

By M E Northwood

Ruby heard the door-bell, moments after she had plunged her hands into the gooey mixture of flour and lard.

"Just a minute," she called, staring at her sticky hands in dismay. "I'll be right there."

Waddling to the front door, she peered cautiously through the gap between the door and the safety chain.

"Yes, can I help you?" She suspiciously eyed the solemn individual standing on her doorstep.

"Hi, I'm Sue Bingham," the woman said, curtly. "I rang yesterday. We arranged to see the house."

"Oh, yes, how silly of me!" Ruby took the chain off. "Come in, come in. I'd totally forgotten about it." She clapped a hand to her head and deposited a sticky blob of white goo on her forehead.

"And I can't blame the menopause, at my time of life!"

Her visitor, refraining from comment, stared distractedly at the gooey forehead and sticky hands.

"Well, you'd better go on through." Ruby said.

The young woman smiled uncomfortably, stepped inside and ran a critical eye over the hallway decor.

Ruby ushered her guest into the living room, hastily wiping her hands down the front of her apron.

"Take a seat, dear," she said, indicating the worn sofa. "Would you like a cup of tea?"

The woman, now perched uneasily on the edge of the sofa, nodded: "That'll be fine, thank you."

Ruby heard the disdain in the woman's voice.

'Better get my best china out', she thought, as she plodded down the hallway. 'I bet she's never drunk out of a mug in her entire life!'

Within the solitude of the kitchen, Ruby quickly ran a comb through her hair and removed the apron from her ample hips. She felt under-dressed in her old clothes and slippers, compared to her smart, slender visitor.

'Remember those evening classes, Ruby! You must be more assertive', she silently chastised herself, as she returned to the lounge. 'You mustn't let this woman unnerve you'.

"Sorry, I didn't introduce myself," she said, holding out her hand for a formal handshake. "I'm Ruby."

The woman, pleased by the lack of pastry mix, took the proffered hand.

"Pleased to meet you."

There was silence; both women, having no common ground, were suddenly lost for words.

"Well, I guess you could take a look at the house now, if you like. Or do you want to finish your tea, first?"

"No, that would be fine." Sue replied. "I mean, I'd like to look at the house now, if that's all right with you."

"Yes, yes, of course!" Ruby laughed nervously. "Well, this is the lounge, as you can see. It's quite a good-sized room I think. Plenty of space in here, for all the family!"

Sue nodded in agreement,

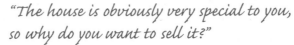

FOR SALE

trying to stifle a yawn. Ruby pretended not to notice.

"Moving on then, to the kitchen. As you can see, it's all in working order," Ruby continued. "You'll find all the mod cons in here! Washing machine, fridge, cooker…"

"Am I right in thinking that all your furniture is included in the price?" Sue asked.

"That's right, dear. What you see is what you get!" Ruby smiled, flicking a switch on the wall to illuminate the kitchen.

"The whole house was rewired only last year and most of the light fittings have been replaced."

"Well, that's good," Sue commented, looking at the kitchen table, neatly set with plates and glasses.

Ruby studied the woman's face for a sign of approval. The thought of all her possessions being replaced filled her with dread.

'It's taken you years to accumulate all this, Ruby', she thought sadly to herself. 'Too many memories are locked inside these walls. Are you sure you can bring yourself to sell it?'

"The house is obviously very special to you, so why do you want to sell it?"

"I suppose this is the main bedroom," Sue prompted.

"Oh, sorry! I was miles away!" Ruby smiled wistfully. "Yes, you're right, of course. This is the main bedroom. The wallpaper has been replaced in here and the same carpet has been laid in all three bedrooms."

"How quaint!"

Ruby noted the hint of sarcasm and sniffed.

"Well, it's good quality and durable. It should last for a good few years!"

"Oh, look at the crib in the corner!" Sue exclaimed, her manner softening slightly. "My daughter would love this!" She gave it a little push, then smiled as the delicately laced cot rocked gently from side to side.

Ruby smiled too. Memories of buying the cradle all those years ago filled her head.

"Forgive me for asking," Sue questioned, "but the house is obviously very special to you, so why do you want to sell it?"

"My husband Frank and I are retiring to Spain. He has arthritis and we thought the sunshine would help."

"Oh, I see," Sue smiled. "How nice. I hope I can do the same thing, some day."

Ruby found herself warming to the young woman before her. Suddenly they were chatting like old friends. Forgetting her fears, Ruby regaled her visitor with several anecdotes about the house; personal stories, dating back almost fifty years.

As the two women finally returned to the sofa, Ruby was overcome with nostalgia.

Sipping stewed tea from her best china teacups, she sensed her visitor was unimpressed with the drink, but happy with the house.

"Now," Sue began, "I'm honestly enchanted by the house and I'm prepared to put in an offer."

Ruby faltered, unsure of how to handle the situation and uncertain now that she could actually part with her pride and joy. There were a lifetime's memories in the house.

"I'm glad you like it. It's always been special to me and I must admit, I'm rather averse to selling it. But, I can't take it with me, can I?"

"I quite understand," Sue replied. "Ultimately, it will be my decision if I decide to buy, but, obviously I have to take my daughter, Ellen, into consideration," she explained.

"Oh, of course!" Ruby agreed.

"Naturally, it's really important that she likes the house."

"Naturally."

A short while later, as Sue finally walked down the driveway, Ruby wiped a tear from her eyes.

'You silly old fool!' she thought, crossly.

Yet her insides ached as the dolls' house was driven away in the boot of a car, taking with it, a piece of her childhood.

April 2004

PIC: REX FEATURES

A flavour of the month

One of the most indulgent months of the year, April is heaven for the sweet-toothed and provides a good excuse to indulge in all things naughty but nice.

On average each person in the UK eats a staggering 9.4kg of chocolate every year and, lb for lb, we actually eat more confectionery per head than any other country in Europe.

As chocolate contains the stimulant, phenylethylamine, which creates a 'feel-good' factor, it's not surprising that most of us crave a chocolate treat from time to time, but it's not all bad. Apart from tasting glorious, a little bit of chocolate – especially the dark variety – can actually be good for us. Chocolate contains high levels of phenol, a chemical that is thought to reduce the risk of heart disease, and it's also rich in magnesium and iron.

Shop shelves will be stacked with Easter eggs but, for a more personalised gift, why don't you have a go at creating these chocolate truffles, which are easy to make. Melt 4oz (110g) of chocolate with 1oz (25g) of butter over a pan of boiling water. When melted, remove from the heat and add 2oz (50g) of cake crumbs, 1oz (25g) of sieved icing sugar and a tablespoon of rum (optional). When cool, form into small balls and roll in a broken chocolate flake.

THURSDAY	1	1-3 Grand National meeting All Fools' Day
FRIDAY	2	
SATURDAY	3	
SUNDAY	4	Palm Sunday
MONDAY	5	
TUESDAY	6	
WEDNESDAY	7	
THURSDAY	8	
FRIDAY	9	Good Friday (Bank Holiday)
SATURDAY	10	
SUNDAY	11	Easter Day
MONDAY	12	Easter Monday (Bank Holiday, except Scotland)
TUESDAY	13	
WEDNESDAY	14	
THURSDAY	15	
FRIDAY	16	
SATURDAY	17	
SUNDAY	18	

MONDAY	*19*	
TUESDAY	*20*	
WEDNESDAY	*21*	Queen's birthday
THURSDAY	*22*	
FRIDAY	*23*	St George's Day
SATURDAY	*24*	
SUNDAY	*25*	
MONDAY	*26*	
TUESDAY	*27*	
WEDNESDAY	*28*	May YOURS on sale
THURSDAY	*29*	
FRIDAY	*30*	

PIC: EMAP GARDEN PICTURE LIBRARY

★ READER'S TIP ★
Maureen Blair in Belfast sticks a lollypop stick in the middle of her pots before putting a plastic bag over the sown seeds. It holds the plastic bag away from the compost surface and her fast developing seedlings.

A year in your garden

Outdoors, sandy soils are warming nicely, while the polythene covers on clay soil will be speeding up the process nicely. So much so that many seeds can go in now. If you are sowing into long straight drills in the soil, it is a good idea to refill over the seeds with compost. Invariably the compost is a different colour to the soil and you will see exactly where the seeds have been sown. It can save time when weeding. That's the only problem with April – the weed seeds also want to get growing. It's also busy on the windowsill and in the greenhouse now. Lots of seed need the protection of warmer conditions before moving outside, and pots full of compost placed in a propagator is a great start to life. Propagators can be simply a tray with a plastic lid, or an all singing, all dancing affair with temperature controls and humidity rectifiers. Money buys optional extras. Whatever you buy, the lid should have vents to allow moisture to leave the area around the pots.

This will prevent rotting. The lids should be as deep as possible. This will mean the seedlings can stay under protection longer, and you can use your propagator for taller cuttings. Temperature control is often important for more delicate seeds. Set it for a particular temperature and whatever the outside conditions are like, you know the seeds are growing in a prefect environment. Saying all that, many seeds just need a place to get started, a first time buyer's kind of propagator. A pot, enclosed by a plastic bag is all that some seeds need. Remember to never allow the leaves to touch the sides of the plastic, as condensation could cause fungal problems.

March 29-April 4

PIC HULTON ARCHIVE

▲Two little girls and their dog (suitably labelled) wait at Euston Station in 1935 for their train to Scotland during the Easter holidays

WHAT'S COOKING?

Calabrese Quiche
(Serves 6)

- 1 x 10-in pastry flan (ready-made)
- 8 oz/225 g ham, cut into thin strips
- 8 oz/225 g cooked calabrese
- 1 large onion, thinly sliced
- 1 oz/25 g butter
- 3 eggs
- ½ pt single cream
- 3 oz/75 g grated cheddar cheese
- Salt and pepper

1 Thinly slice the calabrese heads.
2 Melt the butter in a frying pan and cook the onion until soft.
3 Beat the eggs and cream together, add half the cheese and season with salt and pepper.
4 Arrange the onion in the pastry case and cover with the calabrese and strips of ham. Pour over the beaten mixture, sprinkle with the remaining cheese and bake in a moderate oven 180°C/350°F/Gas Mark 4 for 20 minutes until the filling is set and the top is golden in colour.

PIC: FRESH PRODUCE CONSORTIUM

DID YOU KNOW THAT

The top three unusual places to store winning lottery tickets are:
A) In underwear
B) Under the floorboards
C) Sticky-taped to the body

AT THE MOVIES

Who said?
'I don't like lobsters. I have a long list of dislikes, and it's getting longer'.
(Answer below)

Answer: Joan Crawford playing hard to get with Jeff Chandler in Joseph Pevney's *Female On The Beach*

ON GROWING OLDER
'It's not the years in your life but the life in your years that counts'.

Adlai Stevenson

MY ADVICE IS...
'Live every day as if it were your last'. This was given to me by my mother who lived to be 101.

Mrs E Clark, Blackpool

Out & About To...

The Fan Museum, Greenwich, London

Unless you're a fan of fans, chances are you're unaware of their social and historical significance. Rarely seen in modern times, in days gone by fans were used as essential cooling devices and status symbols. You can see how they developed from the 11th century to the present day at this fascinating museum, housed in two beautifully restored 18th-century town houses. This is the world's most important single collection of fans and includes many rare examples.

Records of the earliest designs date from around 3000 BC, and some of the early folding fans, which appeared relatively recently, were exquisite creations made from materials such as ivory, mother of pearl and tortoiseshell, decorated with silver, gold and precious stones.

In the grounds, you'll find a secret, Japanese-style garden with a fan-shaped parterre (formally arranged flowerbeds), pond, stream and oriental architectural features.

● *Adults £3.50, concessions £2.50, children (under seven) free, free entry for senior citizens and disabled visitors from 2pm*
● *Open Tuesday to Sunday*
● *Refreshments; gift shop*
Tel: 020 8305 1441
(Internet: www.fan-museum.org)

A DAY TO REMEMBER

Chris and Pete finally had a honeymoon in September 1959, a caravan holiday in Norfolk

It was a wedding day with a difference for Christine Brunt from Kent…

Christmas 1958 and we were getting married on December 20. The head office of the jeweller's shop I worked for said I couldn't have the day off work as it was the busiest time of year. I couldn't afford to lose my job, so my dear Peter and I got married in my lunch hour. It was never going to be a big flash 'do' but it was so rushed.

I ran from the shop and down the road to Sidcup Register Office and met Peter and his mum and dad there. We were married in a rather sombre panelled room and Peter was so nervous, he was told off by the lady registrar!

We didn't have any wedding photos, as father-in-law (the only one with a camera) forgot it in the rush. After a quick sherry to wish us luck, Peter ran me back to work on his motor bike.

I just made it in time and Peter bought me a tiny gold cross and chain which I wear to this day. During the afternoon, a lady customer heard I'd just got married, so came back with a 'lucky heather' pot plant and I was so touched.

The working day finished at 9pm in the lead-up to Christmas but my boss relented and let me go half an hour early to prepare for a celebration. We had a good knees-up with the family, with wedding cake and dancing in the street.

Sadly, I lost Peter in April 2000, 42 years and two days from the day I met him. We had lots of memorable days but none so happy and life-changing as my wedding day.

OLD FASHIONED REMEDIES

When my brothers and I were growing up in the 1930s we had the usual winter coughs and colds, for which mother had her own remedies. For ticklish coughs, it was soft brown sugar beaten to a cream in butter. To soothe sore throats, it was blackcurrant tea made from home-made jam. My favourite was a mixture of glycerine, honey and lemon.
Margaret Crompton, Birmingham

Dr Henderson replies: It can be seen from this how popular glycerine and honey is as a combination in many old-fashioned remedies, with lemon added to flavour it. Blackcurrants are rich in vitamin C that helps with colds, but sugar and butter is of little use in this regard, however.

April 5-11

WHAT'S COOKING?

PAUSE FOR THOUGHT

Carol Ann Massey sent in these charming words to share with readers: 'I noticed this verse on a china mug, which I thought was a perfect description of my own cottage and – I hope – the way people think of me':

Home is where the heart is
I love a house that's 'lived in'
With clutter here and there
A magazine left open
A jacket on the chair.
A smell of something cooking
A special recipe?
An over-eager offer of hospitality.
I love a house that's 'lived-in'
It seems to stand apart
For in it is a woman who has a loving heart

SNACK
Pineapple Toasties
(Serves 2)

- 4 oz/110 g grated cheddar cheese
- 4 slices of ham
- 4 pineapple rings
- 4 slices of bread

Grill one side of the bread. Turn and place the ham on the bread. Put a pineapple ring on top of each slice of ham. Cover with cheese and grill slowly until the cheese is melted.

Mrs A Grecco,
Hillingdon, Middlesex

Top tip

Try growing seeds in cardboard egg boxes. Simply bury the egg box when the shoots are ready for planting and the tray will disintegrate into the soil.

WHAT A COINCIDENCE

Many years ago, my late husband and I were travelling home by coach from an Italian holiday and the itinerary included a half-day and overnight stay at a lakeside hotel in Switzerland. We arrived just before lunch and after being allocated our rooms, were told to make our way to the dining room for lunch.

We did this and no sooner had we sat down at the table, than somebody touched my shoulder and I turned to find a cousin of mine. Neither of us had known that the other would be on holiday at that time.

Lily, my cousin, was staying at the hotel with a friend and, even more of a coincidence, just before they went to lunch, Lily had said to her friend: "You go in, I'm just going to the foyer to post this card to Vera,"– (me!). As she joined her friend at their table, she looked up and saw me walking through the room. We all spent a pleasant evening together!

Vera Bartram, West Sussex

DID YOU KNOW THAT

Skin is the body's largest organ, weighing between 2.5 to 4.5kg

OLD WIVES' TALES

White spots on the fingernails means you're calcium deficient.

Dr Henderson replies: Actually, it may be more of a sign you could be deficient in zinc rather than calcium. However, a true calcium deficiency can lead to soft, brittle nails and white marks can be a part of this so it is always worth having this checked if you seem to be suffering from this problem.

A DAY TO REMEMBER

Gretchen Morgan remembers three little flowers…

This photograph was taken at Stapleford in Hertfordshire on Coronation Day in 1953.

My three girls were all dressed in crêpe paper costumes, made by my late mother-in-law. The eldest, Lauren, was a poppy, the youngest, Roberta, was a daisy and Sally, my middle girl, was a cornflower.

There was such excitement at the church fête that day!

Gretchen's red, white and blue girls, Lauren, Roberta and Sally on Coronation Day

ON GROWING OLDER

'Old age isn't so bad when you consider the alternative'.

Maurice Chevalier

AT THE MOVIES

Who said?
'Oh those idiot producers! Those imbeciles! Haven't they got any eyes? Have they forgotten what a star looks like? I'll show them! I'll be up there again! So help me!'
(Answer below)

Answer: Gloria Swanson vowing to return to the screen in Billy Wilder's Sunset Boulevard

PIC: THE NATIONAL TRUST PHOTO LIBRARY

OUT & ABOUT TO…

Biddulph Grange Garden, Biddulph, Stoke-on-Trent, Staffordshire

Chocoholics old and young and garden lovers alike will have an egg-stra special time here over the Easter break (phone first to check dates and times). The highlight is an Easter trail, which comprises a walk through the charming Victorian garden, in search of Easter bunnies. After successfully completing the trail, children are rewarded with a scrumptious chocolatey treat.

The garden was designed in the mid-19th century by James Bateman to display specimens from his extensive plant collection. He divided the grounds into a series of small, themed gardens inspired by different countries and featuring rare and exotic plants. The gardens are connected by tunnels and paths and include an imitation of the Great Wall of China, an Egyptian Court and a formal Italian garden. And don't miss the upside-down tree!

● *Adults £4.60; children £2.30; plus £1 for Easter trail (on April 11 and 12 – call first to check dates)*
● *Tearoom; picnic tables; National Trust shop*
● *Not suitable for wheelchairs*
Tel: 01782 517999
(Internet: www.nationaltrust.org.uk)

April 12-18

OLD FASHIONED REMEDIES

When we were young, my mother kept a small cardboard box of pure tar. (I don't know where it came from). She said it was very good for 'cleaning the blood'. It was invaluable during the war as, with a poor diet, we were always getting boils.

At one time during a very bad winter, I managed to have three boils on my face at once. So out came the box full of shiny black tar and she would dig out a small pellet or two, rubbed into little pills and we swallowed them with a sip of water – they certainly seemed to do the trick!

Mrs W Cokayne, Leicestershire

Dr Henderson replies: I haven't heard this one before, and am glad I haven't! Tar is potentially harmful to health and will have had no beneficial effect on you that I can think of. Boils — especially teenage ones — have a habit of coming and going by themselves anyway so I suspect this is why it seemed to work. As for 'cleaning the blood', tar would be worse than useless I'm afraid.

MY ADVICE IS...

'When through the world you wend your way, of these three things beware:
Of whom you speak, to whom you speak and how, and when, and where'.

Patricia Peters, Surrey

A new life for Margaret Harris from Oxfordshire...

My day to remember was 22 years ago this September when I had a phone call to say the Churchill Hospital had found a kidney for me. And it's still going strong after all these years.

Margaret, who's life was changed forever

ON GROWING OLDER

'Age is strictly a case of mind over matter. If you don't mind, it doesn't matter'.

Jack Benny

DID YOU KNOW THAT

Jellyfish are more than 95 per cent water.

WHAT'S COOKING?

SUPPER DISH
Sweet Honey Chops
(Serves 4)

- 2 tbs clear honey
- 2 tsps cider vinegar
- 4 spare rib chops
- 2 level tsps ground ginger
- A pinch of nutmeg

1 Mix the honey, ginger and nutmeg and coat the chops thoroughly. Marinate for a few hours.
2 Cook in a casserole dish (190 C/375 F/Gas Mark 5) for an hour, basting occasionally.
3 Remove the chops, stir the vinegar into the pan juices and boil until it forms a glaze. Pour over the chops, and serve with new potatoes.

OUT & ABOUT TO...

Beck Isle Museum of Rural Life, Pickering, North Yorkshire

PIC: BECK ISLE MUSEUM

Want to see how your granny used to live? Look no further than this excellent museum on the edge of the North Yorkshire moors. It reflects social and domestic customs from the early 19th century onwards, and the 27 rooms have been laid out with great attention to detail, helping you get a sense of how past generations lived.

In the village shop, you'll see the scales that were in constant use in the days before pre-packaged food. Those were the days when youngsters seized upon treats such as sugar pigs and home-made ice-cream wafers with delight.

The costume room shows how much times have changed, with items such as glove stretchers and skirt lifters displayed alongside underskirts and nightgowns, which were often extensively decorated by hand, although they were rarely seen! And there's lots more to see in the Victorian parlour and pub, print shop, dairy, cobbler's shop, chemist and cottage kitchen.

● *Adults £3; concessions and children £2.50*
● *No café, but several close by; picnic area; shop; wheelchair access*
● *In mid-June (telephone for dates and details), there's an Old Games Day when you can try your hand at ancient pastimes and hobbies*
Tel: 01751 473653

Top tip
Clean chrome taps by rubbing down with a little toothpaste.

AT THE MOVIES

Who said?
'Did anyone ever tell you that you have a dishonest face – for a priest, I mean?'
(Answer below)

Answer: Ingrid Bergman being suspicious of Bing Crosby in Leo McCarey's Bells Of St Mary's

WHAT A COINCIDENCE

Diane outside 'Betty's bungalow'

About 20 years ago I became a home help to Betty, who lived in a bungalow near to where I lived. I loved the bungalow and the garden because it was so peaceful. All you could hear was the rustling of the trees in the park behind the back garden and the birds singing.

The years went by and Betty died, also my mother. My husband passed her bungalow and saw a For Sale notice outside, and I started thinking how lovely it would be to live there. But my husband went by again, and a Sold notice had been put up – it was not meant to be after all!

Within a week, I received my inheritance money from my mother; we walked past the bungalow again and, to my delight, the For Sale notice was up again. And guess what? We bought it and within two months we had moved into 'Betty's bungalow'. What a coincidence that everything fell into place at the right time!

Diane Clarke, Bristol

April 19-25

OUT & ABOUT TO...

PIC: TWINKLE TEFREY

Caerhays Castle Gardens, St Austell, Cornwall

Put a spring in your step with a timely visit to this wonderfully wild woodland garden. Best known for its stunning display of enormous magnolia trees, it's beautifully set in a sheltered valley around the back of a 19th-century castle. The 60-acre garden contains rhododendrons, camellias and many rare and unusual shrubs and trees – including 37 record-breaking specimens – originally created from material discovered by plant hunters in China 100 years ago. The estate has belonged to the Williams family since 1853, and the present owner and his son are constantly conserving and improving the plant collection.

You can follow one – or all if you're feeling sprightly – of the four suggested routes around the gardens, admire the splendid Asiatic magnolias, which should be in their prime, sit and enjoy the lovely sea views, then head to the tearoom for a restorative cuppa and some cake.
- *Adults £4, children £2*
- *Refreshments; small gift shop; wheelchair access*
Tel: 01872 501310

A DAY TO REMEMBER

Brenda Darby from Birmingham remembers a day in New Zealand...

One magical, sunny, blue-sky day, our New Zealand tour took us on a scenic cruise to Milford Sound, a glacial carved fjord.

The scenery was breathtaking – sheer wooded cliffs, many cascading waterfalls, rainbows, too, and flowering peaks in the distance. Nearer, rising straight from the sea, was Mitre Peak, truly awe-inspiring (there aren't enough superlatives to describe it) – and yes, it did look like a Bishop's mitre.

Close by, there was a special surprise – Fairy Falls – with its pure alpine water, while at the entrance to the fjord, some seals lay asleep on the rocks.

OLD WIVES' TALES

Wet a matchstick and rub it on a wart to help get rid of them.

Dr Henderson replies: Of all the old fashioned remedies I hear, there are probably more about how to get rid of warts than any other. Warts are caused by a virus and tend to have a limited life, so even if you do nothing most of them will go at some point and often quite quickly too. This is why it may appear a remedy is working when in fact the wart is simpy going away by itself anyway.

Top tip

Pick flowers first thing in the morning or last thing at night to ensure their longest life-span – flowers picked during the warmest part of the day will not last as long.

DID YOU KNOW THAT

Nearly one million earthworms can be found in one acre of land.

PAUSE FOR THOUGHT

Some wise words from Cynthia Brown of Suffolk:

Never judge by appearances, or first impressions. You never know what unfortunate lives some people may have suffered which results in them probably being a little off-putting at first. Get to know them, then decide.

WHAT A COINCIDENCE

I was born and brought up on a hill farm in north east Scotland and trained to be a nurse at Aberdeen. I served with the Princess Mary's Royal Air Force Nursing Service and in 1944 was posted abroad. Prior to embarkation I had to go to Austin Reed in London's Regent Street to be fitted out with tropical kit and tin trunk.

Afterwards I decided to have my photograph taken for my family and set off towards Picadilly Circus. There, walking towards me, was my brother, Captain Peter Ellis. It was unbelievable, as we had last heard he was a prisoner of war in Italy. He had made a miraculous escape using his knowledge of Gaelic to bluff his way through enemy security! He was off home and I was off to India!

Hilda Stewart Bruce, Northants

Above: Hilda in nursing uniform in 1944
Left: Hilda with Peter (right) and brother Arthur

AT THE MOVIES

Who said?
'Very funny. Ha, ha, I like an associate of mine to have a sense of humour. A good laugh does more for the stomach muscles than five minutes' sitting-up exercises'.
(Answer below)

Answer: Robert Morley commending Humphrey Bogart's wit in John Huston's Beat the Devil.

WHAT'S COOKING?

A MEAL ON A BUDGET
Crispy Cod Crunch
(Serves 4)

- 4 cod pieces
- Salt and pepper
- 1 oz/25 g butter
- 1 oz/25 g white breadcrumbs
- 1 oz/25 g cheese, grated

1 Season the fish, dot with half the butter and grill for 5 minutes.
2 Mix breadcrumbs and cheese together. Turn the fish and cover with cheese mixture, dot with remaining butter and grill for another 5 minutes.
Serve with a seasonal salad and new potatoes.

ON GROWING OLDER
'A beautiful lady is an accident of nature. A beautiful old lady is a work of art'.
Louis Nizer

Go wild in the garden

With the right plants, your garden will become a haven for wildlife

Many of us are put off creating a 'wild' garden, because they appear messy, unloved and overgrown. However, a beautiful garden will attract wildlife – it just needs a little more planning.

Think nectar
Nectar is the main source of energy for insects such as butterflies, bees and hoverflies so include nectar-rich plants in a sunny part of the garden. Choose plants with simple, open, flat flowers such as *Limnanthes douglasii*, solidago, rudbeckia, yarrow and phacelia.

Choose year-round colour
Select a range of different plants, so your garden is packed with nectar all year round. Start off in spring with primroses and follow with plants such as grape hyacinth, honesty, red campion, candytuft, buddleia, lavender, teasels, knapweed, *Sedum spectabile*, Michaelmas daisy and ivy.

Plant a native hedge
A well-balanced native hedge will contain a mixture of plants and provide flowers and fruit for most of the year. Use plants such as privet, pyracantha, spindle, barberry, beech, blackthorn, wild rose and hazel, but buy them bare root by mail during autumn from a specialist nursery.

Grow wildflowers
Many wildflowers are in decline, so give them a boost by growing them in your garden.

Leave the mower in the shed
Unless you have a bowling green lawn, then you'll already have wildflowers among the grass. Simply stop cutting it for a while and natives such as yarrow, daisies and clover will soon bloom. Stop feeding the grass and plant wildflower plugs in holes cut in the turf. If you cut the grass, just mow pathways across the garden.
Gareth Salter

The things we miss

Spring cleaning

As the bright sun of spring started to show up the grime accumulated in houses over the winter, it was time for the annual spring clean. This usually started with a visit from the chimney sweep who cleaned the fireplace.

All furniture, pictures and carpets would be taken from the front room or covered with dust sheets. Children would be told to stand outside in the street and watch to make sure the sweep's brush had popped out of the top of the chimney

Then it was down to scrubbing and the carpet was taken outside and hung over the washing line. Frustrations soon evaporated as you beat the carpet to dislodge all the dust and dirt. Next the walls and pictures rails were washed down.

Furniture was polished to a brilliant shine – often with home-made polish – ornaments were washed and pictures dusted. After such a mammoth operation, the family hardly dared set foot in the gleaming room, and woe betide a hint of sticky fingermarks!

But of course there were other cleaning jobs to be done all year round. Remember blackleading the grate with Zebrite? And not forgetting the fiddly job of cleaning the brasses. This meant going round the house armed with rags and a can of Brasso and cleaning all the doorknobs, the number on the front door (taking care not to leaves white smudges on the paintwork), and the decorative brass candlesticks on the piano.

Cleaning the front of your house was as important as the interior and you could see lines of women scrubbing doorsteps with a donkey stone and washing windows and windowsills.

Puzzles

PIC: REX FEATURES

Where on Earth?

See if you can navigate from Cornwall to Cuba in our globe-trotting grid.
You may just need your atlas before you're home and dry.

ACROSS

7 Archipelago in the South Atlantic, known as Malvinas in Argentina (8,7)
9 Large area of flat unforested grassland in SE Europe or Siberia (6)
10 Country which boasts 277 Munros – mountains over 3,000ft high (8)
11 State of western Brazil, or an industrial seaport of Israel (4)
12 North-western part of the Indian Ocean (7,3)
15 Town in Umbria, central Italy, famous as the birthplace of St Francis (6)
17 Capital of Albania, on the Ishm River (6)
18 Name of a New South Wales river, and a suburb of Sydney (10)
20 Town in Tuscany renowned for the pictured landmark (4)
21 Industrial city in SE France, on the Isère River (8)
23 Sea of northern Europe, linked to the North Sea by the Skaggerak, Kattegat and Öresund (6)
24 Area of the western Atlantic notorious for unexplained disappearance of ships (7,8)

DOWN

1 Sugar and tobacco-producing city in W central Cuba (5,5)
2 Capital of the republic of Macedonia, on the Vardar River (6)
3 Capital of the Maldives (4)
4 City and port on the south coast of Ukraine (6)
5 Scandinavian capital city formerly known as Christiania (4)
6 Port in Yemen at the mouth of the Red Sea (4)
8 US state capital of Georgia, host of the 1996 Olympics (7)
12 State in NE India, famed for tea production (5)
13 Westernmost of the Balearic Islands (5)
14 US city in Indiana, on the Ohio River (10)
16 South American country formerly known as Dutch Guiana (7)
19 Cathedral city on the Adige River in northern Italy, on the route to the Brenner Pass (6)
20 Country, with a 23 Across coastline, whose chief port is Gdansk (6)
21 Desert of southern Mongolia and northern China (4)
22 Resort town of north Cornwall, popular with surfers (4)
23 Region of France, south-east of Paris, famed for its soft cheese (4)

Solution on Page 159

Short story

The gift

By Claudia Napier

The tissue paper was brittle with age and crackled as Katherine opened the box. Nestled inside were five beautifully preserved pieces of horse manure. A chuckle rose in her throat as she remembered the day when Gerhard first gave them to her. Such a silly man he was – horse manure!

He asked her what she wanted for her 50th birthday and she jokingly replied 'horse manure'. Sure enough, that's exactly what she got. The five pieces were presented to her the morning of her birthday, thinly bronzed and wrapped. Five pieces, Gerhard explained, one for each decade of her life. She laughed and swore to keep them for the rest of her life.

That was twenty years ago, and he was gone now, her Gerhard; he had died three months ago. She didn't think he'd mind if she threw them out. Leaving this house that they had shared for the last forty years felt like the end of her life anyway, so she wasn't really breaking any promises, was she?

The chair creaked as Katherine moved to get a better look at the remnants of her life that lay scattered on the lounge floor: dried flowers from long-ago dances; Valentine's Day cards; a half-burned candle from their first dinner together; and a mountain of photo albums. All this had to go, she knew, because there would be no space in the new apartment. She picked up one of the photo albums and flicked through the pages of the past with a hesitant hand.

Memories returned, filling her mind with camcorder accuracy. He was a handsome man, her Gerhard, with his fine, blond hair and blue eyes – a good husband. They never had any children. Not because they didn't want to, but because she couldn't have any.

What a blow that was! Years of tests and negative results left her feeling less feminine somehow; empty, like a beautiful racing car without an engine. Infertility was different in those days – something private, not to be discussed with anybody, not

Now she could finally throw it away… moving house with a box full of horse manure didn't make any sense

even your own partner.

But Gerhard had intuitively known how she felt. He tried to fill the gap in her life by making it as interesting and exciting as possible – holidays in exotic places, expensive clothing, dazzling jewels, fast cars and a luxurious home. It was all that which made the horse manure so hard for her to understand.

He could have given her anything; a scarf, perfume, even a bunch of flowers, but no, it had to be what she asked for – horse manure!

She never told Gerhard, but she secretly felt hurt by his gift. Oh, she laughed with him that day, swallowing her outrage and a certain amount of disgust. But later, when he was asleep, she cried a little and then shoved the box and its horrible contents into the bottom of a bedside cupboard. He woke to find her sitting on the edge of the bed with the tears still fresh on her face and she made light of it all, brushing them aside as a silly fear of age.

Gallant as ever, Gerhard had rushed to reassure her of her everlasting youth by making love to her. Katherine tried to lose herself in his love, but the knowledge of the little box not a foot away from her head, kept intruding.

Over the years she worked around that box, never touching it again, until today. It was with relief that she had pulled it out of the dark recesses of the cupboard this morning. Now she could finally throw it away, because moving house with a box full of horse manure didn't make any sense.

The album slipped off Katherine's knees, leaving only the box with its 'treasure'. Slowly and against her will, she reached out and for the first time ever, picked up one of the brown balls. It was dry with age and started crumbling in her hand, showering her lap with stalks of grass. Her hand snapped shut, turning Gerhard's gift into chaff. This is what she always wanted to do – to destroy the one act of her husband that had upset her.

Disgust unlocked her clenched fingers and Katherine turned her head away, not wanting to see what she had done. Something hard dropped into the box with a thud – something that shimmered and sparkled from under the straw. Reluctant and unwilling to reveal its secret of twenty years, the sapphires and diamonds played a final game of hide-and-seek with Katherine's reality. An invisible band closed itself around her heart as she lifted the earring out of the dung.

"Gerhard, oh Gerhard," she whispered, feverishly crushing and searching for what she now knew with certainty would be hidden in the other four balls. One for each ten years of her life, he had said. Two earrings, a pendant, a bracelet, and a ring – all in sapphire and diamonds, her favourite gems.

"You should have said," she admonished her dead husband. "No, I'm sorry – I should have known. The shame is all mine." Katherine lovingly clutched the broken bronze balls to her chest, silently begging forgiveness from one who had already given it.

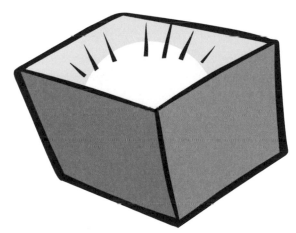

Disgust unlocked her clenched fingers and Katherine turned her head away…

May 2004

PIC: REX FEATURES

A flavour of the month

As we move into spring, the world lights up with a rainbow of colours that symbolise new hope and re-birth.

Lambs skip in the fields, blazing yellow daffodils dance by the roadside and, up above, cherry blossom trees burst open, raining down their pink confetti. Spring has sprung.

This month, look out for one of the most beautiful flowers of the season – the lovely lilac. Originating in the Balkans and China, lilac has been widely planted in Britain since the time of Henry VIII and became a popular cottage garden plant in the 19th century.

Lilacs provide a beautiful display of late-spring flowers, which are irresistibly aromatic. The clusters of small tubular petals come in more than 500 varieties, from pure white to deep purple.

May is a good month for adding colour to your home, too. So if your living room looks a bit drab, try adding some fresh spring colours. Whether it's a lick of paint or some new accessories, you can revitalise a room relatively cheaply. If you don't want to paint, a plain sofa can be transformed with a colourful throw, a bare wall with a cheerful print, or just add a vase or two of spring blooms to your rooms.

SATURDAY	1	
SUNDAY	2	
MONDAY	3	May Day Bank Holiday
TUESDAY	4	
WEDNESDAY	5	
THURSDAY	6	
FRIDAY	7	
SATURDAY	8	
SUNDAY	9	
MONDAY	10	
TUESDAY	11	
WEDNESDAY	12	
THURSDAY	13	
FRIDAY	14	
SATURDAY	15	
SUNDAY	16	
MONDAY	17	
TUESDAY	18	

WEDNESDAY	19	
THURSDAY	20	
FRIDAY	21	
SATURDAY	22	
SUNDAY	23	
MONDAY	24	
TUESDAY	25	25-28 Chelsea Flower Show (provisional)
WEDNESDAY	26	
THURSDAY	27	
FRIDAY	28	June YOURS on sale
SATURDAY	29	
SUNDAY	30	
MONDAY	31	Spring Bank Holiday

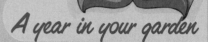

A year in your garden

Panic can set in during May. Every garden centre, nursery and supermarket is full of tempting displays of bedding plants and everyone else seems busy planting them out. But calm down, take a deep breath and check the weather forecast. In most parts of the country a late frost arrives in May. In some places this happens at the end of the month. So, there's plenty of time to plant out that bedding but if you haven't grown your own it's worth buying a few trays. But once at home do take time to acclimatise your seedlings to outdoor life.

Gardeners call this hardening off, and without it, seedlings will be shocked by the relatively cold outdoors and could succumb to slugs, snails and damage from the cold. All you have to do is to place the trays of bedding outdoors on a warm day, and bring them back inside when the evening draw in. Do this for a couple of weeks, then leave your seedlings out all day and night, but this time covering them with sheets of newspapers. Remove the paper first thing the next morning and let the seedlings grow.

By the end of the month they will be ready for planting out. It's also galling to see a neighbour's lovely tulip display, when you know you forgot to plant them last autumn. Never fear, as pots of bulbs in full bloom can be bought and planted straightaway outdoors. If you take them out of the pots chances are the plants will collapse. It's much better to plant the whole lot, container and plants, in the soil. They are then easily lifted and put in an inconspicuous part of the garden once the show is over. All container-grown flowering shrubs can be planted now – remember to water well before and after planting.

PIC: BMAP GARDEN PICTURE LIBRARY

☀ READER'S TIP ☀
Thomas Ball in Darlington saves all the pots he uses when planting bedding and shrubs and takes them back to his local garden centre. He gets a small refund and the pots get recycled. Try it with your local garden centre.

April 26-May 2

OUT & ABOUT TO...

Spalding Flower Festival and Country Fair, Spalding, Lincolnshire

With their heads held high, the thousands of tulips that adorn the floats in the Spalding Flower Festival are a spectacular sight. Held annually since 1958, the parade was started by local growers using the flowers from tulips grown for bulb production.

You can see the floats on display at the festival site from 9am on the morning of Saturday May 1 (phone first to check date and time), then from 2-5pm they will parade the streets of the small market town of Spalding. Whether or not you have green fingers, these beautiful blooms are bound to inspire you to pick up a trowel and get gardening.

Throughout the May Day Bank Holiday weekend, Spalding plays host to Springfields Country Fair, at Springfields Gardens. The entertainment includes marching bands, stalls selling home-grown produce and a craft fair.

● *Roadside viewing of the floats is free; admission to Springfields Country fair: Adults £5, concessions £4, children free.*
Tel: 01775 724843

Vera Evans from Shrewsbury remembers a day she'd rather forget...

A DAY TO REMEMBER

I was about eight years old and had been sent to the corner shop for a pint of vinegar and a packet of Saxa salt. The salt was put on the counter and Mr Beighton took my bottle to fill with vinegar. He had to go through a door with a curtained window to the kitchen, where he kept the vinegar. While he was away, I took the opportunity to steal a pear and dropped it into my closed umbrella.

When he returned I was – rather nonchalantly – busy drawing on the waxed paper that covered the salt box. "Now," he said calmly, "take that pear out of your umbrella and stand there and eat it."

I had been found out and every mouthful nearly choked me. If Mr Beighton had allowed me to eat the pear on the way home, it would not have bothered me in the slightest. Instead, and looking back, he would have made a good psychologist.

I developed a conscience from then on and have tried my best – although not always succeeding – to live up to my name, Vera, latin for truthful.

DID YOU KNOW THAT

One sheep can supply enough wool to make about 14 jumpers.

Top tip

Give felt tip pens a new lease of life by dipping the tip in vinegar.

MY ADVICE IS...

'Don't worry, there's something better waiting round the corner'. Good advice given to me by a colleague when I was made redundant – I went on to a better paid job that lasted more than 26 years!
Janet Brown, Fife

ON GROWING OLDER

'Childhood: The time of life when you make funny faces in the mirror.
Middle age: The time of life when the mirror gets even'.
M Mansfield

WHAT'S COOKING?

Strawberry and Mango Choux Buns
(Makes 6 buns)

- 4 fl oz/120 ml water
- 2 oz/50 g unsalted butter
- 2 ½ oz/65 g plain flour, sifted
- Pinch salt
- 2 eggs, beaten
- ¼ pt/150 ml whipping cream
- ¼ pt/150 ml low-fat strawberry yoghurt
- 1 mango, peeled and diced
- 8 oz/250 g strawberries, hulled and sliced
- Icing sugar

1 Heat the oven to 220°C/425°F/Gas mark 7. Put the water and butter into a saucepan and heat until boiling.
2 Remove from the heat and add the flour and salt, then beat vigorously until a smooth glossy dough has formed.
3 Cool slightly, then gradually add the eggs, beating well after each addition.
4 Put the choux pastry into a piping bag fitted with a large star nozzle and pipe out six 3 in/7.5 cm mounds on to a wetted baking sheet.
5 Bake in the oven for 20 minutes. Take out of the oven and pierce a hole in each bun to allow the steam to escape and return to the oven for 5 minutes to dry out. Cool the buns on a wire rack.
6 Whip the cream until standing in peaks, then fold in the yoghurt. Cut the buns in half and remove any uncooked pastry.
7 Spoon the cream into the bases, add the mango and strawberries, then replace the lids. Dust with icing sugar and serve.

PIC: FRESH PRODUCE CONSORTIUM

PIC: HULTON ARCHIVE

▲ Schoolchildren raise their flags high during Empire Day celebrations at a school in London, in the 1930s

AT THE MOVIES

Who said?
'Whoever you are, I have always depended on the kindness of strangers'.
(Answer below)

Answer: Vivien Leigh in Elia Kazen's A Streetcar Named Desire

OLD FASHIONED REMEDIES

If you suffer from night cramps, try putting two corks in the bed. It works for me.

Mrs C Beard, Plymouth

Dr Henderson replies: Now, I can't explain this one for a second but hundreds of my patients tell me it works! Apparently two or three old corks are best, placed either under the foot of the mattress or at the bottom of the bed. Who am I to argue?

May 3-9

A new member of the family for Daphne Bryant from Eastbourne…

I will always remember the day our first great grandchild was born. His name is Joshua John and was ten days late arriving. He put in an appearance on July 18, 2002, which happened to be my late mother's birthday.

She passed away 23 years ago but would have been just as thrilled with him as we were.

Daphne and Joshua John enjoying a quiet moment

PAUSE FOR THOUGHT

This lovely poem was sent in by Mrs Parkinson, who lives in Milton Keynes:

Smiling is infectious
You catch it like the 'flu
When someone smiled at me today
I started smiling too.

I passed around a corner
And someone saw my grin
When he smiled, I realised
I'd passed it on to him

I thought about a smile
Then realised its worth
A single smile just like mine
Could travel round the earth.

So if you feel a smile begin
Don't leave it undetected
Let's start an epidemic
And get the world infected.

WHAT'S COOKING?

QUICK SNACK
Spinach-stuffed Pastries

(Serves 4)

- ¼ teaspoon or salt and pepper
- 1 small egg, beaten
- 12 oz/350 g puff pastry
- Beaten egg to glaze
- 12 oz/350 g frozen chopped spinach, thawed and well drained
- 2 oz/50 g ham, cut into ¼-in/5 mm pieces
- 3 oz/75 g cheese, grated

1. Mix together the spinach, cheese and ham in a bowl. Add the salt, pepper and egg and mix well. Chill until required.
2. Roll out the pastry on a floured surface to a ⅛ in/3 mm thickness and cut out about fifteen 4 in/10 cm circles. Roll each one across the centre to form an oval and brush all over with water.
3. Place a heaped teaspoonful of the spinach filling in the centre of each round and fold the pastry over to form a parcel. Seal the edges firmly and brush with beaten egg. Place on a baking sheet and prick with a fork. Chill for 30 minutes.
4. Bake in a preheated hot oven (220°C/425°F/Gas Mark 7) for 15 minutes, until risen and golden. Transfer to a wire rack to cool slightly. Serve warm.

OLD WIVES' TALES

Keep a baby in socks to avoid all sorts of medical problems.

Dr Henderson replies: Socks do one thing for babies, and one thing only – keep their feet warm!

DID YOU KNOW THAT

94 per cent of passenger miles are travelled by road

ON GROWING OLDER

'The young sow wild oats. The old grow sage'.

Unknown

AT THE MOVIES

Who said?
'Dolly Messiter! Poor, well-meaning, irritating Dolly Messiter, crashing into those last few precious minutes we had together. She chattered and fussed and I didn't hear what she said. I felt dazed and bewildered'.
(Answer below)

Answer: Celia Johnson resenting the interruption with Trevor Howard in David Lean's *Brief Encounter.*

Top tip

A bowl of boiling water placed in the bottom of your freezer will help it defrost quicker.

OUT & ABOUT TO...

Ironbridge Gorge Museums, Ironbridge, Shropshire

Three hundred years ago, this beautiful valley was the setting for a series of exciting events that were to change the world: The industrial revolution. The ten museums – set in the gorge on either side of the River Severn – give an insight into the momentous changes that altered the local landscape and people's lives.

The best place to start your journey back in time is the Museum of the Gorge, which features a 40-foot-long model of the gorge showing how it was 15 years after the construction of the town's namesake, the first cast-iron bridge in the world.

Other attractions include Blists Hill, an open-air,

WHAT A COINCIDENCE

In October 2002, I lost my dear wife Betty and eventually decided to return to modern sequence dancing to lessen the pain of my bereavement.

More than 25 years ago, we had been dancing pupils of a couple called Pam and Ivan and I wrote to them to ask what they were doing, not having seen them for ten years.

The next day, I was in a local supermarket and someone tapped me on the shoulder – it was Pam, who had received my letter that morning!

During the conversation, we mentioned another couple, Flo and Nick, who had also been in our learners' clan in 1977. After saying goodbye to Pam, lo and behold, I met Nick in the car park lift. The double coincidence was quite remarkable.

I'm happy to say that since then, I've attended Pam and Ivan's dances which, despite my rusty brain and creaky joints (I'm 85!) are very enjoyable!
Basil Lewis, Chester

PIC: IRONBRIDGE GORGE MUSEUM TRUST

living-history museum of life in a Victorian town and Coalport China Museum, which features regular pot-throwing and clay-modelling workshops. You can even don a hard hat and walk into the Tar Tunnel, which extends 900 yards into the hillside, and see the tar seeping from the rock.

● *A Passport Ticket, which lasts indefinitely, costs adults £12.95, over-60s £11.25, concessions £8.25. Alternatively, individual tickets are available for each of the museums.*
Tel: 01952 432166 (Internet: www.ironbridge.org.uk)

May 10-16

AT THE MOVIES

Who said?
'Oh, I know I must be punished, of course, but not on the hands. Please. Not on my hands. Today is the music scholarship, and if you cane me...'
(Answer below)

Answer: Ann Todd pleading to her headmistress in Compton Bennett's The Seventh Veil

WHAT A COINCIDENCE

The phone rang one afternoon and a voice said: "Is that Ruby? (Or so I thought.) I've got a lovely surprise for you. Your mum wants to speak to you."

My own dear mum had died four years previously in a nursing home. Could it be a hoax?

"Hello," I replied in a small, shaky voice.

"Ruth, where have you been? Why haven't you visited me?" asked the elderly lady.

The penny dropped, the first caller had asked for Ruthie, not Ruby. The call came from a residential home many miles away – I had to sit down to a good strong cup of coffee and gather my wits.

Ruby Ainsworth, W Yorks

ON GROWING OLDER

'The only source of knowledge is experience'.
Albert Einstein

DID YOU KNOW THAT

Birmingham means home (ham) of the people (ing[e]) of the tribal leader Birm or Bearma

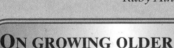

Top tip
Sprinkle salt between your paving stones to prevent grass growing in the cracks.

WHAT'S COOKING?

SUPPER DISH
Pasta Shells
with Tuna and Sweetcorn
(Serves 3-4)

- 12 oz/350 g pasta shells
- 1 tbs olive oil
- 1 medium onion, sliced
- 1 red or yellow pepper, chopped
- 2 x 6½ oz/185 g small cans of tuna in brine
- 14 oz/400 g can of sweetcorn
- 1 tbs lemon juice
- 2 tbs chopped fresh parsley

1. Cook the pasta according to the instructions on the packet.
2. Heat the oil in the frying pan. Fry the onion and pepper until softened.
3. Drain the tuna and sweetcorn, then add to the frying pan. Heat through.
4. Drain the pasta and add to the tuna mixture. Add the lemon juice and parsley. Heat through and serve instantly.

Mrs M Rowling, County Durham

OUT & ABOUT TO...

Ryton Organic Gardens, near Wolston, Coventry

PIC: DAVID LAWSON

If you're interested in finding out about organic gardening, this is a great place to start. Ryton is the flagship garden of the organic association HDRA (Henry Doubleday Research Association), and the 20-acre site has been designed to demonstrate organic gardening methods. All the techniques used can be adapted to your own garden, however small, so those dreams of picking chemical-free flowers, fruit and veg could soon become a reality.

The Herb Garden will appeal if you've struggled to nurture basil and rosemary, only to see your precious plants wither before your eyes. And if your allotment could do with a little TLC, check out the one at Ryton. The same size as a standard allotment, it's mainly used to grow vegetables and shows how recycling, crop rotation and natural methods of pest control work. Plus if you're unable – or unwilling – to wield a spade, the No Dig Garden should offer a few helpful hints!

- Adults £3.95; children £1.50
- Shop; award-winning organic restaurant (using produce grown at Ryton); relaxation and picnic area; wheelchair access
Tel: 0247 630 3517

OLD FASHIONED REMEDIES

For swollen, tired feet and legs: Three-quarters fill a plastic bucket (deeper than a bowl) with comfy warm water (not hot). Add two camomile teabags and soak for a few minutes. Take out the teabags, then bathe the feet and legs for a few minutes. Bliss!

Mrs R Ainsworth, W Yorks

Dr Henderson replies: Bliss indeed! This highlights the beneficial effect in general of warm water on tired feet. Many different substances have been suggested to add to this in different remedies such as mustard, camomile or salt but it is the warmth rather than the camomile which does the trick here.

Pamela Kwiatkowski from Gloucestershire begs some licence for her memory…

A DAY TO REMEMBER

I remember not one, but three days that were milestones in my life, shaping my personality and giving me a comfortable lifestyle as a senior citizen.

I was born in Exeter. loved school and dreamed of going to Maynard High School for Girls. In 1946, when I was 11, the headmistress walked into the classroom and I learned my dream had come true – I'd passed my 11-plus.

Years later, after my family had grown up, I applied to British Telecom for an interview; was successful and had 18 happy years, only leaving to nurse my husband through his terminal illness.

After he died, I applied to become a volunteer with my local Citizens' Advice Bureau. I worked there for eight years, giving back to the community but also learning a great deal.

Pamela (second from left), with her daughter Halina (far left)

May 17-23

PAUSE FOR THOUGHT

Friendship needs no studied phrases
Polished face or winning wiles.
Friendship deals no lavish praises
Friendship dons no surface smile.

Friendship cheers the faint and weary
Makes the timid spirit brave,
Warns the erring, lights the dreary
Smooths the passage to the grave

Friendship – pure, unselfish friendship
All through life's allotted span,
Nurtures, strengthens, widens, lengthens
Man's relationship with man.

OLD WIVES' TALES

Brimstone and treacle are good for 'natural motions'.

Dr Henderson replies: The French have their livers, the Americans their cholesterol levels and the British – well, the British have their bowels! There is something of an obsession with us that we should all be opening our bowels once a day, and if we do not then there is something badly wrong. Three times a day to three times a week is quite normal here, and brimstone and treacle should be avoided at all costs!

OUT & ABOUT TO...

Scottish Crannog Centre, Kenmore, Perthshire, Scotland

PIC: THE SCOTTISH CRANNOG CENTRE

It's not surprising that little remains of the first crannogs, which were built as long as 5,000 years ago. These circular loch dwellings were built of stone in barren environments, and of timber in wooded areas, and were linked to the shore by stone or wooded walkways. Many of the thatched, timber roundhouses were supported on stilts driven into the loch bed.

Although they may appear primitive in comparison with modern houses, according to archaeologists who have been excavating them underwater for years, they were pretty comfortable and some even had double glazing! Made from two layers of woven hazel (wattle) screens filled with bracken (ferns) and moss, this kept in the heat from the central hearth fire so the crannog-dwellers stayed cosy and warm.

At the Crannog Centre, you can explore a reconstruction of an Iron Age crannog, and discover how prehistoric people lived. There's also an exhibition complete with storyboards and some of the finds from the original excavation, plus the chance to try your hand at ancient crafts and technologies.
- *Adults £4.25; children £3*
- *Snacks, shop, disabled access*
Tel: 01887 830583

A DAY TO REMEMBER

Wedding bells for Pearl Dunham from Lincolnshire…

I lost my husband in 1995 and I met John, a widower, in May 1999. We got on really well and, as we lived some way apart, used to see each other at weekends. In the September, on my 65th birthday, we became engaged and almost a year later, we married.

My five grandchildren were my bridesmaids, my eldest son gave me away, my other two sons acted as ushers and John's brother-in-law was best man. We had a lovely reception and one of my granddaughters sang Perfect Moment as we had the first dance. To top it all, my daughter had her wedding ring blessed during the service, as she had lost her original one.

We think we are so lucky to have found happiness again at our age.

John and Pearl with her bridesmaids and best man

WHAT A COINCIDENCE

My coincidence concerns a class mate I hadn't seen for 65 years! My dad used to enjoy filming the family – long before video or colour film came on the scene.

His projector broke and he didn't think he'd be able to get it repaired but, after much phoning around, I found a gentleman who said he'd have a look at it.

When I went to pick it up, we got talking and found that we were at school together. He even showed me a school photograph which I was on. How was that for fate?

Doreen Johnson, London

WHAT'S COOKING?

A MEAL ON A BUDGET
Onion Omelette
(Serves 4)

- 5 fl oz/150 ml single cream
- Salt and pepper
- 1 lb/450 g onions
- 4 oz/100 g butter
- 6 eggs

1 Melt the butter in a fairly deep pan and sauté the sliced onion over a very low heat for about 15-20 minutes. Stir occasionally. Season to taste with salt and pepper.

2 Beat the eggs well and stir in the cream. Season with more salt and pepper. Make the omelette in a shallow pan and use the onion for filling. Serve with a crisp green salad.

ON GROWING OLDER

'Do not regret growing older. It is a privilege denied to many'.

Unknown

AT THE MOVIES

Who said?
'I am writing this to you, and I hope that you read it so you'll know. My heart beats like a hammer and I stutter and I stammer ev'ry time I see you at the picture show. I guess I'm just another fan of yours, and I thought I'd write and tell you so, ho! ho! ho! You made me love you. I didn't want to do it.'
(Answer below)

Answer: Judy Garland reciting a fan letter to Clark Gable in Roy Del Ruth's Broadway Melody of 1938.

May 24-30

OUT & ABOUT TO...

The Manor, Hemingford Grey, Cambridgeshire

A visit to The Manor is an enchanting experience for anyone who's ever read the children's stories about the house of Green Knowe. The late author Lucy Boston's beautiful house and garden provided the inspiration and setting for the series, in which the children who have lived there from the 12th century to the present meet each other.

Built in about 1130, The Manor is thought to be the oldest continuously habited house in Britain, and it's certainly one of the most atmospheric. Visitors can literally 'walk into the books' – the attic contains toys used by the fictional children of the past. Lucy Boston was passionate about her garden, which she planted with nearly three hundred roses, of which more than two hundred remain. In the winter, she also made many exquisite patchworks, most of which are on display in the house.

- *Adults £4, concessions £3.50, children £1.50*
- *The garden is open all year round (but phone first to check), but viewing of the house and patchworks is strictly by appointment*
- *Bed and breakfast is available at The Willows (telephone 01480 494748) and lunch at The Cock (telephone 01480 463609)*
- *Tel: 01480 463134 (Internet: www.greenknowe.co.uk)*

MY ADVICE IS...

'Do things when you think of them, because if you don't do them straight away, you'll forget!'

Hugh Rogers, Cornwall

Top tip

Don't be left in the dark! – always keep a torch and a length of fuse wire near your fuse box.

DID YOU KNOW THAT

It's impossible to sneeze with your eyes open.

OLD FASHIONED REMEDIES

Pour an egg white over burns or scalds to prevent pain and eliminate infection and inflammation.

Mrs R Ainsworth, W Yorks

Dr Henderson replies: The best first aid treatment for first degree burns or scalds – where the skin is reddened and painful – remains cold water and lots of it. If the skin is blistered, white or charred then medical advice should be sought. Egg white probably does little in reducing pain and infection and as a general point it is best to keep the affected area of a scald or mild burn as free of ointments, creams or potions as possible.

AT THE MOVIES

Who said?
'Please don't call me Mr de Winter. I have a very impressive array of first names: George Fortescue Maximilian. But you needn't bother with them all at once. My family call me Maxim.'
(Answer below)

Answer: Laurence Olivier to Joan Fontaine in Alfred Hitchcock's Rebecca

Julie Savides from Middlesex gives thanks for her life…

My day to remember was when I woke up from my colostomy operation to find I was alive and well. The night before I'd prayed to God to look after me and he answered my prayers.

Julie on holiday

WHAT A COINCIDENCE

Emily Street, Vancouver Island

In 1980 I celebrated my retirement by taking a six week holiday in Canada, staying with old friends.

A friend and I visited Banff in the Rockies and stopped for lunch by the side of Lake Louise. We were approached by two couples, one of whom my friend recognised as friends of hers from her home in Vancouver Island several hundred miles away.

I was introduced as a visitor from England and the usual inquiries as to where I came from followed. Imagine my surprise when I found out that the other couple and myself all lived in Gosport only a few streets away from each other, and they had flown to Canada the day before me!

And guess where my Vancouver Island friend lives? Emily Street!

Emily Soper, Gosport

ON GROWING OLDER
'If I knew I was going to live this long, I would have taken better care of myself'.
Eubie Blake

WHAT'S COOKING?

SUPPER DISH
Cheesey Semolina Bake
(Serves 4)

- 8 fl oz/250 ml vegetable stock
- 8 fl oz/250 ml milk
- Salt and white pepper
- Grated nutmeg
- 4 oz/100 g semolina (wholemeal has a nuttier taste)
- 2 eggs
- 5 oz/150 g Gruyère cheese, grated
- 1 oz/25 g butter
- 2 tbs chopped mixed herbs

1 Bring the vegetable stock to the boil in a pan with the milk and a pinch of salt, pepper and nutmeg. Take the pan off the heat and gradually stir in the semolina. Cover the pan and leave to stand for 10 minutes.
2 Beat the eggs with a fork until frothy. Stir into the semolina mixture with half the cheese.
3 Grease a baking dish with some of the butter. Fill with the semolina mixture, then level the top.
4 Bake in a moderately hot oven (200°C/400°F/Gas Mark 6) for 10 minutes. Then increase the temperature to very hot (240°C/475°F/Gas Mark 9) and bake for 10 minutes more.
5 Mix the remaining cheese with the herbs and spread over the dish. Dot with the remaining butter and bake for a further 10 minutes until the top is golden. Serve with salad.

Nature on your doorstep

The shifting seasons

Spring seems to arrive earlier these days, or is it just your imagination? No it isn't, says Anne Jappie from The Woodland Trust

You've probably noticed that things aren't what they used to be. Do you remember when winter began in late October, was bitterly cold and seemed to go on for ever? And that when you were a child, spring sprang with an explosion of blossom, bird song, fresh leaves and bright colours in late March? Nowadays, nature seems to be out of kilter. If you have noticed these things, the Woodland Trust would love to hear from you.

Thousands of people are already helping the Trust by recording the timing of recurring natural events they see in gardens, parks, high streets and woods.

The timing of these natural phenomena – which is known as 'phenology' – has revealed that almost every characteristic of spring 2002 occurred up to three weeks earlier than in 2001. On average, insects such as bumble bees and butterflies were three weeks early, while plants flowered two weeks ahead and many birds arrived a week earlier than usual.

The same phenological research has found that autumn is equally out of sorts. As in the spring, interconnected, complex relationships between plants, insects and animals in woods have been disrupted. For many species, this could affect their survival.

The Woodland Trust believes that climate change is the biggest single threat to what little remains of our ancient woodland.

The phenology project needs your help. Recording what you see is great fun and anyone can do it. The Trust has useful guides to help you identify hundreds of species. Historical records from family diaries would also be most welcome. Records spanning the last 50 years would be especially valuable, because they would help reinforce historic data spanning back to the 1700s.

* A simple recording form is available from the Woodland Trust on 0800 083 7497 or by logging on to www.phenology.org.uk

---

The things we miss

Children's games

As a child your playground would have been the street where you lived. Every day after school roads filled, not with traffic, but with children playing with brothers, sisters, neighbours and friends.

A lump of chalk and a stone was all you needed for a good game of Hopscotch. If it were 'skipping season' mothers would be roped in, literally, to turn a skipping rope stretched across the street while as many girls as possible piled in to skip together – or took it in turns to play skipping games.

You'd have watched your step on the pavements, too, during the whip and top season as you had to dodge the whizzing toys as they careered across the ground.

If you were daring, you could try rigging up an impromptu swing on a lamppost. All you needed was a length of sash cord borrowed from your dad and a cushion pinched from your mum's sofa. You slung the cord over the lamppost and tied the cushion to the end and there was your swing. It was a race to get as many swings as possible before a policeman caught you and ended the game!

PIC: HULTON ARCHIVE

Maypole

May is also the month for traditional dancing round the Maypole. Schools would practise skipping round the pole for weeks before the final show on village greens. The end result would be either a splendid plaited pattern of ribbons round the pole or a tangled cat's cradle, depending on how much rehearsal was done.

The Maypole was originally a pagan fertility symbol. The ribbons would have been vines knotted together to form long leafy ribbons. These were plaited by young girls to ensure the fertility of the land and its people.

Puzzles

Dateline

The answers to these clues are all numbers. Write them in the grid, and the numbers in the shaded squares will represent a significant date for British royalty.

ACROSS

2 Subtract the cube of 88 from 1064449
7 Twenty to midnight on the 24-hour clock
8 Half-a-dozen baker's dozens
9 Double 4975, subtract 1301
10 Add 248487 to 278142
13 Divide 204832 by 296
15 Pre-metric pence in two pounds ten shillings
16 Square 3854
22 Multiply 3999 by 2999
25 Roman CCXX
26 Three-elevenths of 2893
27 Subtract 482928 from 831210
31 Year of the start of World War 2
32 Forty-five per cent of 160
33 Divide 346632 by 39
34 Add 27 Across to 10 Across

DOWN

1 Square 287
2 Add two-sevenths of 518 to a quarter of 628
3 Divide 22356 by 9 squared
4 Multiply 53 by 35, subtract 869
5 Divide 778743 by 987
6 Subtract 43162 from 1 Down
11 Quadruple 546481
12 Add 999999 to 1736059
14 Square root of 441
15 Dozens in five-and-a-half gross
17 One seventeenth of 8177
18 Next in sequence: 300, 373, 446, …
19 Multiply 29 by 18, subtract 159
20 Square of J's alphabetical position
21 Add 36821 to 55893
22 Bingo call – 'Tony's den'
23 Divide 5916 by 348
24 Subtract 20 per cent of 37975 from 47382
27 Double 199
28 Multiply 189 by 5, subtract a fifth of 355
29 Subtract 11 from a dozen score
30 Divide 20232 by 32 Across

Solutions on Page 159

Song and dance numbers

PIC: REX FEATURES

If '10 G B' stands for *Ten Green Bottles*, can you work out the rest of these musical numbers? The list can include anything from pop songs to show tunes, carols and nursery rhymes. The first in the list was a hit for the pictured artist.

1   24 H from T
2   50 W to L Y L
3   3 B M
4   H B S 16
5   T N H a 1000 E
6   W I 64
7   3 T a L
8   2 L B
9   76 T (L the B P)
10 3 L M from S A W
11 5 F 2, E of B
12 16 G O 17
13 3 S to H
14 Y the 1 T I W
15 12 D of C
16 3 C in the F
17 15 M on a D M C
18 1 D at a T

The great adventure

Diane Lindsay and her young family sailed away across the Atlantic to find a new life in Canada in the 1960s, but after the opulence of life on board ship, they were in for a rude awakening...

In a suitcase under the bed, lies a large tattered brown envelope simply marked 'Canada'. Every ten years or so I rediscover it, and drifting away on a tide of memories, I marvel anew at how very quickly the past stops being just the other day, and becomes history.

Faded with age, there are the Canadian Pacific tickets, the 'Wanted on Voyage' labels, the exotic menus and the daily programmes. A frail serviette, marked Empress of England, lies next to playing cards from the Empress of Canada, a tiny baby's shoe nestles against some bedraggled streamers and a postcard of the Jacques Cartier bridge in Montreal. Mementoes from a vanished era, they tell of our Great Adventure, when we crossed the Atlantic twice in one year.

"Tell me about the olden days, Grandma," says Chloe, aged 11, reared on images of two tragic lovers, an iceberg and another great ocean liner. I can scarcely believe that her mum was only five months old in the 'olden days' of 1966. I was only 23 myself, long-haired, mini-kilted and as green as the grass that turned out to be just the same colour on the other side.

My mother cried, my dad looked grim, my Scottish in-laws waved stoically as if they'd seen it all before. As the streamers billowed and the piper's lament echoed the bleakness of the day, we waved a damp goodbye to England and slipped eagerly into opulence. Plush and gilt, morning coffee and bouillon, afternoon tea with thin bread and butter served to the sound of a Palm Court quartet – it was all rather decadent, and worked on the senses like a drug.

It soon felt as if we'd walked on the tilt all our lives, as if the throb of engines and the creaking of bulkheads had been in our ears forever. It's a strange limbo world at sea; there seems no past or future, just a massive circle of sky and heaving water, with the only real reference point the deck, constantly pushing against one's feet.

Our cabins were small and windowless but morning tea served by a steward was both a novelty and a luxury. Breakfast offered an astonishing five courses, while we read the ship's newspaper and planned another leisurely day just like the previous one; a daily promenade around the deck, then, watching from steamer chairs, shipboard romances develop and ephemeral friendships blossom.

While the seas rose and fell, pearling the windows with spray, children played tig, rich American matriarchs patronised the stewards, elderly gents ogled the girls, teenagers ogled each other and sad-eyed drunks came to stare briefly out of the windows before weaving gently back to the bars.

From the various lounges, the strains of the 'Morning Classic' mingled with sounds of betting on the ship's mileage, announcements from the Purser vied with the tap of ping-pong balls, everything inviting you to forget the thrum and the slap and the creak of a relatively small vessel on a very large ocean.

Lunch was superlative, dinner was sumptuous. Once the two children slept, the steward babysat

Diane with Fiona on her knee and husband George with Sam

while we watched a film, danced, or took in a show. We toasted the captain, the ship, the voyage, the future and the ship's cat. Had we been lonely, the Social Hostess would have smoothed our way, had we fancied cards the daily advice was not to gamble with strangers. In case of night starvation, the day rounded off with sandwiches. By the time we sailed up the St Lawrence we were relaxed to the point of pure exhaustion.

Of the Great Adventure I can say little, other than that disillusionment began when there were no grizzly bears prowling the banks of the great river, no Indian Love Call echoed around the pine-encrusted mountains, and no scarlet coated mounties saluted us into Quebec.

Soon after landing, a friend advised me to lengthen my skirts as the Swinging Sixties hadn't yet reached Montreal, and only hookers wore clothes that 'sassy'. Snow fell on Christmas Eve, and every single following day for the next three months, temperatures plummeted, never rising above 28 below zero Fahrenheit during

February. The baby cried all night, and the three-year-old wearily begged us to send her sister back where she came from. When England won the World Cup we knew it was time to go home.

Life is full of little ironies. Circumstances meant we came home on separate sailings. My husband George, with a passion for sea stories, longed for a taste of Atlantic fury. I am a coward. Yet it was during my voyage that a fire broke out in the crew's quarters, an amorous whale speared itself on the ship's bows and a force 12 gale caused us to hove to in mid-Atlantic for 24 hours, losing all radio contact with the outside world. But no, Chloe, we did not hit an iceberg.

I can only describe seas like monstrous green mountains, troughs where the sky disappeared, children sitting on the ballroom floor, and a night of panic when people donned life-jackets and the chairs in the dining room above our cabin rolled back and forth like distant thunder. Metal balustrades twisted, we ate from mismatched crockery, and at Liverpool we were met by a fleet of ambulances. My husband crossed four months later on a millpond.

Some people called it emigrating and commiserated with us when we came back, as if we'd failed some kind of test. It wasn't like that at all. We sold the house and gave ourselves two years to see something of the world. I wasn't to know that soon after leaving the Mersey I would be engulfed by a tidal wave of homesickness that only receded when I sailed back up it six months later. We spent the money, had our adventure, and came gratefully home to earn ourselves another step on the housing market. But while Bob Dylan was singing it out for all he was worth, neither of us realised just how much, and how quickly the times were a-changin'. They still are.

So now we travel the world every year or two in a mere eleven hours to visit our son, our homecoming baby and the only one of our children to miss the adventure. He grew up and went to San Francisco, and although it was too late to put flowers in his hair, when he married his American sweetheart this year, he had orchids round his neck and it was clear that his own adventure had only just begun.

So now it's we who blink back the tears, try not to look grim and wave stoically on a regular basis. Kind of serves us right really.

June 2004

A flavour of the month

PIC PHOTODISC

With the weather warming up, it's time to get outdoors and be active.

A brisk walk can lift your mood, is good for your heart and lungs and can burn off up to 300 calories an hour. And, even small changes can make a big difference. Get off the bus a stop early, park your car at the far end of the supermarket car park, or simply leave your car at home.

Gardening is also a good way to get a dose of fresh air and exercise – just half an hour of gardening can burn up 250 calories. And while in the garden it is worth rabbit-proofing your plants too. Wild rabbits can be a pest. Protect new plants with a collar of wire netting or seal off entire plant areas using chicken-wire – it needs to be more than a metre high, of which a quarter is below ground level.

With your garden looking at its best, why don't you fire up the barbecue for some summer sizzlers? Grilled trout, tuna steaks, corn-on-the-cob and even bananas make for a tasty outdoor meal with a difference.

June is also a great month for herbs. So, accompany your al fresco feast with a summer herb salad of cos, rocket and spinach mixed with chervil, tarragon, flat leaf parsley and tossed in olive oil and lemon juice.

TUESDAY	1
WEDNESDAY	2
THURSDAY	3
FRIDAY	4
SATURDAY	5
SUNDAY	6
MONDAY	7
TUESDAY	8
WEDNESDAY	9
THURSDAY	10
FRIDAY	11
SATURDAY	12
SUNDAY	13
MONDAY	14
TUESDAY	15
WEDNESDAY	16
THURSDAY	17
FRIDAY	18

SATURDAY	19	
SUNDAY	20	Fathers' Day
MONDAY	21	Summer solstice Wimbledon Championships start
TUESDAY	22	
WEDNESDAY	23	
THURSDAY	24	
FRIDAY	25	
SATURDAY	26	
SUNDAY	27	
MONDAY	28	July YOURS on sale
TUESDAY	29	
WEDNESDAY	30	

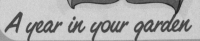

A year in your garden

Plants are roaring away in June, and keeping up with them can be exhausting. Watering is often the primary requirement and containers and hanging baskets should be checked every day. If you have the space, it's a good idea to mix water retaining gel crystals in your compost before planting up bedding. It soaks up water, releasing it when the compost becomes dry. It's best to give shrubs a good soak as this encourages roots to look deep for their own water.

Food is important at this time of year as the production of leaves and flowers takes a lot out of soil or compost. There's a huge range of fertilisers available, but extract of seaweed is one of the best. It's organic and provides many of the nutrients that most plants require. One bottle or packet will feed the whole garden. It also smells like your holidays.

Some plants, such as rhododendrons and camellias are now entering the crucial part of their growing year. It's now that next year's buds are starting to form, and any yellowing of leaves means the plant isn't functioning 100 per cent. Specially formulated ericaceous fertiliser is available to counteract deficiencies in the soil.

Bugs and beasties are also getting cracking this month, and a daily walk around your garden will nip many in the bud. A quick squash between your fingers will stop aphids getting out of control. It saves you buying insecticidal soaps as a cure.

A night stroll, armed with a torch and bucket of salty water will also reduce the slug and snail population.

This is a great month to apply the microscopic worms, available from garden retailers and mail order, as the soil is warm and the pests are active.

PIC: EMAP GARDEN PICTURE LIBRARY

★ **READER'S TIP** ★
Henry Balman in Coventry uses his old washing up water as a spray on his roses. Henry says that the greenfly never get to large enough numbers to cause damage.

May 31-June 6

WHAT'S COOKING?

AT THE MOVIES

Who said?
'It is a far, far better thing I do than I have ever done. It is a far, far better rest I go to than I have ever known'.
(Answer below)

Answer: Ronald Coleman meeting his end in Jack Conway's A Tale Of Two Cities

Goats Cheese and Roasted Pepper Salad
(Serves 4)

- 2 red peppers
- 1 yellow pepper
- 3 tbs olive oil
- 4 oz/100 g continental lettuce
- 1½lb/675 g tomatoes
- 11 oz/300 g French goat's cheese (such as Chevre du Berry)
- 2 oz/50 g pine nuts
- ½ oz/15 g butter
- 2 tablespoons red wine vinegar
- Pinch of sugar

1 Slice tops off peppers, remove core and seeds and halve. Arrange shiny side up on a grill pan and drizzle with 2 tablespoons of olive oil.
2 Grill until charred and blistered, leave 10-20 minutes, then peel away skin and cut into chunky pieces.
3 Wash lettuce, drain and arrange in base of salad bowl.
4 Cut tomatoes into wedges and carefully slice goat's cheese.
5 Arrange cheese, tomatoes and peppers in centre of lettuce.
6 Fry pine nuts in butter until browned, scatter over salad.
7 Season generously with freshly ground black pepper.
8 Mix together remaining olive oil, red wine vinegar, and pinch of sugar. Season and pour over salad to serve.

PIC: PRODUCE CONSORTIUM

A DAY TO REMEMBER

Two special days for Mrs M English from Essex...

My daughter was diagnosed with curvature of the spine and was in plaster for nearly five years. We cheered the day she was discharged and didn't have to go to hospital any more. She was so good and so brave and was only nine when we found out.

My second special day was when I had a phone call from the hospital to say I could fetch my new baby home from hospital. I'd had to leave him as he was premature and only weighed 4lb 4oz. I left my ironing and ran with his pram to fetch him – thank goodness the hospital was only walking distance.

You should have seen his brother and sister's faces when they came home from school. He's now 30 years old and so tall!

OLD WIVES' TALES

Make a jacket from soft brown paper, coat with wax from a tallow candle and it should help a patient with bronchitis.

Dr Henderson replies: It should also take hours of work, make you look and feel silly and be of no use whatsoever! I suppose people thought this would somehow 'soften' chest infections but there is only one good treatment for proper bronchitis, and that is a check-up from your doctor and antibiotics. Still, I suppose by the time you've made this jacket you'll probably be better anyway!

OUT & ABOUT TO...

Topsy's, The Willow Cottage, Stour Row, Dorset

This eccentric garden was created in remembrance of a Mongolian slave girl called Topsy. In the 1930s, she was smuggled out of China and brought to England by three missionaries who owned The Willow Cottage. Topsy lived in the shed that still remains, and developed a love of gardening. She remained at the cottage for many years, until retiring to a nursing home – she died in 1998.

The current owners have gone back to the garden's original, organic roots. Some parts, such as the herbaceous borders, are very traditional, but others are wild; there are also beds made from shredded newspaper, manure and comfrey leaves. You'll find ponds, a stream and inspirational 'self-tensioning' structures made out of baton wood. Owner Jane Montana's latest work in progress is a labyrinth she's fashioning from willow: Topsy would have loved it.

● *Adults £1.50, children free*
● *Topsy's is open on May 30, 31 and June 1, then on some weekends in June and August (important you phone first to check dates and times) as part of the National Gardens Open For Charity Scheme*
● *Teas available; plants for sale; wheelchair access if dry*
Tel: 01747 838088

▲ And they're off! The wheelbarrow race gets underway at a country festival in Devon in 1943

ON GROWING OLDER

'In youth we run into difficulties. In old age, difficulties run into us'.

Josh Billings

PAUSE FOR THOUGHT

Mrs I Rowling of County Durham sent in John Wesley's words – ones that she has remembered for many years:

Do all the good you can,
By all the means you can,
In all the ways you can,
In all the places you can,
At all the times you can,
To all the people you can,
As long as ever you can.

Top tip

Discourage houseflies by sprinkling lavender oil on cotton wool and dotting it around the room.

DID YOU KNOW THAT

Almonds are members of the peach family.

June 7-13

It was a whirlwind romance for Mona Streetley of York…

Mona standing in the place where she met Paul

I was 17 in 1941 and enjoying life despite the war. My mother asked me if I would go to the allotment to get some vegetables for dinner. On my way back I heard a voice say, 'Good morning'. And there he was, a tall, dark, dashing young Army Sergeant.

I was shocked at his approach, so I said, 'I don't know you' and kept on walking. He said he only had three days in our village and wanted to get to know me. Although my parents weren't happy about it, I agreed to meet him.

I brought Paul home to meet my parents and after he went away, our courtship continued by letter. On his next leave he arrived, complete with ring, and proposed to me. We were engaged on June 30 – the same year but we hardly ever saw each other. Then I got a letter to say he was going abroad, so he wrote to my parents asking their permission for us to marry before he went. It was one big rush to get ready but we were married on August 30, 1941. We had two days together, then he was gone and I didn't see him again for four years.

People said the marriage wouldn't last and that we were too young – but they were wrong. It lasted 45 years until Paul sadly died in 1984. He always wrote lovely letters and I still have them – hundreds of them.

OLD FASHIONED REMEDIES

I remember ironing my father's bad back with brown paper. Also putting Belladonna on his back. I didn't like to have to rip it off, though!
Dorothy Nutton, Lincolnshire

Dr Henderson replies: I bet your father wasn't too keen on it either! Warmth can help sore and aching muscles, so there is a possibility that this would give some symptomatic relief to a bad back here. As for the brown paper though – useless I'm afraid.

WHAT'S COOKING?

QUICK SNACK
Salmon Salad
(Serves 4)

- 8 oz/225 g pasta shells
- 4 tablespoons oil
- 1 tb vinegar
- Salt and pepper
- 1 teaspoon mixed herbs
- 1 small tin of salmon
- 1 lettuce
- ½ cucumber, sliced

1. Cook the pasta shells as directed on the packet.
2. Mix oil, vinegar, salt, pepper and herbs together. Pour over pasta, mix and leave until cool.
3. Shred lettuce and arrange around the edge of the 4 plates. Flake the salmon and pile in the centre with the pasta shells.
4. Arrange cucumber between salmon mixture and lettuce and pour over a light vinaigrette.

AT THE MOVIES

Who said?
'One of the gentlemen found time to say, How delicious!'
(Answer below)

Answer: Jean Adair recalling a victim of her poisoned elderberry wine in Frank Capra's *Arsenic And Old Lace*.

We moved from Oldham to Cumbria, and I began to trace my family tree. Wanting to meet people, I started a Wine Appreciation Group and a gentleman who'd joined the group phoned one day to say he'd miss the next meeting. "Oh, off to trace your family tree, are you?" I asked jokingly. He replied no, but asked me which name I was trying to trace. "Thompson," I replied, "a very common name." He continued: "A man in the next village to yours, who is also tracing the Thompson name, turned out to be my third cousin. I'll ask him to give you a ring."

He did and he turned out to be MY third cousin as well – we had a great-grandfather George in common.

A further coincidence was that, although there was quite a difference in our ages, this man had gone to the same grammar school as my husband and – prior to his moving to Cumbria several years after us – had lived within half a mile from us.

Jean Tibbott, Cumbria

MY ADVICE IS...

'Always pull together, never in opposite directions'.
Ivy Jameson, Bedfordshire

DID YOU KNOW THAT

Al Capone's business card said he was a used furniture dealer.

Top tip

Help a stubborn garden hose slide easily on to your tap by rubbing the inside with soap.

ON GROWING OLDER

'Growing old is mandatory; growing up is optional'.

Unknown

PIC: BUCKINGHAMSHIRE COUNTY MUSEUM

OUT & ABOUT TO...

The Roald Dahl Children's Gallery, Church Street, Aylesbury, Buckinghamshire

Remember when your children used to pester you to read Charlie & The Chocolate Factory just one more time? Chances are you didn't mind a bit – and it's just as well because now your grandchildren are hooked on Willy Wonka too! Roald Dahl's unique brand of storytelling appeals just as much to adults as the generations of youngsters reared on the hilarious exploits of Charlie, James and their peers.

Dahl's tales have been brought to life in this exciting exhibition – and you'll enjoy it every bit as much as your grandchildren. All the exhibits are very hands-on, and are designed to stimulate and entertain. You can discover inventions with Willy Wonka, investigate 'minibeasts' inside the giant peach, touch a mammoth's tooth, explore sound with the BFG and ride in the great glass elevator.

● *There are also lots of things to touch, see and do in the adjoining Buckinghamshire County Museum.*
● *Adults £3.50, children £2.75*
● *Café; wheelchair access*
Tel: 01296 331441 (Internet: www.buckscc.gov.uk/museum)

June 14-20

WHAT A COINCIDENCE

Joan and her husband

One day in 1954, I was teaching a little girl in my class, who told me: "I won't be back this afternoon." "Why not?" I asked. "I'm going with my daddy to Tilbury to meet my uncle, who's coming back from Australia." "How exciting," I replied.

The next day she brought in a little, furry koala bear, given to her by her uncle, which I duly admired.

Some months later, I was at our local square dance club with friends when a good-looking young man with an Australian accent asked me to dance. I thought 'great', as I was single!

The following week he was there again and, at the end of the evening, drove my cousin and me home. While at some traffic lights, he said: "My sister-in-law works in the grocers over there." I replied: "I used to teach a little girl whose mother works there." Then the penny dropped – this was the uncle the little girl had met at Tilbury.

A few years later, I married him but, sadly, he died in 1972. We were both very keen square dancers and this photograph was taken in 1956.

WHAT'S COOKING?

SUPPER DISH
Summer Pie
(Serves 1)

- 1 oz/25 g strong cheese
- 2 level tbs fresh breadcrumbs
- Salt and pepper
- 3 oz/75 g carrots
- 4 oz/115 g broad beans
- 2 oz/50 g button mushrooms
- 1 level tb cornflour
- 2 level tbs milk powder

1 Slice the carrots and cook with the broadbeans for 15 minutes in boiling salted water. Add the mushrooms and cook for a further 5 minutes.
2 Drain and reserve ¼ pt/150 ml water. Blend the cornflour and powdered skimmed milk with 2 tablespoons cold water to make a smooth paste.
3 Stir in the vegetable water then return to the pan. Bring to the boil, stirring all the time, then simmer for 1 minute. Add the vegetables. Heat through on a low heat. Transfer to an ovenproof dish.
4 Grate the cheese and mix with the breadcrumbs. Sprinkle on top and grill until the cheese melts.

AT THE MOVIES

Who said?
'Made it, Ma. Top of the world!'
(Answer below)

Answer: James Cagney shooting it out in Raoul Walsh's White Heat

OLD WIVES' TALES

You can't get one cold straight after another.

Dr Henderson replies: Oh, yes you can! In fact, for many people after they have had a cold they are more, rather than less, likely to catch another because their body's immune system can be rather battered and frail from fighting off the last one. Boost this by taking regular vitamin C and courses of Echinacea.

OUT & ABOUT TO...

Special Plants, Greenways Lane, near Cold Ashton, Wiltshire

PIC: MELANIE ECLARE

Serious gardeners and plant collectors will find plenty to lust after in this unusual garden, which has made guest appearances in the TV series Home Front in the Garden and Gardener's World.

Designed by Derry's architect husband, Peter Clegg, it's on several levels and has fabulous views. It features numerous exotic plants, many from South Africa. There are also spring-fed ponds, a bog garden, a woodland walk, a grass garden, dazzling Iceland poppies, a vegetable garden and orchard, an apricot-coloured border and a gravel garden.

Derry's personal touch can be seen throughout the adjoining nursery, which is helpfully organised according to the needs of the plants – tender plants; plants for dry sun; plants for damp shade. Resist them if you can.

● *Adults £1.50; children free*
● *Special Plants is open on June 17, July 15, August 19 and September 16 as part of the National Gardens Open For Charity Scheme (phone first to check dates and times)*
● *Home-made teas, plants for sale, wheelchair access if dry.*
Tel: 01225 891686

PAUSE FOR THOUGHT

'When I was a teenager', writes Maureen Knighton of Northants, 'and argued with my dad that I didn't have time to do chores or errands, he would say, 'There's no such thing as I haven't got time. You must make time'. And he was right'.

Maureen goes on to say that her favourite words of wisdom now are: *This is life NOW. It is not a rehearsal. Make the most of it!*

ON GROWING OLDER

'Just remember, once you're over the hill, you begin to pick up speed'.
Charles Schultz

Top tip

You can disguise the smell of garlic on your breath by chewing a coffee bean.

Keith Gregson from Sunderland remembers a great man...

DID YOU KNOW THAT

The average person falls asleep in seven minutes.

A DAY TO REMEMBER

I'll never forget the day I was in the same room as Martin Luther King. To my knowledge, he only visited England once, to receive a Doctorate of Civil Law at the University of Newcastle Upon Tyne.

I was lucky enough to be one of the students selected to attend the ceremony. My seat was close to the front and I can still visualise the great man talking about his Civil Rights work. He was calm and composed – so different from the passionate speaker we remember rallying people to the cause.

June 21-27

PIC: NATIONAL COAL MINING MUSEUM

OUT & ABOUT TO...

National Coal Mining Museum for England, Caphouse Colliery, Overton, West Yorkshire

It won't make the slightest difference if you visit this museum on the longest (June 21) or the shortest day of the year, because the most exciting part of it is underground. After collecting your helmet and lamp from the lamp room, you descend a full 140 feet below the surface in the cage. Down below, you'll be taken on a tour of the underground workings of the mine and discover what it was like to be a miner from 1820 to the present day.

Back above ground, you can visit the last ever working pit ponies, who are now enjoying their retirement, take a train ride, watch machinery displays, see the pit head baths and stroll along the half-mile-long nature trail. This is one underground ride you shouldn't miss!

● *Adults £1.50; children free (under-fives can't go underground)*
● *Caphouse is a real coal mine, so wear warm clothes and sensible shoes*
● *Visitor centre with audiovisual displays; licensed café; picnic area; gift shop*
● *Excellent facilities for people with disabilities (call before your visit)*
Tel: 01924 848806 (Internet: www.ncm.org.uk)

ON GROWING OLDER

'I don't know how you feel about old age, but in my case, I didn't see it coming. It hit me from the rear'.

Phyllis Diller

Top tip

Shine up your gold jewellery with a slice of bread – it really works!

DID YOU KNOW THAT

A cat has 32 muscles in each ear.

AT THE MOVIES

Who said?
'Little girls, I am in the business of putting old heads on young shoulders, and all my pupils are the crème de la crème. Give me a girl of impressionable age, and she is mine for life'.
(Answer below)

MY ADVICE IS...

Give your time –
it may bring to an end
Somebody's troubles
and make you a friend.
C Jones, Brighton

Answer: Maggie Smith's teaching ethic in the last lines of Ronald Neame's The Prime Of Miss Jean Brodie

WHAT A COINCIDENCE

I was travelling through Europe by train with a girlfriend and on one long trip got talking to a man in the same carriage.

He told me he had a great job as a travel journalist for a well-known newspaper. I told him I used to have a boyfriend who worked at his paper, in the library. The journalist told me he'd worked his way up to become head of the library.

When I got back to England, I phoned the newspaper and asked to speak to him. When I mentioned the rambling club we used to belong to, he remembered me right away. We met and spent a delightful evening, reminiscing.

Can you imagine, meeting a stranger on a train in Europe would lead to meeting a friend of years past, with whom I'd completely lost touch!

Jean Buzan, Bucks

WHAT'S COOKING?

A MEAL ON A BUDGET
Spinach Surprise
(Serves 4)

- 4 oz/110 g cottage cheese
- 1 oz/25 g Parmesan cheese
- ½ oz/10 g powdered milk
- ¼ pt/150 ml water
- Salt and black pepper
- 8 slices white bread
- 2 oz/50 g butter
- Packet of spinach
- 1 oz/25 g margarine
- 2 eggs

1. Remove crusts from the bread, butter each slice and place, buttered side down, in 8 patty tins.
2. Cook spinach in the margarine, drain and place in cup cases, spreading it carefully up the sides to make a nest.
3. Whisk eggs and remaining ingredients together.
4. Pour into bread cases. Bake in oven (180°C/ 350°F/Gas Mark 4) for 20 minutes. Serve while piping hot. Serving with a tossed green salad.

OLD FASHIONED REMEDIES

Found in a 1934 'medical recipe' book:
Embrocation for athletes etc
Crude Pyroligneous Acid, 10 ounces
Methylated Spirits, 12 ounces
Water, 12 ounces
Turpentine, 1¾ ounces
Add one egg. 'Anyone can make pounds by selling it to Athletes and Horse Owners.'
Kay Goldberger, W Yorks

Dr Henderson replies: The thought of rubbing turpentine and methylated spirits on to your skin fills me with mild alarm! Seventy years on I would hope this is never used, as this could be highly irritating to the skin as well as being of no practical use either. I hardly need tell you to avoid it.

Two memorable occasions in one for Dorothy Bloor from Staffordshire…

A DAY TO REMEMBER

I did not decide to be confirmed until my 60th birthday. On the morning of my confirmation, I received a phone call to say my younger daughter had gone into labour 10 weeks early. I was very upset.

At the church, the Bishop asked the congregation to pray for her and she was safely delivered of a baby girl, Kira, who weighed 2lb 13oz. When we checked the time of her birth, it was exactly the same time I was receiving my first communion. The day will always be a special memory.

Dorothy and baby Kira

Time to try drying

Take your summer garden indoors with a dried flower arrangement

The range of flowers and herbs that you can dry is frankly enormous, so don't sit back and be afraid to experiment.

Air drying is the easiest and most successful method, best done in a place with a constant flow of warm, dry air, such as an airing cupboard.

Flowers and herbs suitable for drying include: Lavender, lady's mantle, marsh-mallow, larkspur, cornflowers, roses, angelica, marjoram, sea holly, strawflowers and wheat. There are lots more! Gather herbs for drying just

before they flower, unless you want to dry their flowers as well. Pick flowers in bud or newly opened: A full-blown flower will never dry well. Make sure those you do gather are absolutely dry when you harvest them – noon on a fine day is an ideal time.

Flowers and herbs can be tied and hung upside down. It's a good idea to strip most of the leaves from flower stalks to allow the air to circulate around the stem and flower heads, so reducing the risk of mildew. Keep the bunches fairly small to speed up the drying time.

To get the best out of your dried flowers and herbs, don't be afraid to use other materials, too: Cinnamon sticks, seed heads, small pine cones and seashells, driftwood can all add real interest to an arrangement. Branches, twigs and moss can also be used while they're still fresh – they're easier to work with if they're still a bit damp. But if you use these items in a display, leave it somewhere warm to dry out.

The things we miss

Seaside memories

When, as a child, you had the wonderful treat of a trip to the seaside, there was the thrill of a whole new wardrobe of clothes, marking you out as holidaymakers. Remember those never to be forgotten shirred elastic swimming costumes that squeezed you like a corset? Or the knitted ones you wore as a child which held the water and stretched to twice their size!

And what about those beautiful swirling sun-ray pleated skirts and dresses, or the dirndl skirt, worn with a an embroidered 'Hungarian' blouse.

On the beach most people would be kitted out in voluminous, wide-legged beach pyjamas, rubber paddling shoes or white sandshoes, brought up brilliant and gleaming with a lick of Blanco.

For entertainment you could delight in the Pierrot shows on the pier, or for the more daring, there were Pedalo boats, which were great fun, as long as you could manage to steer them safely back to shore!

With sun cream unheard of, the only protection you had was a hat or, for the gents, a

PIC: HULTON ARCHIVE

large handkerchief carefully knotted at each corner. Or there was always the newspaper, gently wafting up and down as dad snored!

And what about the sand? No matter how hard you tried, there was always a little bit left between your toes that rubbed like mad as you made your hot and weary way back to your bed and breakfast!

And, just in case there was a chance of showers, you always had your Pac-a-Mac or your plastic hood in its own little carrying case with you, ever prepared for the typical English seaside weather!

Veronyca (back row, far right) with some of her fellow Bluecoats

Pontin's,
here we come!

It's 1971 and it's Veronyca Bates's first season as a Pontin's Bluecoat...

The bus threaded its way through the narrow country lane. Since we'd turned off the main road more than a mile back, we hadn't passed another building, car or person. We were approaching a flat coastline and we could see quite clearly a sprawl of small buildings that was Pontin's Holiday Camp, Morecambe.

Over the camp hung an orange cloud that was ballooning out of a tall chimney stack close by and we could smell the sulphurous fumes. The stack was part of a chemical factory and when the wind blew in the wrong direction, the smell was terrible. The campers didn't seem to mind though, and after a while we got used to it.

The 'we' in question were the 1971 season of Bluecoats. We arrived the week before the season began so that we could devise and rehearse our shows. I'd answered an advertisement in 'The Stage' and was interviewed by the Entertainment Manager briefly over the phone before being offered the job on the spot, and now here I was at the gates of the camp.

We were given tea and some stale slices of pork pie and then sent to our chalets, which we shared; two strangers in a very small room for 13 weeks.

The camp hadn't been occupied since the previous September and there was no heating in the chalets – our rooms were cold, damp and musty smelling. Toilets, baths and showers were situated in blocks at the end of the chalet rows. I remember vividly my first sight of the washrooms. Debris had blown into them over the winter and they were filthy. The cleaners weren't due to start work for another three days and there was no cleaning equipment either.

I had to use one of my own T-shirts and some soap to clean the bath as best I could. Hopeful then of relaxing in a hot tub, I discovered the heating for the water wasn't going to be turned on until the end of the week. The weather that first week in May was cold, bleak and cheerless. How I yearned for a hot bath every evening, but had to settle for a quick sluice down in ice cold water.

It was a chaotic week as we worked on our routines but, amazingly, when Saturday came, everything was done and we stood in reception, trying to look relaxed as we welcomed the first batch of visitors.

Campers were encouraged to be competitive and at dinner every Saturday everyone was allocated to one of two teams.

Inter-team rivalry was fierce and campers were encouraged to enter every competition in order to gain points for their own team. The campers' days were tightly organised from the moment they were woken with Radio Pontin's breakfast countdown until they went to bed at midnight with a communal singsong in the ballroom.

As Bluecoats, we worked up to a 16-hour day, six days a week. Those unlucky enough to be on breakfast radio duty would be woken up by security at 6.30am. We had to sign a book to prove they had woken us up, but as radio duty didn't start until 7.25am we usually went back to sleep again. On one occasion I overslept and rushed to the station.

Normally, I should have played a record just before the half hour and then announce the time at 7.30 and tell campers that breakfast would be in half an hour. This particular morning I put the record on, played about eight bars, yanked the record off and announced the time as 7.30am. Five minutes later I announced the correct time as 7.45am. If anyone noticed no-one said anything.

We'd form a breakfast 'guard of honour' at the entrance to the dining room, and to the tune of Ronnie Corbett singing, It's All Going Up, Up, Up we would bounce up and down, clapping our hands and welcoming the campers in. They appreciated it, apparently.

The mornings were spent in organising sports, or we might get a couple of precious hours off duty. In the afternoon we were engaged in overseeing competitions that today seem hopelessly dated.

It was hard work but there was a tremendous spirit of camaraderie among the Bluecoats and the season was one of the best times of my life.

July 2004

A flavour of the month

Flowers and plants are extremely versatile and offer many opportunities to be creative.

For a unique souvenir of an ever-changing landscape, head into your garden with a pad and pencil and sketch what you see. Take snap shots, too, so you can draw your favourite flowers all year around.

With the UK weather being so unpredictable, take some of your garden indoors, so you can enjoy the fruits of your labour, whatever the forecast. Brighten up your windowsills with bunches of flowers picked from your beds. To keep flower-heads upright, place them up to their necks in cold water for an hour. If the heads droop, prick the stems just below the heads to release any airlocks that could prevent the blooms drawing water.

Pressed petals make even longer lasting keepsakes. Press your favourite flowers between the pages of a heavy book, leave for a few weeks until the flowers are completely dry. Make unique gift cards or pictures by glueing petals to card and covering with iron-on plastic, which is available from most large stationers.

Homemade pot-pourri is also easy to make and has long-lasting fragrant results. Spread a mixture of petals on newspaper (rose petals work well) and store in an airing cupboard until they are crisp. Mix with 1oz (25g) of dried orris root, to fix the scent, and a few drops of essential rose oil.

THURSDAY	1	
FRIDAY	2	
SATURDAY	3	
SUNDAY	4	Final day of Wimbledon Championships
MONDAY	5	
TUESDAY	6	6-11 Hampton Court Flower Show (provisional)
WEDNESDAY	7	
THURSDAY	8	
FRIDAY	9	
SATURDAY	10	
SUNDAY	11	
MONDAY	12	Bank Holiday N Ireland (Battle of the Boyne)
TUESDAY	13	
WEDNESDAY	14	
THURSDAY	15	
FRIDAY	16	The BBC Proms begin
SATURDAY	17	
SUNDAY	18	

MONDAY	19
TUESDAY	20
WEDNESDAY	21
THURSDAY	22
FRIDAY	23
SATURDAY	24
SUNDAY	25
MONDAY	26
TUESDAY	27
WEDNESDAY	28
THURSDAY	29
FRIDAY	30
SATURDAY	31

August YOURS on sale

PIC: EMAP GARDEN PICTURE LIBRARY

A year in your garden

The best way to get the full taste of delicious herbs is to grow them yourself. You have a couple of options – either grow them in well drained soil, in a sunny site in the garden or in a hanging basket.

Hanging baskets are great for herbs because the compost is well drained, as anyone who has reached up to water one knows, and you can hang the basket right outside the kitchen door or window and pluck and snip as the recipe demands.

Start off with a standard basket and line it with a fibre lining. Moss is a good alternative but make sure it hasn't been harvested from the wild. The bag will tell you where the contents have come from. Then the compost – and a John Innes Number 3 is best. It's based on loam and will provide a heavy medium, but the nutrients are relatively low. This suits herbs, as too much fertiliser and the plants will produce lush tasteless growth.

Add a handful of grit to the compost and stir well. This will ensure superb drainage. Firm the compost into the basket and when the level is just above the base, add your first plants.

Mint is well suited to baskets. Plants can grow mad without invading the whole of your garden. Poke plants through the lining into the compost, adding more compost to cover the roots. Keep doing this until the compost level is an inch or so below the top of the basket. Never plant right up to the top of the basket, as water will run off the surface and not soak into the compost. Thymes love a hanging basket, and Catmint will fill a basket in no time at all.

Origanum is a must and basil will survive well if the basket is placed in a hot, sunny position.

✳ READER'S TIP ✳

Catherine Mulvaney in Cirencester uses old jumpers as linings for her baskets. They let water through but keep compost where it should be – in the basket. I suppose they also look colourful while you are waiting for the plants to grow.

June 28–July 4

A DAY TO REMEMBER

It's back to 1933 for Anne Hargreaves of Hampshire…

I walked through the huge wrought iron gates in my green and cream suit to begin my first day at work, and saw the notice, 'General office up two flights of stairs'. I was unsure if my leg would carry me that far, as they felt like jelly.

I arrived at the large, highly polished black door and tentatively pushed it open, looking for guidance. "If you're the new girl, come inside at once!" What a frightening sight. There was the lord and master sitting on his rostrum, glaring down at the 40 or 50 clerks at their desks.

I was given my work for the day and told I would have help with the rules and regulations for a few days, then would be expected to be competent within the week. I was also told to hold my hand up if I wished to visit the wash room.

Well, I managed to hold the fort that first day, and survived it for a couple of years. Today, in places of employment, there is laughter and no sign of a raised hand anywhere, thank goodness!

OLD WIVES' TALES

Feed a cold, starve a fever.

Dr Henderson replies: A very common one this, dating back (I think) to 1574, when a dictionary maker named Withals wrote, 'Fasting is a great remedie of feuer'. Current medical thinking is that you want to keep on an even course when you're sick with either a cold or a fever, and you certainly don't want to stress your system by either eating lots or starving yourself. I have been told by a patient that this proverb really means, 'If you feed a cold now, you'll have to starve a fever later'. A more plausible interpretation is that the feed-a-cold idea arose out of an incorrect understanding of disease, namely that there were two kinds of illnesses, those caused by low temperatures (colds and chills) and those caused by high temperatures (fever). If you had a chill, you wanted to heat up, so you ate a lot. If you had a fever, you didn't want things to overheat, so you ate less. Either way, both are wrong — eat normally and sensibly if you are unwell.

WHAT'S COOKING?

Cheesy Bacon Courgettes
(Serves 4)

- 1 lb/450 g courgettes
- 1 onion, sliced
- 1 stalk celery
- 2 tbs oil
- 6 rashers streaky bacon, chopped
- Seasoning to taste
- 2 oz/50 g grated cheese

1 Fry the onion and diced celery gently in the oil with the bacon. Add the courgettes, sliced lengthways, and season to taste.
2 Cover and cook until the courgettes are just tender. Place the courgettes in an oven-proof dish, top with bacon mixture, sprinkle with the cheese and brown under the grill.

PIC: FRESH PRODUCE CONSORTIUM

AT THE MOVIES

Who said?
'Listen to them. Children of the night. What music they make'.
(Answer below)

Answer: Bela Lugosi in Tod Browning's Dracula

PIC: BENINGTON LORDSHIP GARDEN

OUT & ABOUT TO...

Benington Lordship Garden, Stevenage, Hertfordshire

This Georgian manor house with an Edwardian extension and a picturesque Norman gatehouse and ruined castle in the grounds has been the setting for many films and fashion shoots. However, this being Herbaceous Border Week (call first to check dates and opening times), the real stars of the show are the stunning flowers, of which owner Sarah Bott is justifiably proud.

The seven-acre terraced gardens are a clever mix of formality and wilderness, with interesting plants and flowers and lots of wildlife. They should be looking their colourful best at the moment, so enjoy their loveliness.

Once you've had your fill of the flowers, there's a lovely and well-signposted country walk that starts very near the entrance to the gardens. Depending on how fast you walk, it takes between 30 minutes and an hour and a half, so why not take a picnic and make a day of it?

● *Adults £3, children and disabled free. Tel: 08701 261709 for opening times and dates*
● *Local pub, The Bell, serves good food and is within walking distance of the gardens (Internet: www.beningtonlordship.co.uk)*

▲ What summer elegance! These ladies are sunbathing in Hyde Park in 1952

PAUSE FOR THOUGHT

Sometimes when you're feeling so important
Sometimes when your ego's in bloom
Sometimes when you take it for granted,
You're that best informed man in the room.

Sometimes when you feel that your going
Would leave an unfillable hole,
Just follow these simple instructions,
And see how it humbles your soul.

Take a bucket and fill it with water,
Put your hands in it up to your wrist,
Pull them out and the hole that remains
Is a measure of how you'll be missed.

You may splash all you please as you enter,
You may stir up the water galore,
But stop – and in a moment,
It looks just the same as before.

The moral of this is quite simple.
Do just the best you can,
Be proud of yourself and remember,
There is no indispensable man.

DID YOU KNOW THAT

If you could drive your car straight up, you would arrive in space in just under an hour.

Top tip

Keep a glass marble in the bottom of your kettle to prevent it from furring.

ON GROWING OLDER

'I have everything I had 20 years ago...only it's all a bit lower'.

Lois F Kaufman

WHAT'S COOKING?

QUICK SNACK
Quick Quiche
(Serves 4)

Pastry case
- 4 oz/100 g flour
- Pinch of salt
- 2 oz/50 g butter
- Cold water

Filling
- 2 tomatoes, finely sliced
- 3 eggs
- ½ pt/280 ml single cream
- Seasoning
- 2 tbs Parmesan cheese
- 1 oz/25 g margarine
- 1 onion, finely chopped
- 2 oz/50 g mushrooms
- ½ green pepper, finely sliced
- ½ red pepper, finely sliced

1 Make the pastry by mixing together the flour, salt and butter with your fingertips until the mixture resembles fine breadcrumbs. Add enough water for the dough to make a ball.
2 Roll out to line a 8 in/20 cm flan tin or quiche dish. Prick the bottom lightly with a fork and cook at 180°C/350°F/Gas Mark 4 for 15 minutes. Remove from the oven.
3 Meanwhile, melt the margarine in a frying pan and sauté the onion, mushrooms and pepper until just softened.
4 Arrange the mixture on the bottom of the pastry case, followed by the sliced tomatoes.
5 Beat the eggs and add the cream and seasoning.
6 Pour over the vegetables and sprinkle the cheese on top.
Return to the oven for 35-40 minutes until risen and golden brown on top.

Gwen Dunford from Somerset has rubbed shoulders with the stars…

A DAY TO REMEMBER

My husband had worked on a big estate in Somerset for 40 years, and when his boss died, he was asked to move in to keep an eye on everything. Everyone who came to the 70-roomed Victorian mansion attached to the estate – Orchardleigh House – was vetted first, even the people from the international auction house when they put up for sale £3million worth of valuables!

During this time, the house was used for a film, The 4.50 From Paddington. The cast was there for six weeks and we spent time with such stars as Joan Hickson, Maurice Denham and Joanna David. When it was finished, they presented me with a photograph album of everyone involved in the film.

We were invited to the preview at the BAFTA Theatre in Picadilly. It was wonderful, sitting with the stars and seeing the house that I knew so well.

Incidentally, I also showed Robert Wagner and Jill St John around the house when they filmed there for a week.

Gwen – raising a glass to famous friends

DID YOU KNOW THAT ?

Ten per cent of men are left-handed and eight per cent of women.

OLD FASHIONED REMEDIES

For indigestion, fill one small glass with freshly squeezed lemon juice, another with mineral water and touch of bicarbonate of soda, and sip from both alternately.

Dr Henderson replies: A well-known one this, and quite safe, although I suspect the lemon juice is not strictly needed. Bicarbonate of soda is still commonly used in many over the counter indigestion preparations today, often helping with belching and trapped wind. I think this one will be around for a long time yet!

WHAT A COINCIDENCE

I joined the WAAFS in 1940 and after square bashing, I was posted to Harrogate. We lived in a big house that had been a nursing home. I was on the ground floor with five other girls.

One day a girl called Kay was posted to Harrogate and shared my room. I saw her kitbag and printed on it was, 'LAC Thompson 624991'. I just screamed and said: "That was my boyfriend's kitbag and asked her to swap.

My boyfriend had had to hand over his kitbag at Andover before going to France and Kay had been allocated it while she was there.

Of all the thousands of airmen, I couldn't believe it.

Gwen Thompson, Derbyshire

Top tip
Shine up a rusty key by soaking it in turpentine for an hour or two.

AT THE MOVIES

Who said?
'One morning I shot an elephant in my pajamas. How he got into my pajamas I'll never know'.
(Answer below)

Answer: Groucho Marx giving his African lecture in Victor Heerman's Animal Crackers

PIC: NATIONAL TRUST/GEOFFREY FROSH

OUT & ABOUT TO...

Mr Straw's House, 7 Blyth Grove, Worksop, Nottinghamshire

External appearances can be deceptive, but the inside of this 1930s semi-detached house looks exactly as you'd expect it to – 70 years ago. It belonged to brothers William and Walter Straw, and has been preserved as it was when their mother died in the 1930s. It's a time-warp of 1920s wallpaper, furnishings and locally made furniture. There are displays of clothing and memorabilia, and a typical suburban garden, all providing a fascinating insight into daily life in the early 20th century.

- *Entry is by timed ticket only, which must be booked in advance by phone. The house is small, and there is no wheelchair access, although there is a Braille guide and audiocassette.*
- *Tickets £6 including coffee and cakes*
- *Open Tuesday to Saturday. Tel: 01909 482380*

ON GROWING OLDER
'By the time a man is old enough to watch his step, he's too old to go anywhere'.
Joey Adams

MY ADVICE IS...
'Never argue when you know you are right'.
Mrs J Stephenson, Essex

July 12-18

WHAT A COINCIDENCE

In 1939/40 my friend Joan and I worked with the Observer Corps in Bury St Edmunds. Around Christmas we went to the pictures and saw a recruitment film asking for girls to join the WAAF as cooks and waitresses.

So we decided to do our bit to help our gallant air crew, even though I was only 17 and had to advance my age a little! I was sent to Bridgnorth and Joan to Scotland.

I never saw her again until 1970. My husband and I had a pub in Suffolk and I was serving behind the bar when a voice said: "Hello, Hazel." There stood Joan who was passing through the village, fancied a drink and called into our pub!

By the way, I stayed on in the WAAF until 1944 and never did get to waitress. I served in Weston-Super-Mare, Redcar and Newmarket – all training stations and not a plane or an aircrew in sight! My photograph shows the RAF's idea of waitressing!

Hazel Bigg, Suffolk

Hazel (far right) and friends 'waitressing'

WHAT'S COOKING?

SUPPER DISH
Chicken Waldorf Salad
(Serves 4)

- 4 apples
- 2 tbs lemon juice
- 4 celery sticks
- 8 oz/225 g cold chicken, chopped
- 2 oz/50 g walnuts, halved
- 8 level tbs natural yoghurt
- 4 level tbs salad cream
- Salt and pepper
- 1 large lettuce

1 Core, slice and dice the apples and sprinkle with lemon juice to prevent them turning brown.
2 Clean and chop the celery. Wash and drain lettuce, chop heart and mix with the diced chicken, chopped apple, celery, walnut halves and the yoghurt and salad cream mixture. Line four bowls with outer lettuce leaves and pile in the salad.

AT THE MOVIES

Who said?
'That's what I like – everything done in contrasting shades of money'.
(Answer below)

A DAY TO REMEMBER

A day above the clouds for Diane de Caen from Portsmouth…

At the age of nearly 61 I flew for the first time – on my own – to see my son in Australia. It was a fantastic flight and I stayed awake for the whole journey.

PAUSE FOR THOUGHT

Shirley Newman from Cornwall has these words to ponder:

'Even when you feel that you are doing so much for others and getting little in return, remember – it comes back to you in other ways'.

DID YOU KNOW THAT

There are more than 15,000 different varieties of rice.

Top tip

Wash any knitwear inside a pillowcase to prevent it stretching in the washing machine.

OLD WIVES' TALES

If you rub a wart with half a potato, then bury it in the garden at midnight, the wart will disappear.

Dr Henderson replies: All this will do is keep you tired from staying up, and make a hole in your nice garden! Useless I'm afraid, as are all old wives' wart remedies. Warts tend to go by themselves given enough time in most people, and rubbing them with potatoes – during a full moon or otherwise – will not affect this one bit. Eat the potato instead – you'll get more benefit.

PIC: DAVID MOORE, ANGLIAN WATER

OUT & ABOUT TO...

Barnsdale Drought Garden, Upper Hambleton, near Oakham, Rutland.

It's ironic that this water-free garden lies on the shores of Rutland Water, the largest man-made lake in western Europe. Designed by the late Geoff Hamilton (the much-loved presenter of TV's Gardener's World), it was created for a purpose: To show the wide variety of plants and shrubs which need no extra watering, yet flourish in the British climate. Despite being on a south-facing slope on clay soil, which cracks and dries out quickly, the garden is thriving, although it hasn't been watered since 1986! The Anglian Water region, where it is situated, has the lowest rainfall in the UK, so water is scarce.

This innovative garden contains more than 150 plants, which all thrive without extra watering. If you're guilty of using garden watering devices, such as sprinklers – which use up to 1,000 litres of water every hour – you could learn a lot from the special water-conserving techniques used here.

● *Admission free, car park £3*
● *When the Gwash valley was flooded to create this reservoir in 1977, a small village was submerged. However, the village church was saved by raising its floor level, and now houses the Normanton Church Museum, 100 yards from the shore and reached by a causeway. Here, you can find out more fascinating historical facts from dinosaur fossils, an Anglo-Saxon skeleton and a video of the reservoir's construction.*
Tel: 01572 653026 (Internet: www.rutlandwater.net)

July 19-25

A DAY TO REMEMBER

Christine Touhig from Nottingham turned detective one memorable day…

I opened the door to a persistent knock and there on the doorstep was a handsome gentleman from Holland in his 70s, who was searching for an old girlfriend. She had been with him in the WAAFS during the Second World War and she'd lived in our house 50 years ago.

After many inquiries, it transpired that he had the wrong house but we said we would try to help. He arrived the next day with a huge bunch of flowers for me; and we renewed our efforts.

With the help of the local paper we found his former girlfriend, were treated to a slap-up meal and invited to the Netherlands for a week. Aptly enough, the girlfriend's name was Vera and, as Vera Lynn sang, they did 'meet again'.

MY ADVICE IS…

'Try and swallow your angry words – it's much easier than having to eat them'.
Mary Hickson, Lancs

DID YOU KNOW THAT

Dolphins never fully sleep, as the two halves of their brain shut down alternatively.

Top tip

Spray your vacuum cleaner bag with perfume – it'll lightly scent your room while cleaning.

OUT & ABOUT TO…

PIC: BEKONSCOT MODEL VILLAGE

Bekonscot Model Village, Beaconsfield, Buckinghamshire

Seventy years ago, Queen Mary brought Princess Elizabeth (now our Queen) to Bekonscot for her eighth birthday treat. Since then, the world's oldest model village has delighted visitors of all ages – and all proceeds have been given to charity. It began as a hobby for London accountant Roland Callingham in 1929, who bought a field, dug a pond in it and built a few model houses. The rest, as they say, is history…

In this miniature version of 1930s rural England, time has stood still – and untouched by the impending war, mass unemployment and poverty of the era. The beauty of Bekonscot is in the detail, from the accurate working models of trams and trains to the magnificent Tudor house, which depicts how the local gentry lived in luxury, waited on by servants. Children's author Enid Blyton lived near Bekonscot and often visited the village, perhaps to get inspiration for her book The Enchanted Village. In tribute, there's a replica of her house, Green Hedges, with a model of her typing away on the terrace. Perhaps most intriguing is the garden, in which the miniature trees and shrubs, including dwarf conifers and alpine plants, are grown to scale using the Bonsai technique.

Adults £4.80, concessions £4, children £3
● *Refreshments; picnic areas; playground; wheelchairs available*
Tel: 01494 672919

WHAT A COINCIDENCE

In 1945 I was in hospital in Oxford and, after a three week stay, I and two other chaps were transferred to a convalescent home in Burcott village a few miles away. We got out of the ambulance and as we walked in the front door, the matron was coming down the stairs.

She was surprised to see me and asked why I'd come back. I said I'd only just arrived. "Nonsense," she said, "we only discharged you an hour ago." I explained that we'd come from Didcot, to which my mates added their support.

"You are Arthur Hustler, aren't you?" she asked. I replied that my name was Robert Hustler and she took some convincing that I didn't have a twin.

Strange to say that in all my 85 years, I've never met anyone, other than my family, called Hustler, although I know there are lots of them.

Bob Hustler, Surrey

Bob in 1944

WHAT'S COOKING?

A MEAL ON A BUDGET
Cheesey Fish Topper
(Serves 4)

- 4 oz/100 g grated cheese
- 2 oz/50 g margarine
- 4 pieces of fish
- 1 onion, grated
- 2 tomatoes, sliced

1 Grill the fish under a medium grill for 5 minutes. Turn and grill for a further 3 minutes.
2 Meanwhile mix together the cheese, onion and margarine.
3 Spread on the fish steaks, place tomato slices on top, and grill for a further 5 minutes.
4 Serve with a green salad.

AT THE MOVIES

Who said'?
'Even as a kid, I always went for the wrong women. I feel that's my problem. When my mother took me to see Snow White, everyone fell in love with Snow White. I immediately fell for the Wicked Queen'.
(Answer below)

Answer: Woody Allen in his Annie Hall

OLD FASHIONED REMEDIES

Splinters were commonly covered with a bread poultice made from a piece of bread dipped in hot water and covered with a piece of pink lint and a bandage.

Dr Henderson replies: The key here is warmth, as this is undoubtedly of benefit with boils and splinters in helping bring things to a head, and which forms the basis of all poultices. The bread is really superfluous here, although it may have acted to hold some of the warmth in, and a more modern version of this is to apply cotton buds dipped in hot salty water to achieve the same effect.

July 26-August 1

PAUSE FOR THOUGHT

If God should go on strike

How good it is that God above has never gone on strike
Because He was not treated fair, in things He didn't like,
If only once He had sat down, and said, 'That's it, I'm through,
I've had enough of those on earth, so this is what I'll do.

I'll give my orders to the sun – cut off the heat supply
And to the moon, give no more light, and run the oceans dry.

You know he would be justified, if fairness was the game
For no-one has been more abused or met with such disdain
Than God, and yet He carries on, supplying you and me
With all the favours of His grace and everything for free!

We don't care who we hurt or harm to gain the things we like,
But what a mess we'd all be in if God should go on strike!

Mrs S Smith, Herts

AT THE MOVIES

Who said?
'Fasten your seatbelts. It's going to be a bumpy night'.
(Answer below)

Answer: Bette Davis in Joseph L Mankiewicz's All About Eve

WHAT A COINCIDENCE

Top tip

A stiff lock can be loosened by rubbing your key with a little vaseline, margarine or butter.

DID YOU KNOW THAT

The largest weed in the world is the giant hogweed. Left on its own, it can grow to 11 feet (3.5 metres) high.

Around four years ago I moved to St Annes and got talking to the couple who lived in the flat above me.

They were originally from Eccles, near Salford and I said I went to school in Eccles and lived in Patricroft. The man – Bill - said he too had lived in Patricroft when he was a schoolboy.

It turned out that he'd lived in the same house that my family had rented – his parents had rented it after we moved.

But he'd puzzled about one thing – why there were only three electric lights in the house. I explained to him that mother had only been able to afford three – one each in the living rooms and one in the hall. The rest of the house had oil lamps and candles – but this was going back to 1936.

Mrs Riley

D Riley, Lancashire

Rosemary Medland from Hertforshire ponders what a difference a year makes…

A DAY TO REMEMBER

Our special day was October 2, 2001 when my gorgeous granddaughter, Denise, arrived safe and sound. Her arrival was even more memorable to us because we had lost my beloved mother only 12 months before.

We were all sad and despondent and when Denise arrived our darkness disappeared and we could see the sunshine again.

Lovely Denise brought happiness to Rosemary and her family

ON GROWING OLDER

'Life's tragedy is that we get old too soon and wise too late'.

Benjamin Franklin

OUT & ABOUT TO...

Snowshill Manor, near Broadway, Gloucestershire

PIC: NATIONAL TRUST/NICK MEERS

Organic gardens are all the rage, and this one is particularly lovely. Small but beautifully formed, Snowshill was designed in the Arts and Crafts era of the 1920s by owner Charles Paget Wade and Baillie Scott, who admired the craftsmanship of medieval England. Its highlights include old roses, old-fashioned flowers and interesting herbaceous borders.

The Cotswold manor house contains Wade's collections of curios including musical instruments, weavers' and spinners' tools, clocks, toys, bicycles and costumes. He loved dressing up, and visitors to Snowshill – who included Virginia Woolf, Graham Greene and JB Priestley – were often persuaded to join him!

You can also see Wade's cottage, plus the charming garden he created from the muddy farmyard.

- *Adults £3.60 for the grounds, restaurant and shop (or £5.60 for the house too), child £1.30 (£3.20)*
- *Restaurant using organic fruit and vegetables grown in the kitchen garden; gift shop*
- *Braille guide and audio tape of house and garden*
- *Limited wheelchair access; a buggy is available for the elderly and people with disabilities*
Tel: 01386 852410

WHAT'S COOKING?

SUPPER DISH
Cider Sausages
(Serves 1)

- 2 sausages
- 2 slices of ham
- A little oil
- Garlic (optional)
- Dried or fresh mixed herbs
- ½ pint cider
- Salt and pepper

1 Fry the sausages until golden brown. Add the garlic (sliced), salt, pepper and cider.
2 Sprinkle with herbs and simmer for 10 minutes.
3 Remove the sausages from the pan and wrap a slice of ham around the sausages, securing with a cocktail stick.
4 Return the wrapped sausages to the pan and simmer until the sauce is reduced by half.
5 Serve with mashed potatoes and green vegetables, remembering to remove the cocktail sticks from the sausages.
Cynthia Brown, Suffolk

OLD WIVES' TALES

An apple a day keeps the doctor away.

Dr Henderson replies: The classic remedy! Actually, there is some half-truth here because apples contain flavonoids, antioxidants that improve immune function and prevent heart disease and some cancers. Green apples can act as a liver and gall bladder cleanser and may aid in softening gallstones. Because of their high water content, apples are cooling and moistening and assist in reducing fever. Unpeeled apples provide their most plentiful nutrients just under the skin and apples are a good source of potassium, folic acid, and vitamin C.

Painting in the garden

Let's go into the garden with artist Maureen Ward...

The Surrey countryside of my childhood is where I learned to love nature. At 14 years old, I won a junior art award and studied at Epsom and Ewell School of Art. I now live in Lincolnshire and teach art at a local technology college and currently teach watercolour in Adult Education.'

A garden is an everchanging picture, from spring to winter with a host of subjects to draw. All you need is a pad of cartridge paper and pencils – I suggest a 'B', '2B' and '4B' (the higher the number, the softer and darker the mark), a kneadable eraser and something to rest your pad on for support.

You can introduce colour by using coloured pencils, as illustrated in my drawing of snowdrops. There are more controllable than watercolour.

To begin, choose a single flower

or leaf, maybe an empty snail shell. Look carefully at your subject before you begin to draw, understand its shape. If drawing a flower with small florets, draw larger than life, this gives you more scope for effective shading and detail.

Keep your pencils sharp, especially coloured ones. Work lightly at first and build up detail. It can be difficult to remove a pencil mark applied too heavily. Shading can be produced by by following contour lines. Try not to 'over-work' your drawing. Keep it fresh. If your subject is light coloured, shade behind it so the white paper remains.

Oh, and have a comfortable seat, you can't do your best work if you ache!

Happy drawing

The things we miss

Coach-built prams

Any baby looked like a prince or a princess in a coach-built pram. Their traditionally styled, large hard bodies and big-spoked wheels with a shopping tray underneath, made them look more like some kind of infant throne.

They were very comfortable and their suspension allowed you to walk your baby for miles without getting tired. They were also large and sturdy enough for tired toddlers to clamber up into, in their own little 'chair' on the end.

But they weren't without their difficulties. Their weight and size made them a horror to take on to public transport and they were also a real chore to manoeuvre up and down steps. You had to be very careful not to park them anywhere near a slope or you could find your baby taking off on an unplanned ride!

But despite these apparent setbacks and the convenience and lightness of today's modern baby equipment, it seems that the beauty and style of 'heritage' prams are making a comeback – if new mums can afford them!

PIC: HULTON ARCHIVE

Evening in Paris

It was a scent that defined an era. It was launched in 1929 and packaged in a midnight blue half-moon shaped bottle with a silver stopper and was the perfume of choice for young women everywhere. It had a sweet, floral and fruity scent made up of violets, clover, lilac, rose, jasmine, vetiver, styrax, cedar and vanilla notes. Its feminine fragrance and chic good looks ensured its popularity for years to come.

Puzzles

Jigsnip

With the help of just three columns of Down clues, see if you can fit the blocks into the empty grid to form a complete, symmetrical crossword. All of the Across words are Olympic sports.

DOWN COLUMNS
1. Accompanied by • European volcano • Ship's front
2. Jewelled headdress
3. Organ of sight • Tiny round mark

```
H . .    S T L    . I .    W R E
. C A    . . .    B A S    . I . Y
E . .    K W O    . R .    T A E

T O N    T R I    M I N    A T H
W . D    N . .    . . .    L . O
O L O    A T H    E R P    L E T

I W .    . T .    . I .    . B .
N O E    L L .    I N G    E B A
. P .    . U .    . G .    L . W

I N G    B A D    L O N
N . O    O . O    . . E
N D O    W A T    I C S
```

Solutions on Page 159

Pathfinder

Starting from the red letter 'A', and moving up, down or sideways (but not diagonally), one letter at a time, find a continuous path through the names of all but four of the cities that have hosted the summer Olympics? The pictured city is the first on your trail. Can you also identify the four missing cities?

```
K N I S O M I C O D N
I R E L Y E X I C Y E
M O H S K A N T Y S Y
E T W N O T O A B O B
A N E E H T L R E U L
L P R O S A E C N R E
O O N L A E R M M L M
N D E L N T D A U A E
L R S E G S S I N I R
I E B U L M A U H C T
N S E O S T L O M O N
```

PIC: REX FEATURES

Short story

The breakaway

By Anne Harvey

Mavis had never felt so lonely in her life. Sitting in the busy hotel lounge, surrounded by groups of people chattering about their day only intensified her solitude. Why hadn't she guessed it would be like this?

It had all seemed so simple at the time. For years, ever since George had started his own plumbing business, she had urged him to take a holiday. His reply had always been the same. "I can't, Mavis. You know what it's like when you're self-employed. You've got to take the work when you can, while you can." Over those same years, as summer arrived, she found her senses stirred by curtains fluttering in a warm breeze; the sound of music from an open window; the smell of new-mown grass or night-scented stock; the sting of sunburned skin after long hours in the garden. Yet, although she loved the gentleness of an English summer, she also longed for golden shores by an azure sea, lazing on a beach, an exotic drink by her side, a cool breeze caressing her bare skin. Or being serenaded by a gypsy band over a simple meal on a hot Mediterranean night. Or dancing a steamy tropical night away to the rhythm of a Caribbean steel band. She knew them all, those faraway places. She'd seen them countless times, not only in her dreams, but in travel programmes on television or in articles in the weekend supplements.

This summer, when George turned her down again and suggested she went on her own, she rebelled and decided to do just that. Only she'd booked the holiday without his knowledge. And she wasn't at any of those exotic destinations she'd dreamed of. After being cushioned by marriage for so long, she lacked the courage to go alone and chose the English hotel where they had honeymooned years ago.

So, added to her guilt at not telling George where she was, was her own shame that she didn't have the courage of her dreams. If this were a magazine story or a movie, she would have gone to one of those distant shores. Here in genteel Lytham St Anne's, she'd made herself go on excursions; walked along the promenade for miles in either direction; passed the time of day and other pleasantries with her fellow guests. Yet none of it meant anything without George there to share it. Although they'd been married for more than 30 years, he was still her best friend; they always managed to find something to talk about and to laugh over.

When she saw him walking towards her from the reception desk, she thought she'd conjured him up out of her imagination but, dressed in casual summer wear, he was real enough. "Hello, Mavis."

"George! What are you doing here?"

"I came to be with you." He sat across from her in one of the comfy armchairs.

"But how did you find me?"

"I called in at the library. They told me they'd had a postcard from St Anne's. Wasn't too hard to guess where you were staying."

"What would you have done if I hadn't been here?"

He grinned. "I'd have gone all round the hotels in St Anne's. My turn to ask a question. Why didn't you tell

me you were going away?"

"I was angry. I wanted to punish you."

"Because I wouldn't take a holiday?"

"Yes. Every summer it's the same. Well, this year I'd had enough. I only wish I'd had the courage to go to Paris. I've always wanted to."

"You wouldn't like it. It's not all it's cracked up to be."

"How can you say that? You went there on a school trip when you were fifteen. And anyway, I'd like to find out for myself."

He looked uncomfortable. "Maybe next year, love."

"You always say that too. Has it ever occurred to you that there might not be a next year?"

"What do you mean?"

"You're not getting any younger, George. Look, you work long hours, you don't eat regular meals, you're overweight…"

"Thanks for the vote of confidence."

"And you're a prime target for a stroke or a heart attack," she carried on relentlessly.

"Don't be ridiculous!"

She leaned forward. "See that youngish woman sitting with her teenage son? Her husband had a heart attack last year. Ask her if the idea's ridiculous."

In the face of his silence, she grasped his hands. "I want us to spend more time together before it's too late."

He examined her closely.

"Is there something you're not telling me? You're not ill, are you?"

"No," she laughed. "I'm perfectly healthy. But I've been offered early retirement from the library – the usual thing; cuts in the budget – and it's made me reassess my life. Like, what am I going to do with the rest of it?"

He looked stunned. "Why didn't you tell me before?"

"You've been so wrapped up in this new job," she replied.

"But how will we manage without your wage, especially if you want me to take more time off?"

"When will you realise that time spent together means more to me than money in the bank?" she sighed. "We'll manage. And you…" she prodded him with her finger, "can learn to delegate. Jim's good at his job, eager to get on. Why don't you give him more responsibility?"

"I suppose I could sound him out, gradually ease up a bit."

"Start by taking Friday off every week, don't take on any weekend work."

"I've already started. If you'll have me, I've told Jim I won't be in till next Monday."

"And today's only Thursday. George, that's wonderful!" She leaned across to kiss him.

Taking her hand in both of his, he said: "Come September, why don't we enrol at the college for French lessons."

"French lessons?"

"Yes. They'll come in handy when we go to Paris next year."

August 2004

A flavour of the month

PIC: REX FEATURES

Chances are the sun will have its hat on by now and, to make the most of the good weather – while it lasts – why don't you take a trip to the seaside?

There's nothing better than a sea breeze on a sunny day, and a visit to the British coast. Many coach companies organise trips to UK resorts and operate from local pick-up points – check travel agents' windows for details.

Whether here or abroad, make sure you have a happy and healthy holiday. Prevent dehydration by drinking plenty of water and avoiding alcohol if possible. Protect yourself by staying out of direct sunlight between 11am and 3pm, wear a high-factor sunscreen (minimum 15), making sure you cover all your easy-to-forget spots, such as under shoulder straps behind the ears and on the tops of your feet.

And, wear UV-protective sunglasses, a hat with a four-inch brim and clothing made from tightly woven cotton. If you do get burned, soothe with lavender oil or camomile lotion.

Turn beach walks into treasure hunts, collecting pretty shells and seaweed. Seashells can bring a hint of beach life to your home. Use them to decorate your windowsills, as bathroom ornaments or paperweights. Don't collect too many, though, and wash them thoroughly.

SUNDAY	1	
MONDAY	2	Bank Holiday (Scotland)
TUESDAY	3	
WEDNESDAY	4	
THURSDAY	5	
FRIDAY	6	
SATURDAY	7	
SUNDAY	8	
MONDAY	9	
TUESDAY	10	
WEDNESDAY	11	
THURSDAY	12	
FRIDAY	13	
SATURDAY	14	
SUNDAY	15	Edinburgh International Festival starts
MONDAY	16	
TUESDAY	17	
WEDNESDAY	18	

THURSDAY	19
FRIDAY	20
SATURDAY	21
SUNDAY	22
MONDAY	23
TUESDAY	24
WEDNESDAY	25
THURSDAY	26
FRIDAY	27
SATURDAY	28 September YOURS on sale
SUNDAY	29
MONDAY	30 Bank Holiday (Except Scotland)
TUESDAY	31

PIC: EMAP GARDEN PICTURE LIBRARY

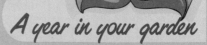

A year in your garden

If only plants would stop growing when you go on holiday. It would save a lot of worry and phone calls to friends and relatives asking them to nip and have a look at your tomatoes. But there are ways to have a stress-free holiday, and still have great looking plants when you get home. Houseplants need water in summer and are best grouped together in a bath or a sink.

Standing the plants on a wet towel will reduce the need for too much watering. The water in the towel will evaporate creating a moist atmosphere, and plants dry out slowly in such conditions. The same trick can be accomplished with trays of pebbles or stones. Wet the stones to create the right atmosphere.

Outside plants are at the mercy of the weather. Wet weather and everything is fine but in a dry climate a hosepipe connected to a timer and outside tap, if local authorities allow it, can be lifesavers. Look out for hosepipes with specially designed perforations. These are laid on to the soil surface, around plants, where the water gently drips or oozes from the pipe. Mulching around the plants will also help conserve water in the soil. But be warned – only mulch on to soil that is already moist. Mulch on dry soil and any rainwater will take time to soak in.

The evening before going away give all your plants a good drink. Your plants will take up water during the night and none will be lost through evaporation in the sun. Soak, and then mulch using anything organic. Make sure the mulch is at least two inches deep. Saying all that, and after installing drip feeder bags in the greenhouse for your tomatoes, the best way of keeping plants looking good while you are away is a good gardening neighbour.

☆ READER'S TIP ☆

Fred Caitlin in Worcester soaks capillary matting in water, dips one end in a bowl of water and stands his houseplants on a flat surface like the kitchen drainer when he goes on holiday. It keeps plants damp enough for weeks of growth.

WHAT'S COOKING?

PIC: HULTON ARCHIVE

▲ 'I'll have a 99 and a fruit lolly, please'.
Excited youngsters gather round a Mr Whippy
ice cream van in 1962

**A dinner dance changed
Harlan Senior from
Sheffield's life forever…**

A DAY TO REMEMBER

*After my 'demob' from National Service with the RAF, I was
enjoying my lifestyle – smart clothes, dining out, theatre
weekends in London, concerts, football on Saturday afternoons
and nights out with the boys. I was into my 30s and everyone
thought I was heading for a life of batchelorhood – until one
fateful evening when it all changed!*

*Every Christmas I went to a dinner dance with friends and
I was introduced to a newcomer – an attractive, smartly
dressed young lady called Christina. We danced together and
as the evening drew to an end, I took my courage in both
hands and asked her out and she said yes!*

*I suffered agonies in the meantime – would she turn up,
what would I say to her? Well, she did turn up and we
enjoyed a lovely meal together.
We arranged to meet again –
and again, and again. I had
fallen in love and suffered more
heartache and agony until I
made my feelings known. I
then found, to my joy, that these
feelings were returned!*

*We married and are still very
much in love after 40 years, and
we have a son, a daughter and
two lovely grandsons. And all
because of that golden evening
that changed my life!*

Harlan and Christina
walking out together

Tomato and Avocado Salad
(Serves 6)

- 12 oz/350 g tomatoes, sliced
- 1 bunch spring onions, trimmed and sliced diagonally
- 2 avocados
- Juice of 1 lemon
- Salt and freshly ground black pepper
- 3 tbs olive oil
- 2 tbs red wine vinegar
- 2 tps Dijon mustard
- 2 tps honey
- 1 packet tortilla chips

1 Place the tomatoes and spring onions
together in a bowl and season generously
with salt and freshly ground black pepper.
2 Peel avocados, halve and slice. Squeeze over
lemon juice to prevent them browning.
Gently mix with the tomatoes and onions.
3 Place olive oil, red wine vinegar, honey and
mustard together in a screw top jar, and
shake vigorously to mix. Toss into salad to
serve. At the last minute stir in tortilla chips.
Serve immediately.

PIC: FRESH PRODUCE CONSORTIUM

ON GROWING OLDER

You know the years are passing when:
- *People call at 9pm and ask:
"Did I wake you?"*
- *You get into a heated argument
about pension plans*

OUT & ABOUT TO...

Mechanical Music & Doll Collection, Portfield, Chichester, West Sussex

Roll up, roll up for this magical musical tour. If you've ever lamented the demise of old-fashioned musical boxes, you'll love this unique exhibition. Housed in a Victorian church, it's a real feast for the eyes – and ears. You'll be taken on a guided tour of 100 years of mechanical musical instruments, beautifully restored and playing exactly as they did when new.

You can see and hear barrel organs and wind-up gramophones, marvel at the first juke box, and listen to the coin-operated Polyphon music box, which played out the last years of the 19th century to a much rowdier audience in its first home, a Victorian public house.

The other half of the church hall is devoted to more than 100 beautiful china, wax and fabric dolls dating from 1830-1930, all in perfect condition and many still in their original clothes.

- *Adults £2.50, children £1.25*
- *Open Wednesday, 1-4pm only*
- *Disabled access*

Tel: 01243 372 646

MY ADVICE IS...

'Never let the sun go down on an argument – it's not worth it'.

Lynn Head, Yorks

DID YOU KNOW THAT

Who's Afraid Of Virginia Woolf is the only film in history to have its entire main cast nominated for the four major acting Oscars.

Top tip

Stick a piece of sticky tape to the wall before hammering in a nail – it'll help prevent the plaster cracking.

AT THE MOVIES

Who said?
'Someone would strike up a song, and the valley would ring with the sound of many voices – for singing is in my people as sight is in the eye'. (Answer below)

Answer: Irving Pichel in John Ford's How Green Was My Valley

OLD FASHIONED REMEDIES

For a sore throat and bunged up nose. Take a large onion and slice it thinly into rings and place on a saucer. Then cover it with a very generous helping of brown sugar. Leave overnight for juice to collect in the saucer. The patient should sip the juice.

Dr Henderson replies: Sore throats and blocked noses are a sign of an old-fashioned cold which are caused by a virus. Onion juice and sugar will have no effect on this and, I can imagine, would be very antisocial if you can stomach drinking it! At least it will do you no harm, though.

August 9-15

OUT & ABOUT TO...

Canonteign Falls, near Chudleigh, Devon

If you're feeling lively, slip on your sturdiest walking shoes and head for this idyllic country park. Covering 80 acres of ancient woodland in the beautiful Teign Valley, Canonteign Falls boasts England's highest waterfall (220 feet), plus lakes, cascades and spectacular rock formations.

The nature trails are great fun, and if you've got your grandchildren in tow, you'll be on to a winner with the junior commando assault course. There are animals to see, plenty of places to paddle and all manner of wonderful walkways to explore – you can even bring your dog, as long as you keep him on a lead.

When you're all exhausted, you can relax and refuel at the Lakeside Café/Restaurant, where delicious home-cooked meals are the order of the day.

- *Adults £4.25, children over four £3*
- *Refreshments; gift shop, picnic tables; play areas*
Tel: 01647 252434
(Internet: www.canonteignfalls.com)

ON GROWING OLDER
Remember when it took five minutes for the television to warm up?

WHAT'S COOKING?

WHAT A COINCIDENCE

Needing extra money when bringing up my five children, I was working for the Chief Maintenance Engineer in a large car manufacturers in Birmingham.

We had a young man named Peter sent to us for training – a very bright 18-year-old but conversation, apart from work, was very limited.

My husband and I decided to spend four days sightseeing in Paris and after an evening at the Moulin Rouge, who should we meet after coming out of the show but Peter!

It was a great talking point back home – we laughed when it was mentioned and said that at least Peter knew I was with my husband. We didn't ask who he was with!

Irene Bell, Warwickshire

Salad Nicoise
(Serves 2)

- French dressing
- $^1/_2$ small cucumber, sliced
- 1 tb chopped parsley
- 1 small tin anchovies or tuna
- 2 boiled eggs
- $^1/_2$ lb/250 g green beans, cooked and chopped
- $^1/_2$ lb/250 g tomatoes, sliced
- Grated rind 1 lemon
- A few black olives
- 1 level tsp basil

1 Arrange the tomato and cucumber in a dish and sprinkle with herbs and lemon rind.
2 Top with the boiled eggs (halved), fish, olives and beans before pouring over the French dressing.

PAUSE FOR THOUGHT

'When I was little', Dr Sharon Cox from the West Midlands, writes, 'I learnt these lines from Anna Sewell's book, Black Beauty:

Do your best,
And leave the rest.
'Twill all come right
Some day or night.

'I have repeated this quote to myself many times; before going into exams, preparing for job interviews, and when worrying how to cope with the unforeseen events that life throws at us.

'When I was worried, my mom would always say, 'you can only do your best', and she was so right – in the end, everything works itself out. This saying took me through O-levels, A-levels, a degree and a PhD. Today, I still rely on this quote when I catch myself worrying'.

AT THE MOVIES

Who said?
'*Here, take my handkerchief. Never at any crisis of your life have I known you to have a handkerchief.*'
(Answer below)

Answer: Clark Gable leaving a weeping Vivien Leigh in Victor Fleming's Gone With The Wind

DID YOU KNOW THAT

Customs officials at Manchester Airport found two tiny tortoises in cigarette packets lined with lettuce. A woman had brought the endangered species from Tunisia. They couldn't be returned because another flight might have killed them.

Top tip

A pot of nail varnish will last longer if you store it in the fridge.

A DAY TO REMEMBER

A degree of happiness for Hazel Ratcliffe from Lancashire...

Over the years my husband Tony and myself have had two extra special days. The first was the birth of my beautiful granddaughter Alex in February 1995, the second, the graduation ceremony of our son Stuart in September the following year.

None of my immediate family had been to university, so when Stuart got a 2:1 degree we were elated. The icing on the cake was that the graduation ceremony was to be made in the glorious York Minster.

We were bursting with pride as Stuart went up to receive his degree. It was a wonderful day – so many talented young people.

Proud mum Hazel and Stuart on graduation day.

OLD WIVES' TALES

Fish makes you brainy.

Dr Henderson replies: Possibly. There is some evidence that nutrients that are found at high levels in oily fish are important in brain development. The brain is very rich in a fatty acid called DHA which the body can produce but not very efficiently. The best source for DHA is diet. It is found in meat and eggs and particularly high levels in fish. Oily fish (like mackerel, sardines, herring, tuna) are very high in DHA, whereas white fish (like cod, plaice, monkfish) only have high levels of DHA in their livers. It won't turn you into Einstein but eating oily fish is good for you in general!

August 16-22

WHAT A COINCIDENCE

When I was getting to know the man who was to become my second husband in 1980; we were talking about numbers.

He said you always remember your Army number, to which I replied that the only number I remember was my identity card number given to us in the war. He knew his too, and we both started to say them and were amazed to discover they both followed on from each other.

We then compared notes; we were both evacuated at 12 years old in 1939, to Beach Road, Cleveleys and when we went back to look, we'd been next door to each other!

Iris Hulme, Manchester

An Italian date for Betty Hancock from Hertfordshire…

Betty and her husband en route to Rome

One of the most memorable days of my life was when we were touring Italy by coach 24 years ago – my birthday.

We left Sorrento after an early breakfast, calling at Monte Casino for lunch, then on to Rome for dinner and an overnight stop. The weather was perfect, the scenery magnificent and we reached the hotel, exhilarated but exhausted.

We were certainly ready for a meal, at an exclusive restaurant in the centre of Rome. I'd always had strawberries and cream as a treat for my birthday for as long as I could remember and although it was June in Italy, the restaurant had no strawberries. They did manage to find a delicious chocolate gateau, decorated with candles and brought to my table by four La Scala opera singers who just happened to be dining there, and they broke into song with Happy Birthday in Italian and English. Never has the name Betty sounded so romantic!

After this, I was rewarded with a kiss from two of the male singers, both with thick lustrous beards – a somewhat ticklish sensation! What a delightful ending to a truly magnificent day.

PIC: THE JENNER MUSEUM

OUT & ABOUT TO…

The Jenner Museum, Berkley, Gloucestershire

It's thanks to the pioneering work of one man, Edward Jenner, in the late 18th century that the killer disease smallpox was eventually eradicated in the 1970s. An English family doctor, Jenner practised at his elegant Queen Anne home, The Chantry, which has been turned into a museum to commemorate his life and work. Today two rooms on the first floor house an exhibition of modern immunology.

In the attractive grounds of his home, Dr Jenner had a small, thatched hut built, which he called the Temple of Vaccinia. Here, on certain days the poor would be given vaccinations free of charge. The hut was originally decorated with bark from forest trees and has been carefully conserved. You can also see the Black Hamburgh grapevines planted by the doctor in 1818, which still thrive.

- *Open Tues-Sat and Bank Holiday Mondays*
- *Adults £3, concessions £2.30, children £1.50*
- *No refreshments are available in the museum, but there's a coffee shop within two minutes' walk*
- *Wheelchair access ground floor only; disabled toilet*

Tel: 01453 810631 (Internet: www.jennermuseum.com)

AT THE MOVIES

Who said?
'*Et cetera, et cetera, et cetera*'
(Answer below)

Answer: Yul Brynner in Walter Lang's
The King And I

MY ADVICE IS...

'Never assume that you've nothing to
learn from your children – you never
know, they may surprise you!'
E Waters, Scotland

ON GROWING OLDER

'Inside every person is a younger person
wondering what the heck happened.'
Unknown

OLD FASHIONED REMEDIES

Whipped egg white left on nappy rash
overnight beats all the expensive creams
you can buy.

Shirley Newman, Cornwall

Dr Henderson replies: I have had this one
said to me before and was frankly sceptical but
in that particular case it did seem to work.
The important point is that it will not further
irritate a baby's sensitive skin and may be
worth trying but modern nappy rash
treatments are so effective that I would prefer
these every time here.

WHAT'S COOKING?

SUPPER DISH
Stuffed Pork Parcels with Cider Sauce
(Serves 4)

- 1 level tsp dried sage
- 2 level tbs sultanas
- 3 tbs unsweetened apple juice
- 1/2 pint/275 ml dry cider
- 1 level tbs cornflour
- 4 pork fillets
- 1 oz/25 g toasted flaked almonds
- 1 medium eating apple
- 3 oz/75 g fresh wholemeal breadcrumbs

1 Cut the pork fillets lengthways through the middle,
  almost all the way through, and open out. Beat out
  until flat, using a rolling pin.
2 Peel, core and grate the apple. Mix together the flaked
  almonds, apple, breadcrumbs, sage, sultanas and apple
  juice. Season with salt and pepper.
3 Spread the stuffing over the middle of the fillets. Tuck in
  the sides and ends to make a meat parcel. Tie in place
  with string.
4 Place in a roasting tin and pour over the cider. Cover
  loosely with foil and cook at 180°C/350°F/Gas Mark 4
  for 45 minutes. Remove the foil and cook for another
  20 minutes or until cooked through. Lift out the pork
  parcels on to a serving dish and remove the string.
5 Pour the juices into a small pan. Blend the cornflour
  with a little cold water until smooth, then stir into the
  cider. Bring to the boil, stirring all the time, and simmer
  for 1-2 minutes.
6 Pour a little sauce over the top of the pork and serve
  the rest separately, along with new
  potatoes and seasonal vegetables.

DID YOU KNOW THAT

Budgies can turn their
heads 180 degrees

Top tip

Bring dried out
paintbrushes back to
life by soaking them
in warm vinegar.

August 23-29

OUT & ABOUT TO...

PIC REX FEATURES

Quince Honey Farm, South Molton, Devon

Bees might not be everyone's cup of tea, but there's a certain satisfaction involved in watching these diligent workers going about their daily toil. Quince Honey Farm has been producing the sticky sweet stuff for 55 years and is the biggest wild-bee farm in the world.

It has observation hives, which open at the press of a button and look straight into the centre of the colonies, so if you're lucky you'll see the queen bee holding court. You can also see how honey is made as it progresses from hive to jar. And honey tasting is included in the admission fee, so there isn't even a sting in the tale!

- *Adults £3.50, concessions £2.50; children £2 (under-fives free)*
- *Restaurant; shop (lots of honey and the farm's own beeswax skin and hair-care products); picnic area.*
Tel: 01769 572401
(Internet: www.quincehoney.com)

WHAT A COINCIDENCE

Visiting Swansea after an absence of 17 years, I thought it would be nice to look up an aunt (my father's brother's wife by marriage). I knew her address but couldn't remember where it was.

So passing by a park, I asked directions of the lady in charge of the miniature golf. Of all the people in Swansea to ask, she turned out to be my aunt's sister!

• Also, while sitting outside my caravan on holiday in Holland, a colleague of mine from the school where I worked walked past me!

Mrs S Dunn, Oxon

PAUSE FOR THOUGHT

Let the sun shine into your heart
Listen to the song the birds sing
Watch the butterflies with their beautiful colours
Enjoy the day as if there will be no others.

Let the sun shine into your heart
Feel the warm wind touch your skin
Feel the love which it brings
For this is life, the little things.
                                    Anon

DID YOU KNOW THAT

The first bomb dropped by the Allies on Berlin during World War Two killed the only elephant in Berlin Zoo.

Top tip

Sprinkling talcum powder inside your rubber gloves will make them easier to remove.

OLD WIVES' TALES

Carrots help you see in the dark.

Dr Henderson replies: Not as such, but propogated during World War Two in night fighter pilots and 'Doctor Carrot' was a familiar sight to wartime children, his posters publicising the benefits of eating carrots. Night blindness is one of the complications resulting from a deficiency of vitamin A and carrots are a good source of this vitamin. So, someone deficient in vitamin A with this problem could benefit from eating lots of carrots, hence the old wives' tale.

A DAY TO REMEMBER

You could hardly describe Ruth Hill from Dorset's memorable day as 'just the ticket'...

I'd just finished my bus conductress training, a job I knew I was going to love. Dad had been a driver and mum, a conductress, so I was following the family tradition.

On my first day, I collected my money bag, my 'setrite' ticket machine, ticket rolls and emergency tickets and checked the destination board was correct. "Hold tight, please," I shouted, pressed the bell twice, and we were off.

All went well for ten minutes until a load of children got on. One playfully pulled the ticket sticking out from the machine and jammed it – so I had to switch to emergency tickets which had to be hand-written.

When we reached our destination, I explained my plight to the inspector, who gave me a spare machine. This one jammed too, so it was another half-hour rush with emergency tickets. I don't know how many people travelled free that trip, but one thing's for sure, I'll never forget my first day as a conductress!

WHAT'S COOKING?

A MEAL ON A BUDGET
Vegetable Risotto
(Serves 2)

- 8 oz/225 g each of peas, sweetcorn, carrots, cauliflower
- 1 medium-size aubergine, diced
- 8 oz/225 g rice
- Salt and pepper
- 6 tbs vegetable oil
- 3 onions, sliced

1 Heat the oil and fry the onions for 5 minutes.
2 Add the rice and stir again. Add water to cover and simmer until cooked (see direction on packet).
3 Add the rest of the vegetables about 7-10 minutes before the end, so that they do not become too soft.
4 Check the seasoning and serve.

AT THE MOVIES

Who said?
'Well, we movie stars get the glory. I guess we have to take the little heartaches that go with it. People think we lead lives of glamour and romance, but we're really lonely – terribly lonely.' (Answer below)

Answer: Gene Kelly spouting malarkey in Gene Kelly and Stanley Donen's Singin' In The Rain

ON GROWING OLDER

'I don't date women my age – there aren't any'.

Milton Berle

Easy does it!

Gardening needn't be hard work if you choose colourful low maintenance plants

Gardening can be a joy but there are times when it's simply hard work. However, you can cut the labour to a minimum by choosing plants that not only add colour and year-round-interest, but will require very little attention.

Evergreens
Create a backbone to your borders with colourful evergreens. The golden-leaved *Choisya ternata* 'Sundance' is a great example. This wonderful shrub thrives in sun or shade but is best in dappled light where its leaves take on a beautiful lime-green colour.

Partner it with the shiny, green-leaved *Viburnum tinus* 'Eve Price' which has lovely pink-flushed buds and white flowers.

Coloured stems
Late winter and early spring are dull times in the garden but the colourful stems of dogwoods will brighten your borders with a fiery display. Try *Cornus alba* 'Elegantissima' which not only has vibrant red stems in winter but also lovely variegated leaves in summer. The yellow stems of *Cornus stolonifera* 'Flaviramea' and the orange-red stems of *Cornus sanguinea* 'Midwinter Fire' make a fantastic combination.

Grasses
A border of grasses and sedges can be effective and low maintenance. Evergreen sedges such as the green and cream *Carex oshimensis* 'Evergold', bronze *Carex buchananii* and black *Ophiopogon planiscapus* 'Nigrescens' require no attention.

Low maintenance tips
● Mulch with gravel, bark or slate as this will reduce weed growth.
● Lay landscape fabric over the ground before you plant.
● Lay a seep hose among needy plants so you don't have to water as regularly
● Plant up containers of seasonal bedding and bulbs but mix them with small, colourful evergreens.

Gareth Salter

PIC: GA PICTURE LIBRARY

The things we miss

The rag-and-bone man

Rarely seen now, the rag and bone man would walk up and down the back lanes of the rows of terraced houses blowing his battered trumpet to announce his search for old clothes from householders. Children would be given exciting gifts of a goldfish, balloons, a tin whistle or a paper windmill in exchange for a bundle of old clothes, woollen jumpers or bags of assorted rags.

PIC: HULTON ARCHIVE

The corn harvest

The heat and dry weather of August meant it was time to harvest the cornfields. The golden stalks were cut by farmers and collected into bulging sheaves, which were then stacked into stooks of six to ten sheaves. Even today, the sight of a field dotted with stooks – some straight and neat, others leaning drunkenly in the blazing sun – is an enduring image of the English countryside. Above them the sky couldn't be anything but the purest blue and the warm air was filled with the scent of grass and wildflowers.

Rag rugs

Old clothing that was no longer good enough to wear would find a new lease of life as a rag rug, also known as a peg rug. Starting off with a hessian sack, it was slit open, washed and cut to size.

Then you would cut up the odd scraps of clothing into pieces. You found a stick about eight inches long and sharpened it, then pushed the pointed end through the weave of the sack and followed it with a strip of cloth. Most children found this a boring, thankless chore but we all had to muck in to get it done.

A pickled egg and a packet of crisps, please

Eating in a pub's just not the same anymore, moans Ray Martin. It's all far too fancy!

Have you tried to buy a crusty ham or cheese roll in a pub just lately? Is it me, have I been unlucky, or have these traditional mainstays of pub cuisine vanished forever, along with skittles and dominos?

You can get a lasagne or a moussaka. You can easily find curry or chicken tikka. Avocado sandwiches, chive dips, date and walnut bread... but cheese or ham crusty rolls? No chance.

There was a time when cheese and ham rolls were the top-notch items on the menu of any self-respecting pub. Of course, they didn't have a lot of competition. There were crisps. Up until the 1960s crisps were ready salted rather than prawn, smoky bacon, grilled chicken or baked bean flavours.

They were delivered to pubs in tin boxes that had a hundred other uses once emptied, so there was no need to think about waste disposal or recycling. Each packet of crisps was supposed to contain a little twist of blue paper with salt inside. Sometimes there was no blue bag but at other times there might be two, three, or even four.

Those blue bags of salt could also be found in small cellophane packets of Brazil nuts. These were hung behind the bar on a card. Peanuts came on a card as well. It usually had a picture of a pretty girl on it and every time a packet of nuts was removed more of her was revealed. It wasn't worth it – she was always wearing a swimsuit.

Another favourite item of pub fare was the pickled egg, now nearly as rare as the Dodo. These came in huge glass jars that could only be lifted by barmaids working in pairs. Sometimes there were similar jars containing pickled onions but these were apt to cause problems because the onions weren't of uniform size. It made no economic sense to have a barmaid armed with a long-handled spoon chasing one-penny onions round the jar for ten minutes while a customer pointed out the one he wanted as if he was choosing a lobster at the Savoy Grill.

Who remembers those strange jars with the lid set off to one side at a 45 degree angle that held arrowroot biscuits the size of small cartwheels?

Nearly every pub had them, yet you hardly ever saw anybody eat one. Ah, but lots of people bought them. And why? Because every pub had an ancient dog in the public bar who was constantly fed arrowroot biscuits by the regulars. Those same dogs also drank huge quantities of mild beer out of ashtrays.

I spent hours of my childhood sitting in cars outside country pubs with a biscuit or a packet of crisps and a bottle of ginger beer.

Ginger beer always tasted better if it came in the traditional stone bottle and even after the stone was replaced by glass, the bottles kept their original squat shape. There's no getting away from it, the container does make a difference to the taste of the drink. Like those bottles of Corona the man used to deliver door-to-door which had complicated spring-clip caps that looked like a medieval instrument of torture. It never tasted the same when they introduced the screw top.

Some pubs had a glass case containing bars of chocolate or nougat. One of my aunts, who liked to appear well-spoken, always pronounced it 'noo-gar'. We all called it 'nugget'.

It's all changed now. The Hot Meat Pie Cabinet was the first sign that things were changing. Pale, flat pies containing an unidentifiable dollop of brown goo. The centre of the pie was more often than not lukewarm. It's a wonder a whole generation of pub-goers weren't wiped out by salmonella. And there were all sorts of legends about what was actually inside those pies. How did we ever bring ourselves to eat one?

My parents had a pub in the 1960s and introduced a miniature hot dog machine. Little did they realise it was the beginning of the end – pub meals, waitresses in white blouses, a restaurant where the saloon bar used to be. A table of condiments and sauces instead of the dart board or shove-halfpenny board. Hot pots, pastas, pancakes, fish and chips, scampi in a basket and full roast dinners. A gastronome's dream.

But you can't get a crusty ham or cheese roll!

September 2004

The harvest of the land is growing fast now. And, to celebrate, harvest festivals and services of thanksgiving will be held in churches and schools across the country. Your grandchildren will be busy making corn dollies and as harvest time is traditionally the time to give food to those less fortunate, they'll probably be decorating baskets to fill with tasty treats for the needy too.

This is also the time for local produce shows or country fairs.

Chutneys, pickles, preserves and jams always go down well, and this easy-to-make marrow chutney is bound to be a winner with your family.

Coarsely chop 4lb/1.8kg of marrow and 1½lb/675g of apple and add to a saucepan containing 1lb/450g of onion, 4lb/1.8kg raisins, 2oz/50g of salt, plus 2 tablespoons of peppercorns, mustard seed and cut up ginger root tied in a muslin bag. Cover with vinegar and simmer for one to four hours until soft.

In a separate pan, dissolve 1lb/450g of sugar into 2½ pints of vinegar and add to the marrow. Cook gently, stirring until the consistency is like jam. Fill airtight jars and store for two months before using.

WEDNESDAY	1	
THURSDAY	2	2-5 Burghley Horse Trials
FRIDAY	3	
SATURDAY	4	
SUNDAY	5	
MONDAY	6	
TUESDAY	7	
WEDNESDAY	8	
THURSDAY	9	
FRIDAY	10	10-19 Southampton International Boat Show
SATURDAY	11	Last night of the BBC Proms
SUNDAY	12	
MONDAY	13	
TUESDAY	14	
WEDNESDAY	15	
THURSDAY	16	
FRIDAY	17	
SATURDAY	18	

SUNDAY	*19*
MONDAY	*20*
TUESDAY	*21*
WEDNESDAY	*22*
THURSDAY	*23*
FRIDAY	*24*
SATURDAY	*25*
SUNDAY	*26*
MONDAY	*27*
TUESDAY	*28* October YOURS on sale
WEDNESDAY	*29*
THURSDAY	*30*

A year in your garden

This is a great month to be taking cuttings. Flowering has slowed down in many plants and as autumn approaches, roots are itching to get growing. It's also good to take cuttings from plants that may have problems getting through the winter. The new plants will be full of vigour and bursting with energy next spring.

The basic principles of taking cuttings is to select a strong growing shoot, one without a flower, and cut it from the parent plant just below a pair of buds. This allows the buds left on the plant to grow. The cutting should be a workable length, bearing in mind it will need a few trims before it is ready for rooting. Put the cutting in a plastic bag and carry it back to a potting shed or greenhouse. Here you need to remove any leaves that will be under the compost surface. If left on the cutting they will rot, causing the whole cutting to die. A quick slice through the base of the cuttings and the whole thing is ready to be inserted into compost.

The compost must be well drained. Add grit to all shop bought composts to ensure success. Then fill pots with the compost but don't over firm. Push your cuttings into the compost. Water the compost and place the pot and cutting in a plastic bag or propagator. The plastic bag should not touch the cutting.

Hormone rooting compounds are available to increase the chances of your cuttings forming roots. These are available as powders, liquids and gels. Always read the instructions and never apply too much of the hormone to the cuttings. Excess hormones will reduce the chances of success. It's broad principle stuff, but it works for most plants – give it a try now.

PIC: EMAP GARDEN PICTURE LIBRARY

★ READER'S TIP ★
Helen Fielding in Preston carries plastic bags with her whenever she visits a garden. She always asks permission, and most garden own-ers are only too pleased to give Helen cuttings, to put in her bags and root when she gets home.

August 30-September 5

MY ADVICE IS...

'Never marry for money, but love where money is', was my mum's tip. I'm not sure she followed this herself so, maybe, that's why she passed it on.

Sylvia Webb, Cambs

DID YOU KNOW THAT

Pop singer Engelbert Humperdinck's real name is Arnold Dorsey.

Top tip

Placing a sheet of tinfoil under your ironing board cover will reflect heat and save energy.

OLD FASHIONED REMEDIES

Save all cabbage and sprout water. (Do not add salt to the greens when cooking.) For serious skin problems in children and adults keep the water in a cool place and drink a small glass, night and morning.

Joan Shea, Galasheils

Dr Henderson replies: I don't know too many children who would drink cabbage and sprout water – mine certainly wouldn't! I am afraid I can't see how this could work at all, although we do know that several large glasses of water a day are very important for a healthy complexion. Once again though, this is harmless and that is important here.

PIC: CHARLES HAWES PHOTOGRAPHY

OUT & ABOUT TO...

Veddw House Garden, The Veddw, Devauden, Monmouthshire

Ever dreamed of escaping the rat race and moving to a land where the flowers smell sweeter, the skies are bluer, the grass is greener... and the pace of life less stressful? The owners of this idyllic garden did exactly that 17 years ago – and they haven't looked back. Set in a valley with four acres to plant and maintain, Veddw was a far cry from Anne Wareham and Charles Hawes' small London garden, but they took to the challenge like the proverbial duck.

A visit to this garden is a real treat, as Anne and Charles have put their hearts and souls (not to mention their backs) into making it a special place to be. The history of the house and land was a big influence: Anne used the local Tithe

Map of 1841 as the basis for a pattern of hedges on one side of the valley; and hazel tree-lined Elizabeth's Walk is named after Veddw House's former resident, Elizabeth Evans. Other areas reflect Anne's love of wild flowers, with a corner full of buttercups, bluebells and poppies – even weeds are welcome in this garden. Not to mention the fish and parrots...

● *Veddw House Garden is open on Aug 30 and 31 as part of the National Gardens Open For Charity Scheme (phone first to check dates and times). Private visits welcome by appointment at other times between April and October.*

● *Home-made teas; plants for sale.*
Tel: 01291 650836

PIC: HULTON ARCHIVE

▲ It's the first day at school and the children are finding it all a bit bewildering. Never mind, it will be home-time soon!

WHAT'S COOKING?

PIC: NATIONAL SUMMER FRUITS

Blackberry Tartes Tatin
(Serves 4)

Berry Base:
- 11½ oz/340 g fresh blackberries
- 2 oz/50 g butter, melted
- 2 oz/50 g light brown muscovado sugar
- 1 tbs lemon juice

Pastry Topping:
- 2 oz/50 g softened butter
- 1¾ oz/45 g icing sugar
- 1 egg beaten
- 4½/125 g plain flour
- 1 tsp powdered cinnamon

1 Preheat the oven to 200°C/400°F/Gas Mark 6. Divide the berries between a lightly-buttered Yorkshire pudding baking tin.

2 Stir the butter and sugar together over heat, with a squeeze of lemon juice, stirring until a butterscotch mixture forms. Pour this equally over the berries. Set the tin in the hot oven.

3 Mix the butter, icing sugar, egg, flour and cinnamon together to make a soft pastry. Divide it into four. Pat and roll each ball out to give four discs about 7.5 cm/3 in across.

4 Remove tins from the oven and drop one pastry disc on the top of each of the hot berry portions, pushing pastry well down.

5 Bake undisturbed for 15-20 minutes or until the pastry is set. Remove from the oven. Leave to stand for 1 minute. Cover the pudding tray with a large platter. Invert each pudding, tipping out each tatin and its juices. Serve hot with ice cream or pouring custard.

AT THE MOVIES

Who said?
'Once I tried to let a smile be my umbrella. I got awful wet'. (Answer below)

Answer: Celeste Holm in Elia Kazen's Gentlemen Prefer Blondes

ON GROWING OLDER
'Of all the things I've lost, I miss my mind most'.
Unknown

September 6-12

ON GROWING OLDER

'Few women admit their age. Few men act theirs'.
Anon

OLD WIVES' TALES

A bowl of celery soup at your bedside to inhale at night will cure rheumatism.

Dr Henderson replies: This is a new one on me, and if it works I will be rich in a week! Inhaling celery fumes is not going to do the slightest good in any illness, let alone something as severe as rheumatoid arthritis and rheumatism. Instead, just eat the soup, which will be good for you!

PAUSE FOR THOUGHT

Petal paradise

To spend an hour of any day
Arranging flowers for hearth or sill,
Is quite the nicest task for me
And one I tackle with a will.

They have power, of this I'm sure,
To ease the burdens of the day,
They soothe the anxious thoughts of those
Who lovingly arrange their sprays.

They cheer a sick room with their gay
And happy faces glowing there.
In life or death they play a part,
They ease anxieties and despair.

Some blossoms bring back memories
Of face, or place, or point in time,
Where you had loved or worked with joy
A reminiscence so sublime.

Joan Hammond, Suffolk

WHAT'S COOKING?

QUICK SNACK
Corn Fritters
(Serves 4)

- 5 oz/150 g tinned sweetcorn
- 2 oz/50 g self-raising flour
- Pinch of salt
- 1 egg
- 4 tbs milk
- Oil

1 Cook the corn according to the directions on the tin.
2 Make a batter with flour, salt, well-beaten egg and milk and stir in the cooled corn. Fry tablespoonfuls of the mixture in a little hot oil until crisp and golden brown on both sides and drain. Serve hot with a mixed salad.

A DAY TO REMEMBER

It's the first day at work for Violet Whitehead from Essex...

I walked into Chadwell Heath Mill at 8am on a Monday morning in January 1939, as a little 14-year-old, to begin my first day's work. Orders were shouted at me from all sides, and I was put to work as the 'run-about' in the Box Making Department.

My job was to put the new rolls on machines, sweep the whole of the department, get the teas and bread rolls from the canteen, get buckets of hot water to wash the gum off the rollers of the covering machine, and much, much more.

In the winter it was so cold in the mill, people would come in and put on another coat. I worked from 8am until 6pm, five days a week, for 8s 6d. Out of this was deducted one old penny for pension, one penny for sports fund and two penny stamp. We had one week's holiday a year, the first week in August, including the Bank Holiday.

I worked in the Box Making Department for 40 years – so I must have liked it!

Above: Violet in 1935
Left: Violet today

WHAT A COINCIDENCE

When studying my family tree, I wrote to the Derbyshire Records Office with an inquiry. A swift reply provided the information I wanted. I was also told that a gentleman from Leicester had been in the office that very day, studying the same family.

I wrote to him and discovered that my great-great grandfather and his great-great grandmother were brother and sister. Together, we were able to trace the family back to the 15th century.

Keith Gregson, Sunderland

AT THE MOVIES

Who said?
'The girls call me Pilgrim because every time I dance with one I make a little progress'.
(Answer below)

Answer: Bob Hope to Paulette Goddard in George Marshall's The Ghost Breakers

DID YOU KNOW THAT

It's impossible to lick your elbow.

Top tip

Keep a gardening diary – it'll remind you when to harvest and sow and what grew well and where last year.

PIC: BRIAN CHAPPLE

OUT & ABOUT TO...

Brodick Castle, Garden and Country Park, Ayr, Isle of Arran, Scotland

This is the perfect time of year to admire the wonderful rhododendron collection at Brodick Castle Garden. There's also a gorgeous woodland garden, which was created in 1923 by Lady Mary Louise, 6th Duchess of Montrose; and a walled garden dating from 1710 which has been restored in the Victorian style.

You can easily spend a day exploring the Country Park, which has walking trails, woodlands, waterfalls, gorges, wildlife ponds, a nature room and a wildlife garden. The castle was built on the site of a Viking fortress and parts of it date back to the 13th century; it was extended in

1652 and 1844 and is open to visitors.
● *Adults £3.50 (garden and country park only), concessions £2.60*
● *Restaurant selling home-made food, gift shop, adventure playground*
● *Limited wheelchair access, but one woodland trail is specially designed for use by wheelchair (there's a battery-operated car available to borrow)*
Tel: 01770 302202
● *Getting to the Isle of Arran involves taking a ferry (01475 650100), which takes around an hour, then a short bus ride (0870 6082608)*

September 13-19

OUT & ABOUT TO...

Last Of The Summer Wine Exhibition, Holmfirth, Yorkshire

The world's longest-running TV comedy series is filmed in the small Yorkshire village of Holmfirth. Incredibly, after 28 years of 'lights, camera, action', this quaint corner of the Pennines remains relatively unspoilt by its time in the spotlight. True fans wouldn't dream of missing the Last Of The Summer Wine Exhibition, where in surroundings reminiscent of Compo's house, you can watch video out-takes, browse through photographs of the characters and see some of the props used in the series.

Visit for a day and you'll have time to drink in the breathtaking scenery, then repair to Sid's Café or The Wrinkled Stocking Tea Room for a restorative cuppa and a tasty home-made snack. And while you're here, why not pop into Steps Gift Shop and treat yourself to a Nora Batty peg bag, or even a set of Wrinkled Stocking China?
- *Adults £2, concessions £1.50, children 50p*
- *Refreshments, gift shop*
- *It's worth bearing in mind that Holmfirth is less crowded on weekdays*
Tel: 01484 681408

ON GROWING OLDER

'Old age is not for sissies'.

Malcolm Forbes

AT THE MOVIES

Who said?
'Youth! Stay close to the young and a little rubs off'.
(Answer below)

Answer: Maurice Chevalier advising Louis Jourdan in Vincente Minnelli's Gigi

A DAY TO REMEMBER

It was a grand send off for Joyce Swinburn from Northumberland when she left work...

In 1988 my husband and I returned to the north east to live after 14 years away from 'home. I'd been working with some really nice girls. We always had a laugh about things and got on very well as a team.

At last the time came for my last day at work and I was in quite a weepy state all day. There was a toast to my departure and a presentation of a beautiful picture of the street where I'd worked – and one of the girls had made up a poem about me and my little ways. Here's an extract:

You're leaving with style
You've not got the sack
So keep the receipt – we might have you back!

You're very loyal and you've been a good friend
We're all very sorry this has to end.
But you'll be all right with your darling Ron
You've had to leave but life goes on.

OLD FASHIONED REMEDIES

Arnica was always to be found in the medicine chest in a little ridged bottle. It was marvellous at preventing bruises and after a fall, the brown liquid was dabbed on the offending area, with soothing results.

C High, Lincs

Dr Henderson replies: I've used this myself! Arnica can still be found either as a rub or in homeopathic remedies and, I have no doubt, it can be highly beneficial in the treatment of simple mild bruising. Safe, simple and natural and I still recommend this to some patients!

MY ADVICE IS...

'If you're stressed, close your eyes for ten minutes every day – either sitting or lying down – and empty your mind'. My doctor advised this when I was getting over depression after the war years.
Irene Ball, Warks

DID YOU KNOW THAT

Queen Elizabeth I owned 150 wigs.

Top tip

If some of your rooms have condensation, put an egg cup full of salt on the windowsill

WHAT A COINCIDENCE

In April 1936 I was on a bus, going to the cinema. A young man got on, who I thought was quite 'dishy'. He gave me a glance and that was that. The next week I was on the bus again, when the same young man got on. We looked at each other again – and that was that.

Three months later I went on holiday to Wales with my parents and sister. Walking along the beach one day, who should I see but the same young man who'd got on the bus!

In the evening my sister and I went to the fun fair and saw the young man with his friend. They asked us on one of the fairground rides and when the evening was over, we promised to meet each other when we got home. We did so and after four years of courtship, we married.

Unfortunately, after five years of marriage, he passed away at the age of 30 but I am so pleased I had those years with him. They were wonderful.

He said he'd wanted to speak to me on the bus but thought I would think he was too forward. It seemed fate meant us to be together.

I am now 84 but remember it all as though it were yesterday.

S Smith, Swindon

WHAT'S COOKING?

SUPPER DISH
One Pot Hot Pot
(Serves 6)

- Salt and pepper
- Stock
- 1 oz/25 g butter
- ½ pt/275 ml gravy
- 2 lb/900 g lamb
- 2 lb/900 g potatoes, sliced
- 1 large onion

1 Divide the meat into cutlets, trimming off the skin and most of the fat.
2 Grease a heatproof baking-dish and arrange a layer of sliced potatoes. Place the cutlets on top, slightly overlapping each other, and cover with slices of onion. Season well. Add the remainder of the potato slices.
3 Pour over about ½ pt/275 ml hot stock seasoned with salt and pepper. Brush the top layer of potatoes with warmed butter and cover with greased, greaseproof paper.
4 Bake for about 2 hours in a moderate oven (180°C/350°F/Gas Mark 4). Then remove the paper and cook for a further 20 minutes. Serve with lashings of gravy.

September 20-26

WHAT A COINCIDENCE !

I was waiting in a queue at a security gate at Heathrow when we were asked to go to another gate.

I turned round to the lady behind me to query this, when she said: "Are you Bridget's mother?" (Bridget is my daughter.) I said I was, and on my way to Ireland to see her. To me she was a complete stranger but a friend of my daughter's. We must look like each other!

M Gatley, Wiltshire

ON GROWING OLDER

'Whenever I feel like exercise, I lie down until the feeling passes'.

Unknown

PAUSE FOR THOUGHT

Rita Carvill from Coventry writes to say that her mother-in-law left her this small recipe for a happy marriage:

4 cups of love
2 cups of loyalty
3 cups of forgiveness
1 cup of friendship
2 spoons of hope
2 spoons of tenderness
4 quarts of faith and
A barrel of laughs
Mix carefully and serve in generous helpings daily, with a dose of sunshine.

OUT & ABOUT TO...

Chelsea Physic Garden, 66 Royal Hospital Road, Chelsea, London

It's a real joy to find a peaceful haven in the centre of London and this garden is very special. The second-oldest botanic garden in the UK, it was started in 1673 to study plants used in medicine, and is still used for botanical and medicinal research.

Before the Embankment was completed in 1874, the garden went right down to the river, and was most easily accessed by boat. Since then, the area has changed dramatically, and the once rural setting is now surrounded with buildings. These provide welcome protection, radiating heat during winter and keeping out cold winds, so creating a microclimate in which rare and tender plants flourish.

Within the three-and-three-quarter-acre site are lots of interesting, attractive plants (all labelled with their botanical name and country of origin) from around the globe. You'll find a perfumery border, herb garden and historical walk; borders of essential oil plants; plus the largest fruiting olive tree grown outside in Britain. With wildlife to watch and plenty of places to sit and listen to the birds singing, it's easy to imagine you're in an old country garden.
● *Adults £5, students and children (aged 5 to 15) £3*
● *Teas; shop; plants for sale; wheelchair access*
● *Open Wednesdays (12-5pm) and Sundays (2-6pm) from April-October*
Tel: 020 7352 5646

Margaret Willis from Tyne Wear recalls her early days as a nurse…

A DAY TO REMEMBER

From early childhood I'd wanted to be a nurse and in 1952, at 15 years old, I wrote to the nearest training hospital. My mother, who didn't know about my letter, was shocked and horrified. Nevertheless, I was invited to an interview with the Matron who kindly informed me that I needed to stay at school, sit my exams, and if I felt the same when I was 18, I would be considered.

I began my nurse's training in 1955 and soaked up the first three months of theory with no problem, after which I began ward training. I loved every minute of it – the duties, the uniform, even the nurses' home; I was well pleased with myself and it must have shown.

Then I was sent to 'special' a child, which meant staying with the patient constantly. I bounced into a side ward and stopped in my tracks. There in the bed was a desperately ill child, who died not long afterwards.

At the end of that day I was devastated, my happy bubble had burst and I faced one of the tragic realities of nursing. That was the day I grew up and, with the help of the ward sister, learned the true meaning of the words caring, sympathy, compassion and, most of all, humility. I had taken my first small steps towards being a nurse.

OLD WIVES' TALES

If a pregnancy is carried high, it's a boy. Low down, it's a girl.

Dr Henderson replies: There are dozens of stories about how to guess the sex of a child and – as with this one – it's all simple guesswork. After all, you have a 50-50 chance of being right, anyway!

DID YOU KNOW THAT ?

The average hamster, if provided with a wheel, will run up to eight miles a night

Top tip

For shiny hair massage a beaten egg into the scalp and then rinse in warm water

WHAT'S COOKING?

Bubble and Squeak
(Serves 2)

- Cold mashed potatoes
- Salt and pepper
- Cold greens (ie. cabbage, kale etc)
- Vinegar
- Thin slices of cold roast meat
- 2 tbs oil
- 1 onion, thinly sliced

1 Heat the oil in a frying pan and fry the meat quickly on both sides until lightly browned. Remove and keep warm.
2 Fry the onion until browned, add the potatoes and greens, which have been mixed together and season well.
3 Stir until hot and add a little vinegar. Place the meat on top and serve.

AT THE MOVIES

Who said?
'Once I tried to let a smile be my umbrella. I got awful wet'.
(Answer below)

Answer: Celeste Holm in Elia Kazen's Gentlemen Prefer Blondes

Doing what comes naturally

Put away the chemicals and follow these tips for an environmentally friendly garden

Protect precious peat bog by making your own compost

PIC: SCOTTISH WILDLIFE TRUST

● Avoid using slug pellets. They don't just poison slugs but affect birds, frogs and hedgehogs that eat the slugs. Control slugs with a barrier of grit or sand around plants. Or a jar with beer in the bottom, sunk into the ground.

● Epsom salts sprinkled around plants will prevent rabbit damage.

● Diluted household detergent is effective against greenfly and blackfly, and is thought not to harm other insects.

● Tiny creatures need small cracks and crevices to hibernate in. Ladybirds love dry plant debris, loose bark and hollow stems for perfect homes.

● Don't trim creepers back too violently; the gap between walls and plants acts as a shelter for insects.

● Leave fallen fruit where it lands; it provides birds with tasty treats.

● A rock or log pile can offer slow worms and newts shelter during the winter months. A length of drainpipe filled with bamboo canes can also attract hibernating lacewings.

● Frogs and toads swim to the bottom of the pond for a wet winter. Keep an eye on the pond to prevent it freezing over.

● If you're lucky enough to have badgers nearby, remember they don't hibernate but sleep for longer periods of time through the winter months. Provide them with plenty of food.

● Protect precious peat bog by buying compost that doesn't contain peat. Make your own natural fertiliser, using garden waste and vegetable kitchen scraps in a home-made box or bought compost bin. If you don't have much space, make your compost in a small 'worm bin' in your back yard.

With thanks to The Wildlife Trusts for their help and information, www.wildlifetrusts.org

The things we miss

The Lamplighter

A familiar sight of yesteryear was the lamplighter who walked round at dusk, lighting the old gas lamps in streets across the country. The lamplighter with his long pole would bring light to dark corners and was a sign that the evening had started.

As electric lights improved, gas lighting declined and by 1933 half the streets of London were lit by electricity. In Birmingham, the last gaslights were removed as late as 1975.

PIC: HULTON ARCHIVE

A new term begins

September was back to school time and children everywhere were getting used to covering up again. As the weather got colder, classrooms got chillier and the layers of clothing increased. First on was a cotton vest and then the liberty bodice – so called because they were probably more liberating than the boned corsets worn in previous years. The bodice was similar to a vest but with a fleecy back, so it was very warm. On top of this, you would wear several layers of jumpers or blouses and cardigans, to keep the cold at bay.

Then there were the coarse, thick, black woollen stockings, or fawn knee-high socks, held up with garters.

But worse than all this was the uniform you had to wear to do gym. This consisted of a gymslip or a white blouse and navy school knickers with a little pocket in them. Most girls hated wearing them with a passion. They were huge, baggy garments with elastic round the bottom of the legs, which almost reached the knees.

Worse than having to wear them, was the prospect of the boys seeing you in your lovely attire as you went from the changing rooms to the gym. You would just die of embarrassment if one of them saw you!

Puzzles

Alphabet jigsaw

Clue A leads to an answer beginning with A, and so on through the alphabet. Solve the rhyming cryptic clues and then see if you can position all your answers in the grid.

A At the start, one simply ends
  The answer is to make amends (5)
B Change direction (to go blue),
  As Teddy is correct to do! (4,5)
C Criminal has caught the bird
  With what the bishop holds, I've heard (5)
D Sag from feeling tired of it all,
  Use a duck to break the fall (5)
E Let nature act a little, see!
  'Twill blow its top occasionally (4)
F Defend our transformation here,
  We've sunk (or so it would appear) (9)
G Eton guard is newly arrayed,
  The answer must be to evade (3,6)
H When in life one feels the pace,
  Is one firmly ironed in place? (4-7)
I Is one right regarding story?
  Can't be returned to its former glory (11)
J Enjoy rude turn, if you've a mind,
  It's gone some way, I think you'll find (9)
K Upsetting UK parties will
  Bring a certain prestige, still (5)

L Little ant-hill is a bit
  Inclined to be the word to fit (5)
M To fashion you must add a pound,
  A sample copy will be found (5)
N Seriously, let's rearrange
  Noon golf, I need the change (2,7)
O It seems as if there is no back
  To scene for film – it's an attack (5)
P In some dry places there is much,
  It's not sharp fruit, though sharp to touch (7,4)
Q Absolutely certain to confuse
  Letters involved in quiet ruse (5,4)
R An inlet, when it has no start,
  An awful vapour will impart (4)
S Crazy Huns, when they're like this,
  You should avoid – or even miss (4)
T Initially taking half our share,
  Excluding the objects over there (5)
U Neat, ruled arrangement – but it's strange,
  Though change there is, we have no change (9)
V Archdeacon has American love,
  A goddess to be seen above (5)
W This man, when in an awkward spot,
  Proved, crossbow-wise, to be a 'shot' (7,4)
X Of element we're on the track,
  Here ten begin, yet none comes back (5)
Y Hindu with a mystic air,
  He's smarter than the average bear (4)
Z Our zinc I'm turning round – it's meant
  To be another element (9)

Four square

Write the four-letter answers to the clues across the rows of the grid. If you have solved them correctly, you'll find another four-letter word reading down each of the diagonals. Now see if you can rearrange all the letters in the grid to form the title of a film by a famous comedy team.

ACROSS
1 Far up
2 Baby's bottle top
3 Irish knitwear style
4 Bard

A fresher outlook

By Claire M Buckland

It had only been two weeks since Hannah had left for university but for Angela it represented the passing of many years. How could the departure of her only child have left such a chasm in her life? She supposed it was a natural reaction to one's offspring stepping out into the world alone. A mother was bound to feel a sense of loss at such a time.

Angela switched on the television. Another one of those lifestyle shows was on. However, this particular format was not one she had seen before. A consultant was invited along to the home of complete strangers with the purpose of assisting them to 'streamline' their lives. Angela watched with interest as a cluttered house was transformed into an orderly and functional living space.

It was a truly liberating experience, not only viewing the 'before' and 'after' scenes, but also witnessing the huge relief on the faces of the house owners. Angela's mind was reeling with which room in the house to tackle first. Now seemed like an ideal time for her to undertake this sort of liberating exercise.

During the weeks before Hannah had packed up her books and belongings for three years of study, mother and daughter had discussed many things. Their conversations in June and July, when Freshers' Week had been an abstract concept, had been free-flowing and light, full of anticipation. But as August succumbed to the cool whisper of autumn, Angela noticed a change of maternal attitude. Whenever she looked at her daughter now, she wanted to take her in her arms and keep her close as she had done as a child. It seemed so alien to her that, for the first time in her life, a space was being created between them. And it frightened her.

Equipped with black bin bags and a grim determination, Angela entered the spare room. The charming American woman on the programme had started by laying everything on the floor, then had methodically formed two piles, items to remain and items for scrap. Angela set to.

Broken cassette recorder? Out. Various chewed and warped classical tapes? Out. Old but still loved crystal vase? In. And so it continued.

Her progress was swift; Angela was thrilled at her uncharacteristic brutality. It was a real parting of a sea of twenty years' paraphernalia. Angela flushed with delight when she considered how much space would be freed up once all the junk had been removed. She could seriously consider putting in a desk, a chair – creating her own office. But for what? For what, indeed.

Then her hand came to rest on a cardboard box marked 'Baby clothes/Photos'. Tentatively her hand dipped into the box. Pink baby cardigan. Immediately the memories came. But she couldn't bear to part with this tiny garment, so she put it to one side. At the bottom of the box lay a number of yellowing photos. As she put in place her spectacles to examine the shots more closely, she realised they were photographs of herself with her mother. It was a moment that stopped her in her tracks.

In one of the pictures, mother and daughter stood side by side, squinting in the bright summer sunshine. They had always been close, too close some independent-minded friends had said.

Now seemed like an ideal time for her to undertake this sort of liberating exercise

The emptied room with space enough for a chair and a desk now made sense

The emptied room with space enough for a chair and a desk now made sense. She could buy a computer and update her rusty typing skills – a room of one's own. 'Yes, a writing class could be just the focus I need right now', thought Angela.

Climbing the stairs to the spare room, the anguish Angela had suffered these last weeks finally lifted. The wonderful timing of Hannah's letter had clearly shown that, although miles away, her mother was not far from her thoughts. Mother – if indeed it had been Angela's mother who had 'spoken' – had been right. 'I'll be back' were Hannah's words, words she wanted to hear so much.

At long last, Angela felt as if she had done the right thing. She had given her daughter room to be herself and in finding herself she had looked back to see the face of her mother. Since the day she had brought Hannah into this world, she had dreaded the moment she would have to let her go. But all that worrying had been senseless. In fact letting go hadn't diminished the bond between mother and daughter; it had strengthened it.

"Hannah, it's mum. Fine thanks. Oh, I got my first assignment back last night. What mark? Distinction. Don't be daft, they don't give the Booker Prize for a short story!"

Angela knew that she had allowed many opportunities in life to pass her by; chances that might have taken her away from the proximity of her mother. But her refusal of them all had been her own conscious decision. She had cherished her family above all else, at the cost of her own personal journey through life. But it had been her choice. And now, she couldn't expect her own daughter to take that same route. Despite her own sadness, deep down Angela wanted her daughter to lead the life she had given her to the full.

It was a moment of startling clarity for Angela. It was as if her own mother was sitting beside her, counselling her as she always had done throughout her life. She couldn't help feeling as if her mother had, somehow, silently led her to this moment. 'You've not let go forever, Angela. She will be back'. The words followed her down the stairs to a letter, newly delivered, lying on the doormat. The handwriting was Hannah's.

Mum,

Somehow a copy of the local rag found its way into my college gear.

I couldn't help seeing the ad (enclosed) for an evening class in creative writing at the school. You often talked about the prizes you won at school for English Composition. Why not give it a go? I'm sure you'd enjoy it. I'll be back on 26th for Reading Week.

Love as ever,

Hannah

October 2004

A flavour of the month

This magical month of ghosts, ghouls and witches is packed with superstition and trickery.

The tradition of Hallow'een began back in the fifth century BC by the Irish Celts, who organised their year according to the agricultural calendar and marked the transition from one year to the next on October 31.

The story goes that during the transition spirits would return to earth, looking for living bodies to possess for the following year. The Celts would then dress in ghoulish costumes and parade around the community to frighten them away.

Years later, the tradition of trick-or-treating is thought to have grown from a ninth-century European custom, souling, when early Christians would make house calls begging for soul cakes. It was thought that even strangers could help a soul's passage to heaven by saying prayers, so, in exchange for a cake they promised to pray for the donors' deceased relatives.

As winter approaches and the clocks change, there's one habit we can adopt. The sun may be weaker but try to spend half an hour outside during daylight – experts say exposure to light can have a positive impact on our wellbeing. Many folk feel below par during winter and scientists believe it's due to lack of light.

FRIDAY	1
SATURDAY	2
SUNDAY	3
MONDAY	4
TUESDAY	5
WEDNESDAY	6
THURSDAY	7
FRIDAY	8
SATURDAY	9
SUNDAY	10
MONDAY	11
TUESDAY	12
WEDNESDAY	13
THURSDAY	14
FRIDAY	15
SATURDAY	16
SUNDAY	17
MONDAY	18

TUESDAY	*19*
WEDNESDAY	*20*
THURSDAY	*21*
FRIDAY	*22*
SATURDAY	*23*
SUNDAY	*24*
MONDAY	*25*
TUESDAY	*26*
WEDNESDAY	*27*
THURSDAY	*28* — November YOURS on sale
FRIDAY	*29*
SATURDAY	*30*
SUNDAY	*31* — Hallowe'en / British Summer Time ends, clocks go back

PIC: EMAP GARDEN PICTURE LIBRARY

☆ READER'S TIP ☆
Peter Smith in Dundee always throws his daffodils on to the soil before planting. He then plants exactly where they have fallen as it gives a more natural look when they flower.

A year in your garden

If you want superb displays of crocus, daffodils, tulips and a whole host of flowers next spring, then now is the time to get planting. A bulb already has everything it needs to flower. All we gardeners need to do is to supply water, and that's best done via the soil.

Choose your bulbs carefully. They need to be firm, plump with no signs of disease on the outside. Check every bulb in a pack before buying, as often there is a rogue bulb, one riddled with rot that can affect the others. If you can't plant your bulbs straightaway, keep them in a cool, dark place such as a shed.

When you do come to plant them ensure the soil is well prepared. That means removing as many stones as possible and all weeds. Then it's a case of digging a hole, either individually with a trowel, or planting areas with a spade. Bulbs need to be planted to a depth three times their height. This ensures plenty of healthy roots, well anchored in the soil and a great display. Daffodils for example can produce leaves and no flowers if planted too shallow.

So it's dig the hole, put in the bulb – pointy end uppermost – and refill with soil.

That's nearly it, but bulbs can be grown in baskets. These baskets, available from aquatic shops, have slits on their sides. This allows water to pass freely but compost to stay put. Fill with compost and plant your bulbs in the baskets. Then plant the baskets containing the bulbs to the appropriate depth.

The bulbs can then be easily lifted when the display is over or if you have heavy clay soil. Lifted bulbs can then be dried and replanted the following autumn. Most bulbs need a well-drained soil but are not reliant on fertilisers.

September 27-October 3

A DAY TO REMEMBER

A parade to remember for Anne Simpson…

My grandson joined the Navy in 2000, when he was 18 years old. In March that year, he had his passing out parade and all the family went down to Plymouth where he was based.

It was a lovely day and we all got rather excited as we took our seats around the parade ground. It would be the first time we'd seen him in uniform.

The Band of the Royal Marines struck up and then they marched out. We were all trying to find this six foot ,blonde young man and when we spotted him there were tears flowing. When it was finished, we all gave three cheers and the new sailors threw their caps in the air.

It was the best day of my life.

AT THE MOVIES

'I've met a lot of hard-boiled eggs in my life but you – you're 20 minutes!'
(Answer below)

Answer: Jan Sterling to Kirk Douglas in Billy Wilder's The Big Carnival

MY ADVICE IS…

'When you're busy holding forth your views, just remember to pause and be prepared to listen. Other people's views are just as important as your own'.
C Staff, Isle of Wight

OUT & ABOUT TO…

Beamish, The North of England Open Air Museum, Beamish, County Durham

We've all wondered how our ancestors lived and this superb museum offers plenty of clues. It's devoted to recreating life in northern England in the early 19th and 20th century. Set in 300 acres of countryside, the museum is split into five main sections, joined up by working trams and buses. There's a town with streets, shops, houses and businesses; a colliery village with a mine, chapel, cottages and school; a manor house with gardens and orchard; a railway station; and a home farm with animals and craft demonstrations.

Beamish is a great place to bring your

grandchildren because, as well as being allowed to touch everything, they can join in activities from learning to swivel hoops and skip hopscotch to taking part in lessons in the school. There's also a Victorian fairground with rides.
● *Adults £12, over-60s £10, children (5 to 16) £7 (children aged under 5 are admitted free)*
● *Meals and snacks (including period pub); good shops; some disabled access*
Tel: 0191 370 4000

PIC: BEAMISH, THE NORTH OF ENGLAND OPEN AIR MUSEUM

▲ The finishing touches are put to a harvest festival display during the Second World War, in 1941

DID YOU KNOW THAT

Cary Grant donated his entire salary from the 1944 film Arsenic And Old Lace – $100,000 – to the US War Relief Fund.

Top tip

Rubbing the cut side of an onion on to a wasp or bee sting can help reduce the pain.

ON GROWING OLDER

'You don't stop laughing when you grow old; you grow old when you stop laughing'.
Unknown

OLD FASHIONED REMEDIES

During the time of the diphtheria and scarlet fever outbreaks my mother would line all six of us children up and the proceed to blow Flowers Of Sulpur powder through a paper cone, on to the back of our throats. It nearly choked us and many a time mum would end up with the yellow powder on her face as one of us blew it back again! Not one of us ever caught the fever and we were told that the powder acted against any germs.
Beryl Jackson, Essex

Dr Henderson replies: Gosh – you did have an interesting mum! We must remember that diphtheria and scarlet fever were terrible diseases that spread fear in the community and we can forget this now they are so rare. The principle behind this was that sulphur had anti-infection properties, but I suspect the reason you all remained well was more due to luck than anything else, although we will never really know. It would never be allowed now!

WHAT'S COOKING?

Pear and Chocolate Souffle
(Serves 3-4)

- 2 oz/50 g plain chocolate
- Knob of butter
- 150 ml/¼ pt milk
- 2 oz/50 g caster sugar
- 4 tbs (level) plain flour
- 3 oz/75 g pears, puréed
- 3 eggs, separated
- 1 egg white

1. Put chocolate in a bowl with a knob of butter and melt gently over a saucepan of simmering water.
2. Heat the milk, then pour the heated milk on to the melted chocolate, stirring constantly.
3. Blend flour and sugar (reserving 1 teaspoon sugar) to smooth paste with remaining milk. Stir in the chocolate mixture.
4. Return to the pan and bring to the boil stirring all the time, then cook for 1-2 minutes. Remove from the heat, before adding the pear purée.
5. Stir in egg yolks. Whisk egg whites until stiff and fold into mixture carefully.
6. Separate into containers and bake in a moderate oven (180°C/350°F/Gas Mark 4) until risen and crusty (usually about 30 minutes).

October 4-10

OLD WIVES' TALES

Burnt toast is good for your stomach.

Dr Henderson replies: No it isn't. If you have had a stomach upset or gastroenteritis, doctors often advise a simple bland diet for a day or two to allow the body to recover, and this can include foods such as dry toast or bread. However, burnt toast is not a good idea and is not going to be 'good' for any part of you, as such.

WHAT A COINCIDENCE

A couple of years ago I put an entry in Friends of YOURS and received lots of replies. A few days later, I had a phone call from my daughter in Perth, Australia, inviting me to stay for a few weeks. Off I went from my home in Halifax and had a lovely holiday.

There was another batch of mail waiting for me when I arrived home, including a letter from Perth. The first thing I did was put the kettle on, of course, and while I was waiting for it to boil, the phone rang.

"This is Helen speaking, from Perth in Australia. I've been trying to contact you. I wrote to you after seeing your details in the Friends of YOURS section in YOURS magazine, which I'd borrowed from my daughter to read on the plane back to Perth, after my holiday in Halifax."

Unbelievable, but as I was leaving for Perth, Helen was in Halifax. Her letter had been lying on the doormat for a month – and as we talked, it turned out that she lived only five miles away from my daughter's house!

We still correspond and hope to meet on her next visit to England.

Irvin Davison, Halifax

A DAY TO REMEMBER

A family celebration for Beverley Dodd from Bath…

In November 1999, I went with my family to my grandparents Mary and Clement Golledge's 60th wedding anniversary party, at Wollverton House Hotel, nr Bath. It was a wonderful day, with everyone enjoying themselves and taking lots of photographs. My favourite is of my grandparents looking so happy as their cut their cake.

Mary and Clement cutting their 60th anniversary cake

Top tip

If your scissors need sharpening make several cuts through some sandpaper.

DID YOU KNOW THAT

It takes **28** days to replace our outer layer of skin completely.

AT THE MOVIES

Who said?
'I once was so poor, I didn't know where my next husband was coming from'.
(Answer below)

Answer: Mae West in Lowell Sherman's She Done Him Wrong

OUT & ABOUT TO...

Ventnor Botanic Garden, Undercliff Drive, Ventnor, Isle of Wight.

PIC: VENTNOR BOTANIC GARDEN

As you walk around this garden, you'd never guess how devastated it was by the great storm of 1987, which ripped through the 22 acres leaving a path of destruction in its wake. Only a few old and well-established trees survived the storm and the next two years were spent clearing up.

Since then, the garden has been redeveloped to create a place where you can unwind and enjoy seeing plants thriving in their natural habitat. Fortunately, this corner of southern England enjoys a subtropical climate, which has earned it the nickname 'The Garden Isle'. The Botanic Garden lies in the heart of the famous 'Undercliff', which protects it from the north and east – and enables a wide variety of exotic plants, trees, flowers and shrubs normally considered too fragile for much of mainland Britain to flourish. From the New Zealand garden to the Mediterranean terrace and hydrangea dell, there's plenty of colour and interest all year round. The latest attraction is a greenhouse, which has been filled with plants to represent nature fighting back, and features a big waterfall, with lush green ferns.

● *Free admission to Botanic Garden; greenhouse £1*
● *Visitor centre; café; picnic area; shop; plants for sale; children's playground; wheelchair access*
Tel: 01983 855397

WHAT'S COOKING?

QUICK SNACK
Buttery Pumpkin Soup
(Serves 4)

● 1½ lb/675 g pumpkin
● 4 oz/100 g butter
● ¼ pt/150 ml milk
● 5 fl oz/150 ml carton of single cream
● Salt and pepper
● Fried bread croutons

1 Dice the pumpkin.
2 Heat the butter in a pan and add the pumpkin, salt and pepper; cook gently until pulpy.
3 Liquidise with the milk.
4 Add the cream, heat through, season to taste and serve with crispy croutons.

PAUSE FOR THOUGHT

Jean Tibbott from Cumbria sent in some valuable words of advice and explains how they came about:
'As a child, I was given an autograph album and people would contribute with small poems or sayings. I well remember my great Aunt Charlotte writing:

Make new friends but keep the old
One is silver and the other gold.

'I am fortunate to have lots of friends, but I have never forgotten those wise words – and my old friends are dearer to me than ever in retirement'.

WHAT A COINCIDENCE

As a child, I went regularly to Sunday School and on my tenth birthday, my mother presented me with the most beautiful bible, with fine tissue paper pages edged with gold leaf. It had been given to her as a wedding present. From then on, I prayed that someone would give me a bible when I married.

Years later I met Victor – the man of my dreams – and we became engaged in Christmas 1938 but when war was declared, he was posted to Scotland. The day before our wedding in 1940, he and his army pals travelled home by train.

In the carriage was an elderly lady and as the train approached King's Cross, she said: "Give this to your bride and God bless you both." It was a gold-leafed bible just like mum's. My prayers had been answered.

I had my first baby in 1947 and we hadn't a clue what to call her. I blurted out Beryl to the registrar – why, I don't know.

Years later in 1982, I related the story of the bible to my cousin and brought it out to show them. My daughter picked up the box that it had come in and said, 'Mum, have you seen the label on the lid?' I'd never looked but it had the word 'Beryl' on it.

PS We had no wedding presents until after the war. What did I end up with? Five chiming clocks and seven lemonade sets. Well, you can't have everything!

Ethel Edwards,
Suffolk

Ethel and Victor on his embarkation leave, December 1940

OLD FASHIONED REMEDIES

Kaolin poultice was always used for chest ailments. The Kaolin was grey which looked like putty and came in a tin which was put in a saucepan of water to heat. The hot 'slop' was smeared on a piece of lint lined with cotton wool. Then it was slapped on the chest, held in place with a bandage and the 'victim' sent off to bed in the hope that the warmth and fumes would ensure a good night's sleep.

Dr Henderson replies: No use for infections, I'm afraid, but warmth can be generally soothing for chest complaints such as tickly coughs and discomfort. The principle is the same for all poultices, where it is the warm temperature that is said to have all the benefit. I've never come across anyone still using this, and it is highly unlikely to be of much benefit, I think.

Top tip

Instead of buying expensive shoe polish, buff up your footwear with baby oil – it'll shine them up a treat!

DID YOU KNOW THAT

Henry Ford produced his Model T in black because the black paint available at the time was the fastest to dry.

AT THE MOVIES

Who said?
'*I am troubled with insomnia*'.
'*Well, I know a good cure for it*'.
'*Yeah?*' '*Get plenty of sleep*'.
(Answer below)

Answer: W C Fields in Never Give A Sucker An Even Break

ON GROWING OLDER

'You're only young once, but you can be immature forever'.

John Greier

WHAT'S COOKING?

Lamb Casserole with Pears

- 2 lb/900 g middle best end of neck of lamb
- 2 tsps of ground ginger
- 6 medium cooking pears, peeled and cored
- 4 medium potatoes, peeled and diced
- 4 tbs dry cider
- Salt
- Fresh ground black pepper
- 1 lb/450 g frozen whole French beans

1   Trim excess fat from lamb, fry brown the pieces
    in their own fat on both sides then transfer to a
    casserole dish. Sprinkle with ground ginger.
2   Quarter the cooking pears and place in
    layers over meat. Arrange diced potatoes over
    the pears.
3   Add dry cider. Season well. Cover and cook
    in a warm oven (160°C/325°F/Gas Mark 3) for
    1¼ hours.
4   Add French beans for last 30 minutes of cooking
    time. Adjust the seasoning if necessary.
    Mrs Clarke, Harrowside, Blackpool

Joan Shea from Galashiels goes back to 1945...

A DAY TO REMEMBER

*My day to remember is one of many
from a long and exciting life. As a Wren, I spent one
day taking my Poppy Appeal box to every Messdeck
and Wardroom of the Allied shipping anchored in
Aden harbour in 1945.*

*My boxes were constantly overflowing and
replenished from dawn to dusk and beyond.*

*But shinning up and down ladders is rather
beyond me now!*

PIC: HULTON ARCHIVE

OUT & ABOUT TO...

The Laurel & Hardy Museum, Ulverston in Furness, Cumbria

Appropriately situated in Stan Laurel's home
town (he was born in Ulverston on June 16,
1890), this museum was started by the late Bill
Cubin, who was a real authority on his subject.
It's now run by his daughter, Marion Grave, who
says it's 'the hobby that got out of hand'. At least
she doesn't describe her father's unusual legacy
as, 'Another fine mess you've got me into'!

You'll find an amazing collection of
memorabilia – believed to be the largest in the
world relating to the hot-headed bowler-hatted
duo. The items on display include photographs,
all kinds of personal bits and pieces and
furniture. There's also a small cinema showing
free films and documentaries all day. If you're a
fan, you'll find this an entertaining option for a
dull or rainy day in the Lake District.

- *Adults £2.50, senior citizens £1.50*
- *Wheelchair access*
Tel: 01229 582292

October 18-24

PAUSE FOR THOUGHT

As a child, I and three of my sisters spent time in a Church of England Children's home. Being the youngest, they did everything for me. When I was fostered out, aged six, I was on my own. Having been so isolated from normal family life, I had no conception of other people's feelings or thoughts – not unusual in small children.

One Easter Sunday when I was seven, I was taken by my foster parents to church. I can remember hearing the vicar say, 'Do unto others as you would have them do unto you'. It was like a light being switched on and it awoke my awareness of the needs of others. More than 50 years on, I still try to live by these words.

Sheila Crisall, Cheshire

A DAY TO REMEMBER

Barbara Finch from Lincolnshire recalls a holiday experience with a difference…

My late husband and I had a unique holiday experience when we were in Germany years ago, where we enjoyed the company of two lovely couples. Nothing extraordinary in that, you may think but, up until a short time before, these four people had been incarcerated behind the dreaded Berlin Wall.

We met them in a little village on the River Mosel and, although our understanding of each others' language was sparse, we arranged to meet them for the evening and what a joyous occasion it was! It was their first real holiday they had had outside East Germany for many years.

Later, we linked arms and swayed and sang to the music of the band, and we were glad to be able to express our delight and joy at their liberation. I shall never forget that heart-warming experience.

OLD WIVES' TALES

The best medicine tastes the worst and therefore does you the most good.

Dr Henderson replies: Wrong. This dates back to the days when the few medicines available often did taste strong or unpleasant, but modern medicines are powerful and effective and usually pleasant-tasting, if they taste at all.

DID YOU KNOW THAT

The most recorded song is Lennon and McCartney's Yesterday

Top tip

Write your shopping list in the order you visit the shops – it'll save leg power walking backwards and forwards.

AT THE MOVIES

Who said?
'Very stupid to kill the only servant in the house. Now we don't even know where to find the marmalade'.
(Answer below)

Answer: Judith Anderson in Rene Clair's And Then There Were None

OUT & ABOUT TO...

Hever Castle and Gardens, Edenbridge, Kent

PIC: HEVER CASTLE & GARDENS

There's always a period in mid to late October when Hever Castle Gardens really shine. At this time – dubbed Autumn Colour Week (phone to check dates) – the gardens are bursting with stunning bronzes, reds, ambers and yellows. These autumnal shades are reflected in the lake and outer moat, making the display of foliage even more impressive.

During this week, the castle gardeners will be on hand to show you around the grounds and discuss autumn gardening topics. Tours (call to check times) are included in the normal ticket price.

There's also a formal Italian garden, Tudor and rose gardens; topiary; a 110-metre herbaceous border, a yew maze and a water maze – weather permitting! The childhood home of Anne Boleyn, Hever Castle contains many Tudor antiques and paintings. If the heavens open, it's well worth a visit – not least for the curiosity value of seeing where one of Henry VII's doomed wives lived in happier times.

● *Gardens only: Adults £6.70, senior citizens £5.70, children £4.40*
● *Restaurants; gift shop; book shop; wheelchair access*
Tel: 01732 865224 (Internet:)

ON GROWING OLDER

'The more sand that has escaped from the hourglass of our life, the more we should see through it'.

Unknown

WHAT'S COOKING?

WHAT A COINCIDENCE

Last year my brother and his wife were touring Australia and I'd been writing them an airmail, as I knew they would be in one place – Baragara Beach in Queensland for ten days.

Afterwards, I settled down to enjoy the latest copy of YOURS and I read of two sweethearts from the Second World War who had been reunited 40 years later and had married. And they now lived at Bargara Beach, Queensland. I re-opened the airmail and enclosed the cutting.

Isobel Gay, Perthshire

BUDGET MEAL
Cheesyburgers
(Serves 4)

● 4 oz/100 g grated cheddar cheese
● 1 onion, peeled and grated
● 1 tbs chopped parsley
● 8 oz/250 g cottage cheese
● 4 oz/100g breadcrumbs
● 1 egg, beaten

1 Mix all the ingredients together.
2 Form into 8 cakes, roll in a little flour and fry in oil until browned.
3 Serve in sliced bread baps with lettuce and slices of tomato.

October 25-31

AT THE MOVIES

Who said?
'You see, Mr Scott, in the water I'm a very skinny lady'.
(Answer below)

Answer: Shelley Winters in Ronald Neame's The Poseidon Adventure

In 1974 my husband bought a beautiful car – a 1971 Opal Commodore. When he died in 1988, I sold my car and took over the Opal. Each year – sometimes with a few minor adjustments – it passed its MOT. That is, until November 2000.

Now the repairs would be more costly and I only used the car for shopping. I was 82 and it was a big car to drive, so I tucked it away in the carport. It stood there for several months and I began to worry about it– this beautiful car was just going to stand and rust.

I was now having my groceries delivered and one day, to my surprise, a different person arrived on the doorstep. A young lady, who started to ask about the car and said her husband would love it. He came round and fell in love with it, so I sold it to him.

It had not been outside for six months but with jump leads and two turns of the ignition it started – purring away. When it was driven away I was sad, but also happy knowing it would be looked after and loved.

That was the one and only time the young lady delivered the groceries – my own little coincidence!
Irene Williams, Milton Keynes

OUT & ABOUT TO...

Flag Fen Bronze Age Centre, The Droveway, Northey Road, Peterborough

If only ghosts could talk, we'd know all about the spooky customs of our ancestors on Hallowe'ens of the past. Failing that, visit Flag Fen, where you can find out how people lived 3,000 years ago. Set on an archaeological site where numerous Bronze Age finds were discovered, the highlights of this 'living museum' are reconstructed Bronze and Iron Age roundhouses. Each building was thought to house a family spanning three generations.

The artefacts at Flag Fen include weapons, jewellery, pottery, sacrificial items and part of the earliest wheel found in Britain. Also on display is the Seahenge wooden circle – prehistoric timbers that were found sticking out of the sands at Holme-next-the-Sea and brought to Flag Fen to be preserved.

The 20-acre park around the museum offers many more clues about the lives of local people of the past, including native plants and flowers, a herb garden and a rare breed of 'Bronze Age' sheep.

● *Adults £4, concessions £3.50, children/students £2.50*
● *Flag Fen holds regular special events, re-enactments and hands-on activities to celebrate historical (and mythical) times, including Hallowe'en (telephone for details)*
● *Visitor centre; coffee shop; picnic areas; gift shop; wheelchair access.*
Tel: 01733 313414 (Internet: www.flagfen.com)

PIC: RITA HEALANDS, FLAG FEN

OLD FASHIONED REMEDIES

My brother suffered with asthma and the winds in the winter were bitter, so mum made him a brown paper vest to go to school.

Mrs P Jackson, West Sussex

Dr Henderson replies: I feel sorry for your brother here. This would have been no good at all, I'm afraid. Although cold air and winds can indeed make some asthma sufferers worse, a brown paper vest would have been useless in affecting this. Far better to wear an ordinary one and avoid the teasing of class mates!

A DAY TO REMEMBER

Dorothy White from Kidderminster recalls a fête at the local residential home…

The sun shone between the showers on the day of the fête, so considering the weather, it wasn't a bad turn out. A local jazz band gave a great showing in the car park and all the tables were laid out inside. Philamena and May, the care assistants, manned the nearly new clothing stall and Jean was ice-cream vendor. A cake stall, tombola, a book stall, a vegetable stall, white elephant, a stall selling beauty products made of honey and raffles galore.

The funds raised went towards future events and residents' outings – it truly had been a day to remember.

Top tip

Tiny fragments of broken glass can be picked up using damp cotton wool.

DID YOU KNOW THAT

A duck's quack doesn't echo and no-one knows why.

ON GROWING OLDER

'Boys will be boys – and so will a lot of middle-aged men'.

Elbert Hubbard

MY ADVICE IS...

'Don't spend too long planning and dreaming. Go out there and turn your dreams into reality – it applies to us all – whatever our age!'

K Chattington, Lancs

WHAT'S COOKING?

QUICK SNACK
Quick Vegetable Dip
Serves 4

- 8 oz/ 250 g full-fat soft cheese
- ¼ pt/150 ml natural yoghurt
- 1 small green pepper, seeded and thinly sliced
- 2-3 leaves fresh mint, finely chopped (or 1 small teaspoon bottled mint)

1 Beat the cheese to soften, add the yoghurt and beat until smooth. Stir in the pepper and mint, and mix well.
2 Turn into a serving dish and chill

Serve the dip with pieces of raw celery, carrot, red pepper and broccoli.

Variation: The dip can also be used as jacket potato filling, but leave out the mint

Going potty!

Transform some ordinary garden pots into beautiful herb containers with decoupage. Hester Cresswell shows you how...

Hester and her decoupage pots

DECOUPAGE derives from the French verb 'decouper', to cut out. With a little patience and imagination you can apply the following techniques to many different projects.

Painting

With a matt emulsion, give your pot two coats of paint.

Decorating

● You can decorate your pots with birthday cards, magazines or wrapping paper.
● Photocopy your image, as the original may not stick properly.
● Cut out carefully.

Colouring

● To give a black and white picture a sepia look, mix a little acrylic raw umber paint with water and, using a damp cloth, wipe over the picture.
* Leave to dry before cutting out accurately with small craft scissors.

Pasting and gold finishing

● Using Gloy Paste, glue your image to the pot, sealing down with a damp sponge.
● You need to apply several coats of acrylic varnish, which dries very quickly.
● To finish the top edge of your pot, apply Antique Gold. Rub and buff using very little at a time, with your finger.
● Plant herbs and leave to hand in the kitchen for use when you're cooking. Taste and style all in one!
● Products available from arts shops.

Hester Cresswell lives in south Lincolnshire and says: "I do hope this decoupage idea spurs you on to more adventurous projects." For details of Hester's painting workshops, please write to her c/o YOURS magazine, Bretton Court, Bretton, Peterborough PE3 8DZ

The things we miss

Football fans

Remember going to watch the 'footie' with dad? Trotting along, trying to keep up, the excitement building as you got nearer. And if you'd gone to a big match, you could hear the noise of the fans even before you could see them! You always wore your team's scarf – and did you have a flag to wave, too?

The trouble was, when you'd got through the turnstile, it was difficult to catch a glimpse of your team because everyone got in the way. But that's where your dad's mates came in – you had the best view of the lot, as you were passed from shoulder to shoulder. And yes, your lads have scored!

PIC: HULTON ARCHIVE

Hair-raising days

In these modern times of 'hair stylists', 'mega-hold' hairspray and 'styling wax', it's amazing to look back and think of the tortuous lengths we used to go to, to make sure our hair looked just right for the 'Friday night hop!'

If you wanted a 'perm', you'd have to allow at least two hours for the whole tedious process and have to put up with the horrid smell of peroxide!

But if you didn't fancy a head of tight curls, if your hairdresser had been trained well, you could get a Marcel wave, and all styled with the fingers. A dab of hairset and your hair was 'waved' between first and second finger – quite an art. And do you remember those scissors with serrated edges which used to thin out and tame thick hair?

And think back to that momentous occasion when you left school to start your new job, and part of the growing up process was to go and have your pony tail cut off, to be replaced by a short hairdo. And at the end, the deed done, a young lady stared back at you in the mirror.

Puzzles

Code cracker

In this clueless crossword, every letter of the alphabet appears as a code number. All you have to do is crack the code and fill in the grid. We've decoded one letter to start you off, so you can write a 'B' wherever the number 24 appears in the grid. For a further clue, the word in the shaded squares is a drink sold by the pint in your local. Use the smaller grid to keep track of letters you have deciphered.

A	B̶	C	D
E	F	G	H
I	J	K	L
M	N	O	P
Q	R	S	T
U	V	W	X
Y	Z

Code grid:

24 B	6	6	17	■	7	14	18	22	9	20	26	1
14	■	11	■	4	■	2	■	14	■	15	■	3
22	14	18	22	14	4	4	■	17	6	24	6	4
12	■	17	■	24	■	26	■	14	■	3	■	4
24	17	14	21	26	■	13	26	18	3	26	25	■
26	■	■	■	15	■	24	■	■	■	15	■	5
25	26	18	14	17	5	■	25	14	15	19	6	14
6	■	17	■	■	■	19	■	22	■	■	■	22
■	16	14	17	1	26	25	■	10	15	14	19	9
8	■	8	■	26	■	26	■	15	■	21	■	18
3	25	8	6	17	■	26	17	3	1	14	13	3
4	■	3	■	1	■	23	■	18	■	3	■	25
13	14	22	12	6	17	6	4	■	8	4	14	1

1	2	3	4	5	6	7	8	9	10	11	12	13
14	15	16	17	18	19	20	21	22	23	24 B	25	26

Letter set

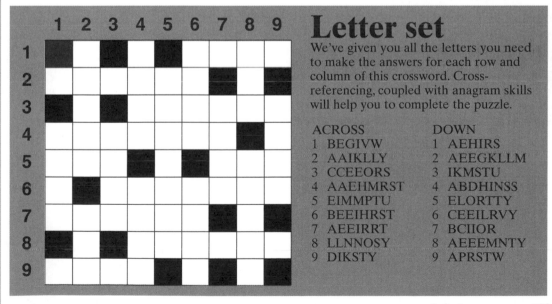

We've given you all the letters you need to make the answers for each row and column of this crossword. Cross-referencing, coupled with anagram skills will help you to complete the puzzle.

ACROSS	DOWN
1 BEGIVW	1 AEHIRS
2 AAIKLLY	2 AEEGKLLM
3 CCEEORS	3 IKMSTU
4 AAEHMRST	4 ABDHINSS
5 EIMMPTU	5 ELORTTY
6 BEEIHRST	6 CEEILRVY
7 AEEIRRT	7 BCIIOR
8 LLNNOSY	8 AEEEMNTY
9 DIKSTY	9 APRSTW

Solutions on page 159

And they're off!

Wyn Terrett had only ever watched the horse racing on the television but now she had the chance to experience the real thing...

"It's yellow ticket number 331 and the prize is a trip to the races." Standing on our village green at the local fête, we all scanned our raffle tickets and – joy of joys – it was mine. Going to the races was one of those things that my husband and I had promised ourselves we would do one day, but the opportunity had never arisen. Now we could put that right.

We wrote to Newbury Racecourse claiming our prize, receiving a letter with a list of racing fixtures and two badges for the members' enclosure. Now all we had to do was go!

On a bright but chilly winter's day, under a cornflower blue sky we set off, well wrapped up against the cold, and each wearing our members' badges. Arriving at the course, once it was known that we were prizewinners, we were waved through to a space in front of the grandstand.

Inside it was much more spacious than we'd imagined. The Long Room had a glass wall to one side leading on to the terraces. There was a bar on the opposite side with a table laid out with a buffet at the end and a stand for placing bets (and, hopefully, for collecting our winnings).

Looking around us during lunch we saw such a cross-section of society. There were young girls in low cut tops which gave us goose bumps just looking at them. There were ladies in fur hats and coats, dripping with gold jewellery, accompanied by handsome men in thick woollen overcoats. Then there were groups of men in dark glasses with slicked back hair, smoking fat cigars – and looking very exotic – they had a bob or two, no doubt!

After lunch we stood at the collecting ring admiring the horses. What a huge amount of time and effort had gone into the training of these beautiful, powerful creatures. Eager to be off, coats glistening in the winter sunshine, they left the ring to canter down the course, which was away in the distance. For the first race of the day we stood on the rails by the finishing post. Being unable to see the start was no problem because there were large screens around the course.

When it was announced that the horses were under starter's orders, the silence was almost tangible. Then, suddenly: "They're off!" With these words the buzz of excitement swelled as the punters roared the names of their favoured horses, urging them on, calling them names that didn't seem to be mentioned anywhere on the race card!

As they approached the finish, the noise rose like the crest of a wave. I was so excited by the thundering hooves – which made the earth beneath my feet shudder – that I completely forgot the name of my horse. Once over the line, the noise subsided and the winners were ecstatic. Hats were thrown into the air, strangers embraced and there was much back-slapping. Losers, on the other hand, stared at the ground, shoulders drooping. Others were angry as they threw their tickets to the muddy ground.

Returning to the warmth inside, I found that my first horse of the day – Royal Hector – had lost. Still, that was the name of the game. I looked around – the bar was buzzing, with the winners treating all and sundry to drinks, Champagne corks were popping. The losers were drinking, too, drowning their sorrows, so trade was brisk.

After a hot drink, we made our way to the row of bookies outside, as I'd always wanted to talk to one – after all, it was my day. The bookies were in a long line with boards displaying prices, none of which we understood. Some were in smart tweed jackets and caps, others wore thick woollen overcoats or anoraks. I approached a jovial man who tried good-naturedly to explain the mysteries of the betting world. The basics I understood but the rest remained (and still does remain) a mystery!

Undeterred, I placed my money on Joly Bey to win. This means that you only win if the horse comes first in the race. With an 'each way' bet you win if the horse is placed, usually first or second, but if there are more runners it can extend to third or even fourth. When you place your bet with a bookie he sets the odds, but on the Tote, the total bets are added and the amount shared out at the end. Are you confused? I was!

I was disappointed that there was very little of the frenetic arm waving that the bookies on TV all seem to do – and was even more so when Joly Bey lost. Having consoled ourselves with a cup of tea, I placed an each way bet for the last race of the day and we made our way to the finishing post.

Having won nothing so far, we had everything crossed. "Come on, come on!" we yelled, raising both arms in the air, "You can do it!" When my horse thundered past the winning post in second place, we threw our arms around each other in wild disbelief, cheering madly. We'd won! Although a very small return for all that we'd lost, we felt like millionaires as we collected our winnings.

With racing over for the day, off we went to the car park. The torn betting slips were picked up by the breeze and tossed on to the course, drifting through the quickly emptying stands like confetti. It felt as if the bride had just left for the reception, there was such a sense of anti-climax.

We so enjoyed our day out at the races that we're going again – to a warm summer meeting. Next time we might understand the system a bit better and return home with full pockets instead of empty ones, and who knows I may even buy a new hat and go to Ladies' Day. That's almost a safe bet!

November 2004

PIC: REX FEATURES

A flavour of the month

With the wind whistling around your ears, you'll probably want to snuggle up by a roaring fire and hibernate. But don't let the winter weather get you down!

It may be cold outside, but there's still plenty to see and do. Create your own central heating system with plenty of hot drinks and winter warming soups. Wrap up well to enjoy the beautiful colours and scenery as autumn turns to winter.

In fact, there's nothing better than a brisk walk to help warm you through. Collect fallen pine cones, dry them out, then brush their scales with essential oils. They'll make attractive scented decorations for bowls..

November is the month when the night sky comes alive with nature. Listen for the sounds of tawny owls, which are particularly vocal in late winter when they vie for territory and mates. And look out for bats. Superstition says they are good luck omens. In China and Poland the bat symbolises a long and happy life. And here, in the UK, it is thought that a bat spotted in bad weather means a good forecast is just around the corner.

If you fancy a trip out this month you can see the Christmas lights being turned on in Regent's Street, be a spectator at the London to Brighton Veteran Car Run or visit the Lord Mayor's Show in London.

MONDAY	1	All Saints' Day
TUESDAY	2	Order YOURS subscriptions now for Christmas
WEDNESDAY	3	
THURSDAY	4	
FRIDAY	5	Bonfire Night
SATURDAY	6	
SUNDAY	7	
MONDAY	8	
TUESDAY	9	
WEDNESDAY	10	
THURSDAY	11	
FRIDAY	12	
SATURDAY	13	
SUNDAY	14	Remembrance Sunday
MONDAY	15	
TUESDAY	16	
WEDNESDAY	17	
THURSDAY	18	

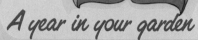

FRIDAY	19
SATURDAY	20
SUNDAY	21
MONDAY	22
TUESDAY	23
WEDNESDAY	24
THURSDAY	25
FRIDAY	26
SATURDAY	27
SUNDAY	28 — First Sunday of Advent
MONDAY	29 — December YOURS on sale
TUESDAY	30 — 30 St Andrew's Day

A year in your garden

As the air fills with the smoke from bonfires, gardeners are at their most excited. This is the time for bare root trees, bargain herbaceous and superb shrubs. In late autumn the soil is still warm, is always wet and perfect for planting. Bare root trees are available from most garden retailers and are exactly that – trees with their roots bare. No containers, no wrapping just tree. And you get a lot of tree for not a lot of money.

Shrubs are the same, and garden centres often have a sale to get rid of shrub stocks to make way for their Christmas bangles and baubles. But it's herbaceous plants where the real bargains can be had because most have finished flowering and are busy bulking up before winter. A pot full can be split and replanted in well-prepared soil.

Existing clumps of herbaceous plants can be lifted and gently teased apart using two garden forks. Each section can then be replanted elsewhere in the garden, or in your garden if the plant belongs to a friend. These divisions, or your new trees and shrubs, will quickly develop strong root systems and next spring will get off to a flying start. Many herbaceous plants have root systems that continue to grow throughout autumn and winter.

This is also a good time to assess your garden. As leaves fall you see the bare bones, and now is the ideal time to fill with evergreens or plants with exceptional autumn interest.

Cotoneasters will be berrying up now and will attract birds into the garden. Smoke bushes will be turning colour and setting the autumn colour scene ablaze with reds, oranges and yellows. Firethorn is a wonderful berrying plant, with birds loving the red and orange berries but leaving varieties that produce yellow berries to the last.

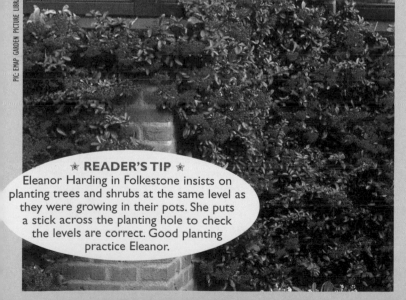

PIC EMAP GARDEN PICTURE LIBRARY

☆ READER'S TIP ☆
Eleanor Harding in Folkestone insists on planting trees and shrubs at the same level as they were growing in their pots. She puts a stick across the planting hole to check the levels are correct. Good planting practice Eleanor.

PIC: HULTON ARCHIVE

▲ Poor Guy Fawkes is off to the bonfire, borne high on the shoulders of children of the Aldersbrook Children's Home, Wanstead, in 1947

A Royal day for Brenda Mitchell from Essex...

I am chairman and standard bearer for Hockley and District branch of the Women's Section of the Royal British Legion and when our branch was asked by the central Essex office to do our bit locally to help raise a million for the millennium, we raised £930.

My proudest day came when I marched past Clarence House for the Queen Mother's birthday celebrations. I am still active and carry the standard now at 80 years old.

Brenda and her late husband Henry, who was also a standard bearer

ON GROWING OLDER

'I'm still chasing pretty girls. I don't remember what for but I'm still chasing them'.

Joe E Lewis

OUT & ABOUT TO...

Museum of Garden History, Lambeth Palace Road, London

There's no doubt that the range of tools and gadgets available to gardeners has improved considerably in recent years. If you'd like to see just how much easier the job is now, visit the Museum of Garden History – housed in a restored church – and check out its extensive collection of historic garden tools.

Alongside the museum is a replica of a 17th-century knot garden, opened by the late Queen Mother 21 years ago. It's a peaceful spot to sit or stroll, but there's also heaps of history here. Officially entitled The Tradescant Garden, it commemorates a father and son, both called John, who made their name in the 1600s as gardeners to King Charles I and II and plant hunters. The flowers, shrubs and trees that they brought back from their travels were used to plant the garden at Hatfield House, home of the

PIC: MUSEUM OF GARDEN HISTORY

Salisbury family. Twenty-one years later, the very same cuttings went back to their roots when the knot garden was designed by the Marchioness of Salisbury, using specimens from her garden. The John Tradescants are now buried in the churchyard at the museum.

- *Suggested donation: Adults £2.50, concessions £2*
- *Refreshments available morning and afternoon*
- *The museum runs seasonal lectures by gardening experts, an annual fair and also puts on art exhbitions – telephone for details*
Tel: 020 7401 8865

WHAT'S COOKING?

Leek and Cheese Pancakes

- 4 oz/100 g plain flour
- Large pinch salt
- 2 eggs, size 3
- ½ pt/300 ml semi-skimmed milk
- 2 tbs chopped chives
- Butter for frying
- 1½ oz/40 g butter
- 1½ lb/700 g leeks, trimmed and chopped
- 2 cloves garlic, crushed
- 8 oz/225 g ricotta or curd cheese
- 4 oz/100 g mature cheddar cheese, grated
- Salt and pepper

1 To make the pancakes, put the flour, salt, eggs and milk into a blender or food processor and blend until smooth. Stir in the chives.
2 To cook the pancakes, melt a small knob of butter in a 20-cm/8-in frying pan. Pour in enough batter to coat the base of the pan. Cook the pancake over a medium high heat until set and golden. Turn and cook the other side until golden. Transfer to a plate and continue to make the pancakes until all the batter is used up – this should make 8 pancakes. Heat the oven to 180°C/350°F/Gas Mark 4.
3 To make the filling, melt 1 oz/25 g of the butter in a pan, add the leeks and garlic and cook gently until tender. Stir in the two cheeses and mix together, season.
4 Place two heaped dessertspoons of the filling on a pancake, fold in half then fold again to make a cornet-shaped parcel. Place in a greased ovenproof dish. Repeat with all the pancakes and filling. Melt the rest of the butter and brush over the pancakes, place the dish in the oven and bake for 12-15 minutes until golden.

PIC: FRESH PRODUCE CONSORTIUM

OLD WIVES' TALES

A dock leaf is good for sprains.

Dr Henderson replies: Yellow dock leaves are said to be beneficial in simple sprains, either simply applied directly to the area or as a poultice. You can also use salves made by mixing the expressed juices of the dock plants in animal fat or vegetable oils.

PAUSE FOR THOUGHT

'I always remember these wise words,' writes Connie Reeve from Hants:

Today is here
Yesterday has gone
Tomorrow has yet to come.
So, let's live for today!

DID YOU KNOW THAT

Happy birthday is the most frequently sung song in the world.

Top tip

When stewing rhubarb add some chopped dates or sultanas, thus using a little less sugar

AT THE MOVIES

Who said?
'You're a real beautiful woman. It's almost kind of an honour sitting next to you. You just shine in my eyes. That's my true feeling, Roslyn. What makes you so sad? I think you're the saddest girl I ever met'.
(Answer below)

Answer: Clark Gable complimenting Marilyn Monroe in John Huston's The Misfits

November 8-14

WHAT A COINCIDENCE

I was an aircrew cadet under training at Newquay, Cornwall in 1943. The Airforce occupied all the hotels, either for accommodation or for training. The beaches were open, which was unusual, as in most places they were mined.

Droves of holidaymakers were making their escape from the bombing and the horrors of war, finding somewhere to stay wherever they could.

It was a peaceful Sunday morning and I decided to go and sit in a shelter on top of the cliffs. I began a conversation with an elderly couple who asked me where I came from. Hounslow in Middlesex, I replied. Yes, the gentleman knew of it, and said they had a relative who worked on London Transport. I told them my father worked for the same company.

His relative's surname was Rix, which is my surname. He realised that I was his nephew and, when we'd both got over the shock, said that he hadn't seen or heard from my parents for 20 years. I spent all my free time with them that week of their holiday, and we had a family reunion.

It always amazes me, with the thousands of holidaymakers and cadets there at the time, that we should meet.

E Rix, East Sussex

Top tip

Save money by diluting your washing-up liquid to half the strength while still in its container – it's just as good and will last twice as long.

MY ADVICE IS...

'When you're angry, either walk away or count to ten before you open your mouth. Much better than saying something you'll regret'.

C Haynes, Powys

DID YOU KNOW THAT

The act of walking requires the use of 200 muscles in the human body. Forty or so will lift your leg and move it forward

OUT & ABOUT TO...

The Shoe Museum, Street, Somerset

Generations of British children have been raised on Clarks shoes… and we mean generations! The firm was founded in 1833 by Cyrus Clark and his brother James, and the museum contains all kinds of footwear made by them, plus shoe-making tools and machinery, and photographs of factory outworkers. There are also shoes worn in Roman Britain and from Mediaeval times until 1950; shoes from other countries; Georgian shoe buckles and costume illustrations and fashion plates from the 18th century onwards.

And if your old shoes were used to kit out your grandchildren's Guy Fawkes and went up in smoke on Bonfire Night, it might be worth paying a visit to the Clarks factory shop, also in Street. Here, you'll find samples and end-of-season shoes, at greatly reduced prices.

● *Free admission
Tel: 01458
842169*

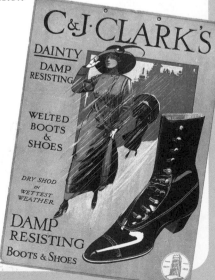

Heartbreak turned to joy for Anne Wilkinson of Gwynedd…

When I was 23 I met my husband and in 1954, expected my first baby. My baby was premature and only lived for five days. I lost two more babies, and was thinking of giving up but then found I was expecting again. This time, when the baby was born, I heard a lusty cry and had a gorgeous girl, with a mass of dark curls. When they put her in my arms it was the most precious moment of my life. I named her Deborah Anne – and she's now 47. I then went on to have two beautiful sons.

Left: Deborah Anne, aged 3.
Below: Anne Wilkinson, mum to Deborah and her two sons

OLD FASHIONED REMEDIES

The quickest way to get a boil to 'boiling point' (as it were!) was to put a plaster over the offending protuberance, with a hole cut out in the middle. Then put another piece of plaster over the 'cut out' hole. It hurt like mad and I yelled when it was taken off but it did seem to do the trick!

C Smith, Lancs

Dr Henderson replies: Boils have a natural tendency to 'point' or come to a head and I don't think this trick would have affected this. However, it would have kept it clean and stopped you from rubbing it, so that would have been a help, although I can understand you yelling when it was taken off!

WHAT'S COOKING?

Bacon, Cheese and Tomato Toastie

- 4 oz/110 g grated cheddar cheese
- 4 rashers of bacon (cooked)
- 400g can of tomatoes (drained and chopped)
- 4 slices of bread

1 Mix together the cheese, bacon and tomatoes.
2 Grill one side of the bread, turn, add the cheesy mixture and heat slowly until warmed through and the cheese is bubbly.
3 Serve with a green salad.

Mrs A Grecco, Hillingdon, Middlesex

AT THE MOVIES

Who said?
'I – I was born backwards. That is why I work in Africa as missionary, teaching little brown babies more backward than myself'.
(Answer below)

Answer: Ingrid Bergman in Sidney Lumet's Murder On The Orient Express

ON GROWING OLDER

'You know you're not in the first flush of youth anymore when you need a rest after brushing your teeth'.

November 15-21

WHAT A COINCIDENCE

Some years ago I drove past my old schoolteacher's home in my car and, clearly saw the well-remembered man who had taught me for some while. I saw him walk up the path to his front door and thought little more of it at the time, my mind being full of other things.

Hours later at home, my scalp suddenly prickled with fear when I remembered that the teacher had died several years earlier. A rather spooky coincidence.

Mrs M Shattock, Bristol

DID YOU KNOW THAT

Elephants are the only animals that can't jump.

PAUSE FOR THOUGHT

*Thank heaven for the happy touch
Of getting joy from nothing much.*

If more people, especially the young, could want less, they might be a lot happier.

Mrs H Simpson, Essex

ON GROWING OLDER

'It's hard to be nostalgic when you can't remember anything'.

Unknown

Top tip

A piece of crusty bread placed under an uneven table or chair leg will stop the offending item wobbling.

OUT & ABOUT TO...

Mount Stewart House, Garden & Temple of the Winds, Newtonards, Co. Down, NI

This 18th-century Gothic mansion is well worth a visit, not least for its over-the-top interior. However, save most of your time for exploring the 300 acres of landscaped grounds and woodland. The formal gardens were created by Edith, Lady Londonderry, as a series of outdoor 'rooms', stocked with plants from all over the world. Thanks to the mild climate of the Ards Peninsula, many rare plants thrive in this spot. There's also an isolated sandy beach, reached via an avenue of lime trees.

- *Gardens only: Adults £3.75, children £2*
- *Lakeside Garden and Walks open daily from October to April, 10am-4pm*
- *Restaurant; gift shop; wheelchair access (there*

PIC: NATIONAL TRUST/STOCKEN-TOMKINS

are two wheelchairs and two self-drive battery-operated cars available to borrow – phone to book)

- *Nearby, on the shores of Strangford Lough, you'll find Exploris (Tel: 028 4272 8062), Northern Ireland's only aquarium. Here, you can get up close and personal with fish in the touch tank, or gaze at the open sea tank, one of the largest in the UK, which is home to sharks and conger eels.*

Sometimes, you can see sick or orphaned seals in the seal sanctuary (phone to check).
Tel: 028 4278 8387 (www.nationaltrust.org.uk)

OLD WIVES' TALES

Olive oil and raspberry vinegar is good for coughs.

Dr Henderson replies: Although an oil-based liquid may give some people temporary relief from a sore throat or the sensation of a tickly cough, this combination will do little to actually stop a cough or clear any kind of chest infection.

WHAT'S COOKING?

Winter Stew and Dumplings
(Serves 4)

- 1 level tbs tomato purée
- Bouquet garni
- Salt and pepper
- 4 oz/115 g flour
- 1 level tps baking powder
- 2 oz/50 g shredded suet
- Water
- 1 lb/450 g lean braising beef
- 1 onion
- 8 oz/225 g carrots
- 8 oz/225 g turnips
- 1 leek
- 1 beef stock cube
- ½ pt/275 ml water

1 Cut the beef into cubes and coat with flour. Place in a casserole dish.
2 Chop the onion, carrots, turnips and leek. Add to the meat. Crumble in the stock cube. Add the water, tomato purée and bouquet garni. Season with salt and pepper.
3 Cover the dish and cook at 150°C/300°F/Gas Mark 2 for 2½ hours.
4 Make the dumplings by mixing the flour, baking powder, suet and a pinch of salt with enough water to make a soft but not sticky dough. Divide into 4 balls.
5 Increase the oven temperature to 180°C/350°F/Gas Mark 4 and place the dumplings on top of the meat and vegetables and return to the oven for 15 minutes. Uncover the dish and cook for another 15 minutes. Serve with seasonal greens.

Eva Shackleton from Kent had a very important appointment to keep…

A DAY TO REMEMBER

It was an occasion to remember, when I met the Queen to receive the MBE for my voluntary work with the Soldiers, Sailors' and Airmen's Association (SSAFA), with which I have been associated since 1945.

I travelled to London the day before with my friends Olive and Bill, staying at the Tower Thistle Hotel. After an enjoyable evening meal and a visit to the theatre, I retired to bed. I woke up at regular intervals, and after breakfast we left for the Palace, arriving around about 10am.

We made our way up the red-carpeted stairs; eventually directed to a large ante-room. The investiture began at 11am, one of the ushers briefing all the recipients. I was then escorted to the ballroom, as part of a group of 12.

When it came to my turn, the Queen asked me where I came from, and for what I was being honoured. Her Majesty shook my hand and, after having placed the insignia on me (on a small hook), I curtsied.

I had bought a dress and matching hat for the occasion but I'm not a hat person, so I took it off as I left the Palace. What a wonderful day, especially as I'd shared it with my helpful friends Olive and Bill.

Eva receiving her MBE from Her Majesty the Queen

AT THE MOVIES

Who said?
'Do you know what I think when I see a pretty girl? Oh, to be 80 again'.
(Answer below)

Answer: Louis Calhern in John Sturges's The Magnificent Yankee

November 22-28

An addition to the family for Eunice Brown from Hertfordshire…

On September 24, 2002, at 9am my granddaughter Michelle gave birth to Ryan Jimmy Cleary which made me a great-grandmother. What a wonderful day! Ryan has made the Browns a five-generation family.

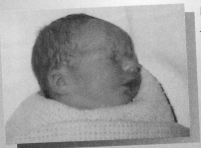

Little Ryan Jimmy Cleary

OLD FASHIONED REMEDIES

Oh, the tablespoon of castor oil on Saturday nights. But what good did it do?

Dr Henderson replies: Probably absolutely nothing! One of the best-known home remedies of all, with the aim of making sure the bowels were kept in good working order for the rest of the week. Tasted foul, did little good and was the bane of many children's lives everywhere! I'm delighted this practice has now stopped!

MY ADVICE IS…

'To thine own self be true'. This is a quote from Shakespeare which I've always tried to follow.
Erin Cape, Worc

WHAT'S COOKING?

MEAL ON A BUDGET
Bacon Jackets
(Serves 2)

- 2 large baking potatoes
- 3 rashers bacon
- Salt and pepper
- 2 oz/50 g cheese, grated
- 3 tbs of tinned sweetcorn
- 1 oz/25 g butter
- 2 tbs milk

1 Prick potatoes with a fork. Bake in a moderately hot oven for 1½-2 hours (200°C/400°F/Gas Mark 6) until soft.
2 Cut potatoes in half, scoop out soft insides and mash with butter, milk and the cooked sweetcorn.
3 Grill bacon until crisp. Chop and add to mashed potatoes and season well. Return to potato shells.
4 Sprinkle with grated cheese and grill until cheese bubbles.

AT THE MOVIES

Who said?
'I wouldn't believe anything you said if you had it tattooed on your forehead'.
(Answer below)

Answer: Jane Russell in Gentlemen Prefer Blondes

OUT & ABOUT TO...

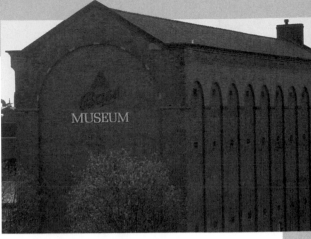

PIC: THE BASS MUSEUM

MUSEUM

The Bass Museum, Burton upon Trent, Staffs

If the prospect of downing a swift half along with buckets of nostalgia appeals to you, you'll love The Bass Museum. Aptly set in Britain's brewing capital, Burton upon Trent, it offers a fascinating insight into the history of this essential tipple. Step back in time into the Chairman's Gallery, where you can see original brewing equipment and learn how, despite the march of technology, the art of brewing has changed little over the years.

There's also a micro-brewery, run by the Museum Brewing Company, which is one of the oldest working micro-breweries in Britain. But there's more here than beer – perhaps the most endearing 'exhibits' are the resident Shire horses, which were used to transport beer before motor vehicles and were still in harness for Bass until the 1960s.

Walking around the museum can be thirsty work, so make sure you visit the Burton Bar to sample the cask ales produced by the Museum Brewing Company. And if you've worked up a hunger, check out The Wheelwrights Restaurant, where you can wash down your meal with a perfectly pulled pint.

● *Adults £5.50, concessions £4, children £3 (includes half a pint sampling or tea/coffee for adult/senior citizen and soft drink for children)*
● *Licensed restaurant; wheelchair access*
Tel: 0845 6000 598

ON GROWING OLDER

You know the years are passing when:

● The clothes you put away until they come back in style… have come back in style
● You sing along to the lift music

DID YOU KNOW THAT

The first woman to play golf at St Andrew's Golf Club in Scotland was Mary, Queen of Scots in 1552. She was the club's founder.

Top tip

Empty film holders make perfect cheap salt and pepper shakers. Simply make the required number of holes with a pin or skewer.

WHAT A COINCIDENCE

My husband and I moved from Kent to Hertfordshire 30 years ago and every Saturday we'd do our shopping in Aylesbury. On this occasion we split up to do our errands and I decided to have a coffee in Woolies.

Looking round, there was only one seat, next to two elderly ladies. We got talking and were bemoaning the new buildings going up in Aylesbury. I mentioned the same thing was happening where I used to live, in Ashford. One of the ladies said she'd lived there, too. After a quite unbelievable conversation, it turned out that she'd lived in the next road to us and had been my mother's best friend until they'd lost touch. As a three-year-old, I'd been bridesmaid at her wedding. She went quite pale at the coincidences.

I'm pleased to say that Mother and I renewed our friendship with 'Aunt Nell' until the day my aunt died.

Jean Kitchener, Herts

Grub's up!

PIC: E JANES

Everyone enjoys feeding the birds in their gardens. It can be as simple as putting out kitchen scraps or scattering a few cake crumbs for a Robin but if you want to attract a variety of species – then a little of what they fancy will work well.

There's a huge range of bird food available so what will your garden birds like best?

Nuts and seeds are the staples for many species:

● Peanuts will attract most of the tit family including, with luck, the delightful Long-tailed Tits, Greenfinches and Siskins.

Nuthatches and Great-spotted Woodpeckers also favour nuts.

● Black sunflower seeds are popularity with tits Greenfinches and the colourful Bullfinch.

● Sunflower hearts – seeds with the husks removed – attract Greenfinches and Goldfinches. House Sparrows, Chaffinches and Robins have learnt how to perch and take seeds from feeders.

● Fat bars and balls are popular with many species. Great-spotted Woodpeckers love them and Starlings make short work of them.

● Mixed table seeds for scattering often contain dried fruits and many birds, enjoy this mix.

● Porridge oats are a favourite with Robins and Blackbirds and can be hidden under bushes for Wrens to find.

● Grated cheese, dried fruit,

Great-spotted Woodpecker at a home-made fat feeder

apples and pears will be also be gratefully received.

Always make sure you buy good quality food – especially peanuts. These can be contaminated with a harmful mould so buy only from a reputable supplier.

It's best to provide food all year, although they will eat less in summer and early autumn when natural food is available. Birds may need extra supplies in winter and late spring when the breeding season begins and natural food is scarce.

Feeding the birds will reward you with hours of pleasure.

The things we miss

Gas irons

Although, in theory, gas irons were quicker and more efficient than the old hotplate variety, they did have some distinct drawbacks. Not least was the speed at which you could move them. If you hurried to get the dreaded ironing out of the way and moved too fast, the flames would spurt out of the sides of the iron and scorch the clothes. Not to mention the risk of singed eyebrows!

Village shops

In every village and town you could buy your daily essentials, plus a few little extras, at the parade of village shops.

There would be a baker, a butcher, a greengrocer and a general store. They were the heart of any community.

Shopkeepers would exchange pleasantries with their customers, asking about their families and troubles and sometimes dispensing advice, along with a pound of sausages.

At the village shops you knew everything was fresh and hadn't travelled miles across the country or even the world to be there for you. The vegetables at the greengrocer's were freshly dug; if you got to the baker's early enough, the bread was still warm from the oven; and the meat from the butcher was fresh in.

If you had a small purse you could buy small portions. Ham was sliced on a hand-slicer and tea, sweets or mixed biscuits were weighed out on 'see-saw' scales.

The butter would be cut from a huge slab and patted into shape with two wooden paddles.

PIC: HULTON ARCHIVE

Puzzle answers

Missing links

```
S N O W . C O P Y .
A . I . H R . I .
B A G . A C A D E M Y
S H . L . B C . O
O U T L E T . M E N U
L . O . U . . R
U N I T . O R D E R S
T V . R . O X . E
E C O N O M Y . A L L
. R . S . A C . F
. T Y R E . L A T E
```

Logic problem

Scarf, Molly, Allergic to material, Damaged stock.
Socks, Dolly, Wrong size, Sale item.
Tie, Polly, Hideous colour, Old stock.

Skeleton

```
. R . O R B I T . P .
L O A F . A . H E L M
. T . F A R C E . U .
L A P E L . I M A G E
O . A R B I T E R . E
R O D . U . A . E A R
I . R A M A D A N . I
S U E D E . E V A D E
. S . A N K L E . E .
D E E P . E . R E S T
. D . T R Y S T . K .
```

Cryptograms

1 'There aren't any real movie makers any more. The business is run by the cornflakes men and they are only in it for the girls'.

2 'I'm an entertainer. This is my job. There are men, women, children and soldiers being killed right now. My job is to cheer them up'. (Peter O'Toole)

Where on Earth?

```
. S . S . M O . O . . A
F A L K L A N D I S L A N D S
. N . O . L . E . L . T . E
S T E P P E . S C O T L A N D
. A . J . . . S . A . A .
A C R E . A R A B I A N S E A
. L . . S . . B . T . V .
A S S I S I . T I R A N A
. R . U . A . . Z . N .
P A R R A M A T T A . P I S A
. I . . R . . . O . V .
G R E N O B L E . B A L T I C
O . A . U . N . R . A . L .
B E R M U D A T R I A N G L E
I . . . E . O . E . D . E
```

Dateline

```
8 . . 3 8 2 9 7 7 . . 3
2 3 4 0 . 7 8 . 8 6 4 9
3 . . 5 2 6 6 2 9 . . 2
6 9 2 . 1 . 7 . 6 0 0 .
9 . 1 4 8 5 3 3 1 6 . 7
. . 8 5 1 6 6 0 . . . .
9 . 1 1 9 9 3 0 0 1 . 3
2 2 0 . 2 . 5 . 7 8 9 .
7 . 3 4 8 2 8 2 . . . 7
1 9 3 9 . 7 2 . 8 8 8 8
4 . 8 7 4 9 1 1 . . . 7
```

The date is: 8/5/1660 – Charles II is proclaimed king at the Restoration of the Monarchy.

Song and dance numbers

1 Twenty Four Hours from Tulsa, 2 Fifty Ways to Leave Your Lover, 3 Three Blind Mice, 4 Happy Birthday Sweet Sixteen, 5 The Night Has a Thousand Eyes, 6 When I'm Sixty-four, 7 Three Times a Lady, 8 Two Little Boys, 9 Seventy Six Trombones (led the big parade), 10 Three Little Maids from School Are We, 11 Five Foot Two, Eyes of Blue, 12 Sixteen Going On Seventeen, 13 Three Steps to Heaven, 14 You're the One that I Want, 15 Twelve Days of Christmas, 16 Three Coins in the Fountain, 17 Fifteen Men on a Dead Man's Chest, 18 One Day at a Time.

Jigsnip

```
W R E S T L I N G
I . Y . N . O .
T A E K W O N D O
H . I . W . I .
. C A N O E I N G
E . P . G .
T R I A T H L O N
N . L . O . E .
A T H L E T I C S
. I . B . T .
B A S E B A L L .
. R . L . W . U
B A D M I N T O N
O . O . W . D
W A T E R P O L O
```

Pathfinder

Athens, Helsinki, Rome, Antwerp, London, Los Angeles, Berlin, Seoul, St Louis, Amsterdam, Munich, Montreal, Melbourne, Barcelona, Tokyo, Mexico City, Sydney.
The four missing cities are: Paris, Stockholm, Moscow, Atlanta.

Alphabet jigsaw

```
. B . N . . Y . P . L . V
X E N O N . J O U R N E Y E D
. A . F . . G . I . A . N
C R O O K . Z I R C O N I U M
. R . O . H . K . T . S
W I L L I A M T E L L
. G . I . R . H . Y . G . U
S H U N . D R O O P . E T N A
. T . G . P . S . E . T . A
. . I R R E P A R A B L E
K . A . E . . R . R . T
Q U I T E S U R E . M O D E L
. D . O . S . E . U . R
F O U N D E R E D . O N S E T
. S . E . D . K . . . D . D
```

Four square

```
H I G H
T E A T
A R A N
P O E T
```

The film is: *A Night at the Opera* (Marx Brothers).

Code-cracker

```
B E E R . W A T C H D O G
A . X . L . P . A . U . I
C A T C A L L . R E B E L
K . R . B . O . A . I . L
B R A V O . M O T I O N .
O . . U . B . . U . . Y
N O T A R Y . N A U S E A
E . R . . S . C . . . C
. J A R G O N . Q U A S H
F . F . O . O . U . V . T
I N F E R . O R I G A M I
L . I . G . Z . T . I . N
M A C K E R E L . F L A G
```

```
G P I L Y E W F H Q X K M
A U J R T S D V C Z B N O
```

The drink is: Beer.

Letter set

```
. G . B . V I E W
A L K A L I . Y .
. F . S O C C E R
H A M S T E R . A
E M U . T . I M P
I . S H E R B E T
R E T I R E . A .
L . N Y L O N S .
S K I D . Y . T
```

Short story

The turnstile

By Martin Aldridge

As the tube train doors closed, it occurred to me that I was starting my thirty-ninth year in the men's department at Ludworth's clothing emporium for men and women. How many journeys had I made in all those years? I looked at my fellow passengers; we were like sheep herded into the same pen.

"Baah!" I said quietly. The man opposite raised his eyebrows. How many of us had previously shared the same carriage, or even sat in the same seats before?

I rubbed my chest trying to shift the painful indigestion I felt. I knew I shouldn't have had that extra portion of double chocolate fudge cake, and I had been doing so well with my diet, losing nearly two stone since I started. I reached in my coat pocket and pulled out some indigestion tablets. I popped a couple into my mouth and started to chew the chalky lumps.

I soon felt better and started to read the posters above the head of the person opposite me. They were quotes. One, by Woody Allen, read, 'On the plus side, death is one of the few things that can be done as easily as lying down'. The one next to it

read, 'For dust thou art, and unto dust shalt thou return'. It was from the Bible, Genesis, Chapter 3. A bit gloomy, I thought. Anyway, what was this preoccupation with death all of a sudden? People needed something jolly to send them off to work in the morning.

As the train slowed down for my stop, my chest pain vanished. I stood up and stepped towards the doors. Strange how no one else was getting off with me, normally there was a big rush to see who could squeeze out first. Even odder, only the doors that I was standing at opened. I stepped out on to the platform and the doors shut behind me. I looked up and down and saw no one else had disembarked. This wasn't my station, no wonder no one else had got off. In fact, I had never seen this station before and looked for its name on the tiled wall. I saw the familiar London Underground logo, 'Welcome', it read. I wondered if this was a new station that had just opened.

Then I heard the train pull off behind me and I turned in the vain hope of getting back on, but it was too late. The passengers in the carriage that I was on only a few

moments earlier were out of their seats and crowding round someone on the floor. But it quickly became a blur as the train gathered speed.

There was a weird feeling in the pit of my stomach. I turned back and looked around the station platform, it was the brightest, cleanest station I had ever seen.

Ahead of me was an archway with a sign above it saying, 'Entry'. I walked through and saw escalators to the left. Stepping on, they started to move. I looked up towards the top of the stairs but they were disappearing in a cloud of light.

Now, I may not be the sharpest knife in the box, but when I started to hear a choir singing in the background, I

Strange how no one else was getting off with me, normally there was a big rush...

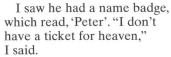

I never thought my last journey would involve escalators at an Underground tube station

knew there was something seriously wrong. I didn't want to admit it, but I realised I was dead. I had died on that train and the person I saw those passengers crowding over was me.

I had read stories about people who claimed to have had a near death experience, and how they had travelled through a tunnel with a light at the end of it. I never thought my last journey would involve escalators at an Underground tube station!

After what seemed an eternity, I finally reached the top and found myself in a large marble hallway. At one end was a turnstile with a ticket inspector waiting.

I assumed this to be my version of the pearly gates. As I reached the turnstile, the ticket inspector, who had a long white beard, said:

"Ticket please."

I saw he had a name badge, which read, 'Peter'. "I don't have a ticket for heaven," I said.

"How did you know this was heaven?" He asked. "Who told you?"

"No one, just a lucky guess," I replied.

"Well, you see, we've been trying to break it to people a little more gently than we have done before – thought it might be less of a shock to them." He seemed a little upset and I regretted spoiling his plan.

"It was very good though, very professional," I said. He cheered up a bit.

"Do you really think it was good?"

"Yes, really."

"You know, it was my idea to put the quotations on the train," he said proudly.

"I thought that was the best part," I said.

"Anyway,' he continued, "I still need to see your ticket for you to enter," He stopped and pulled a small card from his pocket.

"The kingdom of everlasting peace, love and tranquillity."

"But I don't have a ticket," I said.

"Yes you do," Peter said. "Check the train ticket you bought this morning." I fumbled in my trouser pocket and pulled the ticket out.

"Now you probably didn't look this morning, but you'll notice a valid from date, which was the day you were born, and an expiry date, which is when you had a heart attack on the train and died, which is today." I looked

at the ticket. There it was, my life summed up on a train pass. I turned it over and noticed something on the other side. The small print stated that I could only use the pass on London Underground trains within the Underground network, and I knew I was way beyond the network. I pointed this out to Peter who looked at it very carefully.

"Looks like I've over looked something. I told them we'd have teething problems with this new system, but they didn't listen. Right, am I to believe that you don't want to enter the kingdom of everlasting peace, love and er…"

"Tranquillity?" I finished.

"Yes, tranquillity,"

"Well, not for a few years yet. I am only fifty-seven."

Peter thought for a moment and then said: "Right then, perhaps next time I'll have it all sorted out. Remember to keep off those double chocolate fudge cakes!"

The next thing I knew I was on the floor of the train with someone blowing into my mouth, and a terrible pain in my chest.

I heard a voice.

"Keep still, the ambulance should be here soon." It was a passenger who I had seen many times before but had never spoken to.

"Thanks," I said weakly.

When the ambulance men arrived and started to carry me away, I saw another quotation written on the station wall, it read, 'To lengthen thy life, lessen thy meals', by Benjamin Franklin. Point taken, I thought.

December 2004

A flavour of the month

PIC: REX FEATURES

With Christmas just around the corner, it's time for those last minute preparations and presents. Start by making or buying your Christmas cards and decorations at the beginning of the month, as time may be short in the busy run up to the big day.

Tree decorations are simple to make using felt and glue. Cut out felt Christmas stocking shapes, then carefully glue two together around their edges, leaving the top of the stocking open. Decorate with brightly-coloured felt shapes, add a small loop of ribbon for hanging and fill with chocolate goodies.

It's time to be creative in the kitchen too. There's no need to stick to the standard mince pie recipe. For a truly festive dessert, replace the jam in a roly poly or swiss roll with sweet mincemeat. Or make an apple pie with a lattice top, replacing half the apples with mincemeat. Decorate the top with seasonal pastry cutouts, such as stars and trees.

With the shops becoming increasingly crowded as Christmas approaches, why don't you try a armchair shopping? Most big stores offer mail order. Remember to get orders in early, as you don't want your presents still locked up in the store cupboards on Christmas morning.

Wishing you a very happy and peaceful Christmas!

WEDNESDAY	1
THURSDAY	2
FRIDAY	3
SATURDAY	4
SUNDAY	5
MONDAY	6
TUESDAY	7
WEDNESDAY	8
THURSDAY	9
FRIDAY	10
SATURDAY	11
SUNDAY	12
MONDAY	13
TUESDAY	14
WEDNESDAY	15
THURSDAY	16
FRIDAY	17
SATURDAY	18

SUNDAY	19	
MONDAY	20	
TUESDAY	21	
WEDNESDAY	22	
THURSDAY	23	
FRIDAY	24	
SATURDAY	25	Christmas Day
SUNDAY	26	Boxing Day
MONDAY	27	UK (Bank Holiday in lieu of Christmas Day)
TUESDAY	28	UK (Bank Holiday in lieu Boxing Day)
WEDNESDAY	29	January YOURS on sale
THURSDAY	30	
FRIDAY	31	

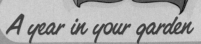

A year in your garden

It's cold, it's wet, it's dark – it's a great time of year. Seed catalogues just won't stop dlopping through the letterbox and the promise of all those flowers and organic vegetables next year is too tempting.

And let's face it, while the garden slumbers you can be plotting next year's display. At last you have a chance to see where the gaps were, to see what was a roaring success and what not to bother with. It's also a chance to get a couple of packets of the new varieties the seed companies have to introduce each year – thank goodness! Growing plants from seeds is the most rewarding part of gardening.

But not everyone has time or room for propagators, pots and paraphernalia on windowsills and greenhouses. What we need are plants. The seed companies know this and have more and more varieties ready grown for gardeners.

Plug plants are cuttings taken from parent plants, grown in small mesh pots and sent out by post in spring. But it's now you need to order as they sell like hotcakes. Same thing goes with seedlings. Geranium seeds are expensive and can be erratic in germination. Ready grown seedlings are already up and running. A packet of cauliflower seeds contains enough for a field of the things – but a strip or tray of seedlings is just right for the average sized garden.

Another benefit of finding time for planning and ordering your seeds and plants is that companies want your orders early and most offer incentives for early birds. It can be in the shape of free plants or discount. So settle down with your favourite drink, surround yourself with piles of next year's catalogues and dream yourself the best ever spring garden. After all, it's only a few months away.

PIC. EMAP GARDEN PICTURE LIBRARY

★ READER'S TIP ★
George Arnold in Exeter keeps a diary. It's a gardening diary where he notes when he sows each and every seed he grows. It's invaluable when assessing how good a plant was.

▲ 'And they laid Him in a manger'. Solemn children in a nativity play in 1937

Barbara Walkling from Kent would like to say thank you…

A DAY TO REMEMBER

More than 60 years ago, as a seven-year-old (pictured below), I stood on a station platform waving goodbye to my favourite aunt and new uncle on their honeymoon. As we waited, a train steamed into the other platform and suddenly the place filled with noise and rushing figures.

Hospital personnel in white coats, Red Cross workers, stretcher bearers, ARP wardens, policemen appeared as if from nowhere. Carriage doors opened to emit a tide of men, some in dirty uniforms, some bandaged, some on stretchers.

Our parents, uncles and aunts dashed about to help. For a seven-year-old it was very bewildering and we children were shepherded into the nearest waiting room and told to stay there. Some time later my father told me that I had witnessed part of the Dunkirk evacuation.

Over the years I have been so aware of the enormous debt we owe these brave men and their rescuers. Navy, Air Force, the little ships crews and, above all, the many, many men who gave their lives. So, after all this time, from one ordinary person to those extraordinary people, may I please say thank you.

WHAT'S COOKING?

Pork and Cabbage Stir Fry
(Serves 4)

PIC: FRESH PRODUCE CONSORTIUM

- 12 oz/350 g lean pork fillet
- 1½ lb/700 g Savoy cabbage
- 1 tbs oil
- 1 heaped tbs chopped root ginger
- 2 cloves garlic, finely chopped
- 6 spring onions, chopped
- 1 tbs soy sauce
- 1 tbs dry sherry
- Large pinch 5 spice powder
- 3 tbs chicken stock
- 1 tsp corn flour

1 Cut the pork into thin strips. Wash the cabbage, discard the outside leaves, then shred the rest, cutting away the hard core.
2 Mix the cornflour with the soy sauce, sherry, chicken stock and spice powder.
3 Heat the oil in a large frying pan or wok, add the pork, ginger and garlic and stir fry until the meat is lightly browned.
4 Add the cabbage and spring onions and toss together in the pan until just beginning to wilt.
5 Add the cornflour mixture and continue to cook, stirring for 2-3 minutes. Serve with rice or noodles.

PIC: STEVEN WOOSTER

OUT & ABOUT TO...

The Beth Chatto Gardens, Elmstead Market, Colchester, Essex

One of those rare gardens that looks amazing in all seasons, this gem began in 1960 as an overgrown wilderness with poor soil and worse drainage. Following their philosophy of gardening with nature, not against her (known as ecological gardening), Beth Chatto and her late husband Andrew transformed it into a superb informal garden that blends in beautifully with the surrounding countryside.

There are blissful surprises at every turn – clearly the result of careful planning and constant planting. You might not have time to see what lies around every corner, but don't miss

the Mediterranean area, as many drought-resisting plants retain their foliage in winter. And at this time of year in the water gardens, when flowers are thin on the ground, the ghost-like branches and blond stems reflected in the ponds look very pretty.

- *Adults £3.50, children under 14 free*
- *Open Monday to Saturday*
- *Seasonal tea room; picnic benches; wheelchair access except for during exceptionally wet weather*
  Tel: 01206 822007

OLD WIVES' TALES

Put pure apple cider vinegar on cuts immediately – it will kill the bacteria and aid the healing process.

Dr Henderson replies: Pure apple cider vinegar has a reputation as a natural antiseptic and does no harm in my book. If you have a small cut, use it on it immediately. It may sting a little, but it does seem to help kill bacteria and speed up the healing process.

DID YOU KNOW THAT

Pandas spend about 12 hours a day eating bamboo

AT THE MOVIES

Who said?
'What can you say about a 25-year-old girl who died? That she was beautiful. And brilliant. That she loved Mozart and Bach. And the Beatles. And me.
(Answer below)

Answer: Ryan O'Neal in Arthur Hiller's Love Story

PAUSE FOR THOUGHT

Jean Wilson, from Cambridgeshire, writes:
'When I lost my dear husband, a very good friend sent me a card with the words, Sorrow is not forever, Love is. How very true these words are and they give me much comfort'.

Top tip
To avoid the bathroom filling with steam when you have a bath, run cold water before the hot.

ON GROWING OLDER

'Youth is the gift of nature but age is a work of art'.

Garson Kanin

December 6-12

WHAT A COINCIDENCE

Doreen and Peter

Our favourite holiday spot has always been Orlando and one day we decided to check out a local bar because the bartender (a fellow Geordie) was supposed to be a real character. After chatting for an hour or so, my husband, Peter, and bartender, Brian, realised that they'd been best friends at school and hadn't seen each other since 1962.

Since that day in 1987 Brian and his wife Lorna have become our very close friends whom we visit as often as possible.

Coincidence number two came not long after the first one. We were browsing in a flea market in Sanford about 40 miles north of Orlando. Suddenly I heard a voice call out: "Doreen!" What a surprise when it turned out to be a lady who had lived next door to me in Newcastle five years earlier. She and her husband had moved to Sanford to start a business. What a small world!

Doreen and Peter Gordon, Newcastle

MY ADVICE IS...

'A kind word or an unexpected thoughtful deed can make someone's day'.
H Anker, Teeside

ON GROWING OLDER

'Grow old along with me! The best is yet to be'.
Robert Browning

OLD FASHIONED REMEDIES

To reduce sweating and body odour, paint your armpits with freshly squeezed lemon juice in the morning.

Dr Henderson replies: As a natural deodorant, some people still swear by this although there is no good medical reason why sweating should be reduced due to lemon juice.

Body odour is caused by the build-up of certain bacteria in the armpits and one theory is that the acidic juice delays this but I find this hard to believe. However, if you are looking for a natural deodorant it is safe and cheap and I would not stop you trying it but don't expect miracles here.

Mrs P Hancock from Boston remembers the day she could kick up her heels...

A DAY TO REMEMBER

I'll never forget my last day at work. I started work at 14 and left on my 60th birthday – and started a new life! Freedom from rules and regulations, I could do what I liked when I liked. I joined voluntary organisations and made new friends. I'm very busy and very happy – it's great!

AT THE MOVIES

At the movies
Who said?
'Nice speech, Eve. But I wouldn't worry too much about your heart. You can always put that award where your heart should be'.
(Answer below)

Answer: Bette Davis congratulating Anne Baxter in Joseph L Mankiewicz's All About Eve

WHAT'S COOKING?

QUICK SNACK
Smoked Mackerel Pâté
(Serves 4)

- 12 oz/350 g smoked mackerel fillets
- 2 oz/50 g margarine
- 2 tbs natural yoghurt
- 2 tbs mayonnaise
- Pepper
- Grated rind and juice of a lemon
- 1 teaspoon dried mixed herbs

1 Remove and discard the skin and any bones from the mackerel fillets.
2 Purée the flesh in a blender (or mash thoroughly with a fork) with the remaining ingredients.
3 Put into a dish. Store in the refrigerator for up to three days.

Serving suggestions:
- Spread the paté on slices of toast and pop under the grill, topped with sliced tomatoes. Grill for 2-3 minutes until thoroughly warmed through.
- Use as a dip with vegetable crudités: çelery, red and green peppers, cucumber and broccoli

DID YOU KNOW THAT

Irving Berlin could only play the piano in one key – F sharp.

OUT & ABOUT TO...

Wensleydale Creamery, Hawes, Yorkshire Dales

PIC: SUE HISCO, WENSLEYDALE CREAMERY

Stuff the turkey: For many of us, the best part of Christmas dinner is a cheese platter, piled high with old favourites and new friends – all washed down with a cheeky red wine or mature Port. So if your palate will feel hard done by this Christmas without some of the ripe, smelly stuff, head for Wensleydale Creamery.

You'll see how the cheese is made, plus, if you're short of a few Christmas gifts for your nearest and dearest – not to mention yourself – it makes the perfect present. Choose from crumbly white Wensleydale, which has a mild, slightly sweet flavour with a honey aftertaste, and the blue-veined variety, which is more strongly flavoured. The latter takes six months to mature and has a smooth, creamy texture similar to Stilton. Special varieties include sheep's milk Wensleydale, created for people who are allergic to cow's milk, and Wensleydale with all manner of additions: Cranberries and kirsch, anyone?

- *Visitors' centre; museum; viewing gallery; shop selling cheese and other foods; food hall; free cheese tasting*
Tel: 01969 667664

December 13-19

WHAT A COINCIDENCE

In 1940 as a 12-year-old I had six penpals in New Zealand – four girls, a boy called Vernon and a dear old man, whom I later called Uncle Jim.

I wrote to Vernon, who lived in Arrowtown, for many years until 1950 when I became engaged. My fiancée took umbrage to my writing to this young man, so my correspondence stopped.

For 62 years I enjoyed writing to the others, never dreaming I would ever visit them. Then in 1992, I had a small windfall and so I went to New Zealand.

I stayed with Doreen, a relation of Uncle Jim, and while there, I lost a lens from my spectacles and had to drive 80 miles to an optician in Dunedin.

While we were waiting, Arrowtown came up in the conversation and I remarked that I used to write to a young man who'd lived there – Vernon Hansen. To my utter astonishment Doreen said: "Oh, I know Vernon – his sister is my best friend." Out of a population of nearly one million people!

Doreen told me he now lived in Dunedin and, despite my protests, hauled me off to the nearest phone box.

"Hello, is that Vernon? This is a voice from the past," I said nervously. "It's Betty, isn't it?"

I went to see Vernon, met his wife and we now write once a year at Christmas, when he sends me an illustrated calendar to remind me of my wonderful trip to New Zealand.

Top: Betty
Above: Vernon – Betty's penfriend from 1940 to 1950

WHAT'S COOKING?

SUPPER DISH
Sherry Chicken Surprise
(Serves 4)

- ½ pt/275 ml stock
- ¼ pt/150 ml single cream
- Oil and butter for frying
- 4 chicken joints
- Salt and pepper
- 4 oz/110 g butter
- 4 oz/110 g mushrooms
- 1 oz/25 g plain flour
- 3 tbs sherry

1. Season the chicken well. Melt the butter and fry the chicken for 25 minutes. Remove and keep hot.
2. Add the mushrooms and sauté for 2-3 minutes. Remove and keep to one side.
3. Add the flour to the remaining fat. Mix well and cook for 2-3 minutes. Remove the pan from the heat, add the sherry and stock gradually. Return to the heat, bring to the boil, stirring continually until thickened.
4. Add the cream, mix and heat through, but do not boil. Return the mushrooms to the sauce, heat through again. Pour over chicken and serve.

DID YOU KNOW THAT

The African bushman, who lives in a quiet environment, has no measurable hearing loss at the age of 60.

OLD WIVES' TALES

To prevent sinus problems from pollen, put sesame oil up each nostril.

Dr Henderson replies: I had not heard of this old wives' tale but on researching it with my patients found it to be very well-known! Apparently the traditional nose drop preparation consists of cold pressed sesame oil that is given as 2-3 drops into each nostril morning and night. Some people can be allergic to this and I would not advise it if you are nut allergic in general, but otherwise many people swear by it!

AT THE MOVIES

Who said?
'In spite of everything, I still believe that people are really good at heart'.
(Answer below)

Answer: Millie Perkins in George Stevens's The Diary Of Anne Frank

OUT & ABOUT TO...

Trebah Garden, Mawnan Smith, Falmouth, Cornwall

PIC CREDIT: TREBAH GARDEN

'This is no pampered, pristine, prissy garden with rows of clipped hedges and striped lawns. You are going to see a magnificent old, wild and magical Cornish garden', promises the Trebah Garden Guide.

At Christmas it's more exciting than ever, especially for children, who can hunt for clues around the garden, and follow a trail that leads to Santa Claus sitting beside a roaring fire in his secret grotto, where they will receive a small present.

Trebah was started in the 1840s by Charles Fox, a Quaker landowner, who imported the rarest, most exotic trees and plants he could find from all over the world. It has grown into an incredibly romantic garden, set at the head of a 25-acre wooded ravine that descends 200 feet down to a private secluded beach.

A walk around the garden takes in waterfalls, ponds of giant koi carp and glades of sub-tropical ferns and palms. You can wind your way down the Zig-Zag slope, past huge 100-year-old tree ferns and gaze in awe at the 60-foot rhododendrons and ancient magnolias.

Trebah is full of nooks and crannies for children to explore, including a tunnel of giant rhubarb and play areas such as Tarzan's Camp.

● *Admission varies depending on the time of year. From November until the end of February: Adults £2.50, concessions £2.25, children £1.50*
● *The Santa Trail takes place on four days in December (phone to check dates). On Santa days, children have free admission to the garden, and pay £2 to follow the trail*
● *Restaurant; gift shop; plants for sale*
Tel: 01326 250448

PAUSE FOR THOUGHT

Cornish gardens

Bright stars fade as morn is breaking
Dewdrops pearl each bud and leaf,
Sun comes up, the lark is soaring
O'er Cornish gardens far beneath.

June musk-roses softly blooming, scented and pure
Emblems of nature, formed to allure,
Vivid, red geraniums planted near the door,
While fragrant tangled sweet peas
Perfume the balmy air.

Happy hours spent dreaming here before the autumn fall
Russet leaves have fallen, scented petals too,
Though Michaelmas daisies still keep flowering through
A sharp and biting frost replaces summer dew.

Our garden sleeps in winter, bulbs and corms all safe below,
Yet we're nearer God's heart in our Cornish gardens
Than anywhere else I know.

Joan Bunt, Cornwall

Top tip

Deliver as many local Christmas cards as you can – keeps you fit and saves on stamps!

A honeymoon with a difference for Linda Gray from West Yorkshire...

A DAY TO REMEMBER

The year 1988 was a special year for my husband and I, as it was the year we were married. We are keen followers of stock car racing and the day we flew back from our honeymoon on the island of Gozo (after a 5am start!) was a day to remember in more ways than one.

It was the World Stock Car Racing Final, so after sorting out a few things at home, we then set off to Coventry to watch the racing. And it was well worth it when our favourite driver won! What an exciting year but most of all, a wonderful way to finish off our honeymoon.

ON GROWING OLDER

'Every man desires to live long; but no man would be old'.

Jonathan Swift

December 20-31

MY ADVICE IS...

'If you make a New Year resolution and don't keep it for long, don't give up – after all, you have the rest of the year to try again!'
Vi Booth, Hants

ON GROWING OLDER

'Cheer up! The worst is still to come!'
Philandeer Chase Johnson

WHAT'S COOKING?

A MEAL ON A BUDGET
Savoury Bread and Butter Pudding
(Serves 4)

- 6 thin slices white bread
- 1 pt/570 ml milk
- 1½ oz/40 g butter
- 3 thick slices ham
- Mustard
- 3 tomatoes, thinly sliced
- 3 eggs
- Salt and pepper

1. Remove crusts from bread and spread with butter. Place slices of ham on 3 slices of bread, top with tomato slices and smattering of mustard.
2. Cover with remaining bread, buttered side up. Cut each sandwich into 4 triangles. Place in a shallow, buttered heatproof dish.
3. Beat together eggs, salt and pepper and milk. Pour over bread and garnish with remaining tomato slices.
4. Bake in a moderate oven for 35-45 minutes (180°C/350°F/Gas Mark 4) or until golden brown.

A DAY TO REMEMBER

Vera Bartram from Lancing was feeling low – but not for long…

At the time of the first anniversary of my husband's death I was feeling very depressed. Then I saw an advert for an Over 55s morning at the local leisure centre. I'd always liked tennis but, due to my husband's illness, had not played for seven years. I wondered if it was possible to take it up again.

It took a great deal of courage to walk on my own through the doors to the Over 55s morning but I'm glad I did because it turned my life around. They were a friendly crowd and we played badminton and tennis. Through one of the ladies I met there, I got a job as a temp, which I did until I retired at 70. I also met an old friend there, so the day I went to that leisure centre is, for me, a day to remember.

Vera, whose life was changed around

Top tip
Patterned paper tablecloths make a cheap alternative to wrapping paper at Christmas.

OLD FASHIONED REMEDIES

Lemon regimes for rheumatism and gout were popular 100 years ago. They began with the juice of one lemon on the first day, upping the dose daily until the juice of 30 was taken in a day, after which the same dose was diminished at the same rate.

Dr Henderson replies: No use, I'm afraid, as rheumatism and gout will be completely untouched by this. Thirty lemons a day is excessive and over-acidic, too, so don't be tempted by this one which fell from favour fairly rapidly for obvious reasons.

AT THE MOVIES

Who said?
'A boy's best friend is his mother'.
(Answer below)

Answer: Anthony Perkins in Alfred Hitchcock's Psycho

DID YOU KNOW THAT

A 'clue' originally meant a ball of thread. This is why one is said to 'unravel' the clues of a mystery

My husband and I often spoke of the magical chance it was, the first time we met. The brass band I went to see in Widnes Park that Sunday attracted crowds from far and near – including my friend and I dressed up in our Sunday best, gloves included!

We were strolling towards the bandstand when I was surprised when a fair curly-haired young chap said, 'Excuse me', very politely and told me I had dropped a glove.

After four years I married the attractive blue-eyed man, enjoyed 53 happy years and we had three children!

The miracle was that my husband-to-be did not live in Widnes and had never been to the park before. And I had not visited the park on a Sunday afternoon for years.

Emily and her husband at a dance festival

OUT & ABOUT TO...

Edinburgh Tartan Weaving Mill & Exhibition, Old Town Weaving Co, 55 Royal Mile, Edinburgh, Scotland

If you're in Edinburgh to celebrate hogmanay, take some time out to see another, quieter, side of the city. A showcase for Scottish crafts, this exhibition tells the story of the country's traditional textile: The kilt. You can see the powerful working mill in action, watch the tartan weavers at work and learn about the history of the kilt and its oldest example, the Falkirk Tartan, which dates from 250AD.

There's also a traditional weaver's cottage, where you can try your hand at weaving fabric for a kilt. And afterwards there's the chance to try on the wares in the colourful Tartan Shop. There'll be no stopping you at the ceildh...

● *Adults £4.50; concessions £3; children £2; family ticket £8*
● *The museum is open daily except for January 1, but for the past few years the shop has opened on New Year's Day (phone to check)*
● *Restaurant; shop; wheelchair access Tel: 0131 226 1555*

PIC: REX FEATURES

A prickly customer

Helen Firminger of the London Wildlife Trust tells us how to attract and look after hedgehogs in our garden

Even in urban London gardens it's marvellous that a creature, unchanged since this country was covered in wildwood, is able to live in small gardens. Railway banks have replaced hedgebank, and shelter will be found in pyrocantha where once it was bramble, but for hedgehogs, it's business as usual.

If you want to attract them to your garden, have a good look at the surrounding area and think about how they are going to move around – they need about a mile to range in. If your garden is fenced, four inch holes cut into the bottom of your fence, and that of your neighbour's (but ask permission first!) will help them move around in safety.

Hedgehogs tend to move around areas of cover, spending the days sheltered among brambles or similar dense plants, so add some leaf piles and twig piles to shelter them. They will use purpose-built homes as well but are fickle in bed space from night to night.

Our prickly friends are well known to more pragmatic gardeners for their slug and snail eating habits. They do eat other invertebrates, too, including small reptiles but they will certainly help a practical, organic gardener to rear slug-free lettuces.

You may have the privilege of seeing the prickly family out foraging in July, with four or five babies following mum to learn the tricks. They all go their own separate ways in August, taking advantage of the summer surplus of food to build up fat before hibernation time arrives.

Any rich garden has lots of summer food for visiting hogs. If you need to supplement this in autumn, use dog food or the dried mixes available from specialist suppliers. Hedgehogs need to drink, too, so a bowl of water is helpful, and do make sure that any ponds or swimming pools in the neighbourhood include an easy exit edge.
More information from The London Wildlife Trust, tel: 0207 261 0447

The things we miss

Christmas traditions

The sound of Away In A Manger drifting down the street or over the fields was a sure sign that Christmas – and the carol singers – were round the corner. With thickly-mittened hands, shaking as they held their carol sheets, and their breath rising in a haze above their head in the cold night air, they walked laughing and chatting from door to door trying to make a few pennies wherever they could. But you had to get the timing right: Too early in the year and people weren't ready to be reminded that they had all their festive preparations ahead of them; too late and people were fed up with pleading faces and off-key tunes.

PIC: HULTON ARCHIVE

Seasonal memories

● Dad would have been keeping chickens since the war, so Christmas was the only time of the year that you ate poultry.
● Remember when Mum boiled up the pud in the Burco boiler? You could smell them cooking when you were in bed!
● What about that crystal set radio you received? All set for Jack Jackson's Record Round Up on a Saturday night.
● In the afternoon, it was all quiet for the King's speech on the radio.
● Oh, the Christmas cake and the trifle, made with Carnation milk, of course!
● And after games like Snakes and Ladders or Monopoly, it was off to bed ready for Boxing Day

Competition!

What was YOUR best day of 2003?

I t's the start of another year and the last 12 months have simply flown by. Judging by your lovely letters we know how much you enjoyed dipping into the 2003 YOURS annual!

Now we would love to hear from you if you had a memorable event in 2003. Maybe it was a wonderful day out, a wedding, a never-to-be-forgotten holiday, a reunion with an old friend, or a loving hello to the newest member of the family!

Tell us about your special day in 2003, in not more than 350 words and we'd really like a photograph or two to accompany it – both of your special event and one of you as author. We'll take really good care of them and return them in due course (but it will be a while).

Send your entries to the address given on this page by Friday February 27, 2004.

And we have a wonderful prize for the best entry

You can win a Rhine Cruise to Switzerland for two – worth £1,000!

You can enjoy the breathtaking beauty of the Rhine valley on a memorable ten-day cruise to discover the unique charm and special atmosphere of Germany, France and Switzerland. With awe-inspiring scenery – snowy peaks, mountain streams, lush forests, combined with modern cities, traditional towns and good food – you'll be assured of a very warm welcome!

This break includes return coaching from selected pick-up points throughout the UK, convenient Channel crossings and nine nights full board accommodation onboard a friendly, family run cruise vessel with a full programme of entertainment onboard.

One of the highlights of your holiday is sure to be an included visit to the French city of Strasbourg – capital of Alsace and seat of the European Parliament. You'll also have the chance to experience the Rhine and Moselle Valleys, the Black Forest of Germany, Heidelburg and much, much more.

We hope to publish the winning entry, along with a selection of the best entries in a future publication.

Please send your entries to: *YOURS magazine, Bretton Court, Bretton, Peterborough PE3 8DZ*, marking your envelope BEST DAY OF 2003. Usual YOURS competition rules apply.

Good luck to you all – and we hope the coming year is equally special.

The prize holiday must be taken during 2004. This prize is supplied by Travelscope Promotions Ltd. If you would like more information about other river cruise holidays on offer please call 0870 7705010 for a free brochure. Or write to Travelscope Promotions Ltd, Elgin House, High Street, Stonehouse, Glos GL10 2NA